# Praise for
# AdoptingOnlin

C000067138

"An Outstanding Adoption Resource!" — Marlou Russell, Ph.D, A

"Mardie Caldwell's book *AdoptingOnline.com* is a valuable resource for couples or singles that are beginning the process of adoption. The contents are well structured and flow easily. I heartily recommend this book."

— Gerald Bowman, LCSW, ACSW, Licensed Clinical Social Worker working with Americans abroad since 1989

"Mardie Caldwell's new book *AdoptingOnline.com* is a wealth of valuable information for anyone considering adoption. This is a resource for every situation and covers every angle you need to know for the best possible outcome. I highly recommend *AdoptingOnline.com* as the definitive authority." — Frank F. Lunn, President Kahuna Business Group, author and adult adoptee.

"*AdoptingOnline.com* is an immense contribution to those searching to complete their families through adoption." — Teresa Sgrignoli, single adoptive mother

"*AdoptingOnLine.com* is a great book! Mardie speaks from her heart and desires the best for both parties in the adoption process. We are a family built through adoption and through Lifetime Adoption." — Amy Brown, adoptive mother

"*AdoptingOnline.com* is informative, well-organized and very entertaining. The information is presented in an easy-to-read format, and the real-life stories will make the dream of adopting seem even more achievable. I can't imagine this book NOT helping anyone considering the option of adoption!"

— Dawn Whitaker, adoptive mother

"As an adoptive mother, as well as a child advocate, few issues touch my heart and soul like adoption. Mardie Caldwell has a talent for matching families longing to raise a child with children who need loving, stable homes. I have benefited immensely from her experience, and now others can reap the rewards of adoption from the information provided in *AdoptingOnline.com*."

— Cheryl Ann Palmer, M.D., Pediatric Neuropathologist, The Children's Hospital of Alabama, adoptive mother

"Mardie's new book *AdoptingOnline.com* gets 2 thumbs UP! Easy reading and packed full of useful tips and information for people interested in adoption! You must read this book if you are considering adoption. Great for adoptive families as well as birth mothers!"

— Linda Logue, adoptive mother

"*AdoptingOnline.com* is a perfect "how-to" guide to adopting using the Internet. Sprinkled with personal stories, it's a breezy and enjoyable read chock-full of useful information."

— Julie Valentine, Founder, Adopting.com and adoptive mother

"*AdoptingOnline.com* puts into writing everything we were told during the adoption process! Plus, we were matched within one month of sending out our *Dear Birth Mother letter!*"
— Sarah Neal, adoptive mother

"Mardie has answered the call to building families and those of us are blessed many times over for it. Her wisdom, insight and expertise, give light and hope to adoptive couples. This is a book of astounding value. The time and research going into *AdoptingOnline.com* is incalculable."
— Renee Runyan, adoptive mother and chaplain

"An awesome book! Mardie has outdone herself! *AdoptingOnline.com* is crammed full of information for the adoptive parent!"
— Michelle Goff, adoptive mother

"Caldwell shares her adoption journey with all the emotion and humor possible. This is an astonishing book for its resource material alone. Everyone in the adoption triad should read this, and for EVERY potential adoptive parent it is a must!"
— Shannon C. Lutz, Sociologist and mother

"To all that value the determination and perseverance that enable one to handle the financial load of adoption, you must read this book! *AdoptingOnline.com* offers practical, easy to follow and SAFE financial advice for those needing to save money and for those about to spend it!"
— Wendy Carrillo, Accountant and mother.

"A resourceful, succinct and practical guide to adoption, *AdoptingOnline.com* is about connecting children with parents. What could be more important? This book is an astounding effort to save time and resources for the potential adoptive couple and any member of the adoption triad."
— Stacy Carroll, M.A., Prudential Teacher of the Year 1999, educator and mother.

"Caldwell's passion for children and adoption are graphically illustrated throughout her book in her own words. The resource section of *AdoptingOnline.com* is unbelievably comprehensive, sure to save time, money, and energy in anyone's adoption." — Nathalia Chayadi, B.A.

"I am amazed at how much good and practical information *AdoptingOnline.com* contains, especially the sections on how to avoid bad adoption situations. It is good advice for anyone looking to adopt and for anyone thinking about adopting, it's a MUST read!" — Eric A. Stovall, Attorney

"Having read the new book *AdoptingOnLine.com* by Mardie Caldwell, I am sure the amount, breadth and quality of this information does not yet exist anywhere else! Not only is it sophisticated, practical, thorough and professional, it is also humorous, sensitive, loving and gentle. It goes well beyond being a technical manual about how to use the internet for adopting; it is filled with almost poetic prose about real-life adoption situations that at times will bring tears to your eyes and at times will fill your heart with warmth. If there was a discipline called "adoptionology" this book could serve as its major textbook—but with lots of soul. I heartily recommend this book for anyone interested in adopting, interested in learning about a friend or relative's adoption or planning to help others adopt. My sincerest congratulations to Mardie Caldwell for a real "labor of love.""
— John P. J. Dussich, Ph.D., Victimologist, California State University, Fresno

Your #1 Guide to a Successful Adoption

# AdoptingOnline.com

## Safe & proven methods that have brought thousands of families together

Mardie M. Caldwell

© COPYRIGHT 2004  All rights reserved

*No part of this book may be copied or transmitted in any form without the express permission of the author.*

AdoptingOnline.com

Published by
American Carriage House Publishing
P.O. Box 1130
Nevada City, CA 95959

Text and art copyright © 2004 by American Carriage House Publishing. All rights reserved. No part of this book may be reproduced or transmitted in any form, by any means (electronic, photocopying, recording, or otherwise) without the prior written permission of the author.

Library of Congress Catalog Card No.: 2004104364

ISBN: 0-9705734-1-3

Printed in the United States of America

Distributed in the United States by American Carriage House Publishing

For general information on American Carriage House Publishing in the U.S., please call our Consumer Customer Service department at (530) 470-0720.

For reseller information, including discounts and premium sales, translations, using books in the classroom, photocopying or authorization, please call (877) 423-6785 or e-mail **info@carriagehousepublishing.com.**

Limit of Liability/Disclaimer of Warranty: The author and publisher have used their best efforts in preparing this book. American Carriage House Publishing and the author make no representation or warranties with respect to the accuracy or completeness of the contents of this book and specifically disclaim any implied warranties of merchantability or fitness for any particular purpose and shall in no event be liable for any loss of profit or any other commercial or personal damage, including but not limited to special, incidental, consequential or other damages. This book is designed for educational and informative purposes only. This information is not intended to substitute for informed legal advice. You should not use this information without consulting with a qualified adoption professional. AdoptingOnline.com does not endorse any of the sites or products discussed herein. You are strongly encouraged to consult a qualified adoption professional with any questions or concerns you may have regarding your adoption. Verify companies through **www.bbbonline.org**. Some of the information contained herein may not be valid in some regions, or may be prohibited by law and should be ignored where it is prohibited, not applicable or inconsistent with local law. The best adoption advice can only be given by a qualified adoption professional who knows you personally and the laws in your state.

*Trademarks: All brand names and product names used in this book are trademarks, registered trademarks, or trade names of their respective holders.*

*This book is dedicated to all the precious children who will be adopted by the "adoptive parents in waiting" reading this book, and to the wonderful birth families who have chosen to help create these new families. Through their choices, they have made so many of us proud parents through adoption.*

*May God bless you and guide you in finding each other.*

# Table of Contents

# About the Author

Mardie Caldwell, C.O.A.P., is a nationally recognized authority on open adoption and adopting on the Internet. An Adoption Facilitator and Certified Open Adoption Practitioner, Caldwell is the founder of the nationwide adoption organization, Lifetime Adoption Facilitation Center, Inc., established in 1986. Caldwell has assisted in over 1000 successful adoptions and was one of the first adoption professionals on the Internet. Caldwell is also the radio talk show host for "Let's Talk Adoption…with Mardie Caldwell" at **www.LetsTalkAdoption.com.**

As an adoptive parent who has experienced many of the challenges prospective adoptive parents face, Caldwell knows the joy, the sorrow and the frustration of dealing with infertility and adoption. She also understands and wants to share the important steps that must be taken to complete a safe and secure adoption.

Caldwell's life work has been dedicated to educating and helping adoptive parents and birth parents find each other. Her greatest desire in life is to build happy families by providing loving and secure futures for the precious infants and children brought to us through adoption. Caldwell works one-on-one with birth parents, medical professionals, adoption attorneys and social service professionals to attain her goal.

Caldwell has been a guest on numerous television and radio talk shows and is regularly interviewed by family and parenting magazines. She has authored numerous articles about the challenges and joys of adoption. She and her husband, Greg, reside with two of their four children in Nevada City, California.

You can contact Mardie Caldwell at **www.MardieCaldwell.com**.

# Acknowledgments and Credits

This book has been years in the making. It often felt like my long journey through infertility: longing to conceive, then impatient to have the baby (book) in your arms and then the joy of adoption once it was finalized. I will be forever grateful for all the wonderful people who have selflessly helped, encouraged, supported and inspired me along the way.

First and foremost, I am thankful for my loving and devoted husband, Greg. Without his encouragement and continual stream of love and support, this book would have never made it into print.

To our precious children, Jesse, Alissa and Julia, for helping everywhere they could and especially to our son Cory; without him, adoption would never have been a part of my life and my passion.

I have a tremendous appreciation for my staff who have been an encouraging team throughout this process, allowing me to work on the book while they took midnight emergency birth mother calls: Rebecca Robinson, Diane Pruss, Heather Featherston, Sanda Evans, Rebecca Gulas, Martha Chambless, Lori Deniz, Vicki Almond, Luke Mertens, Alex and Barbara Lissow, Barbara Raimey, Veronica Hofheinz, Daniel Raiche, Jan Hammontree, and Jennifer Welton.

## Special Thank-you(s) to:

Mary Parton, my faithful assistant, for her tireless support and constant encouragement; she worked harder than any human should in research and balancing the never-ending tasks and calls to help make this book a reality.

To Sushila Mertens for all her suggestions; my college writing professor, Bud Gardner; Dan Poynter for advice and encouragement; Sonja Wells for the sweet, inspirational notes left on my research table early on in the process; Rebecca Faccio, Lindsey Rios, Stephanie Markley, and Charity Warren for their support in keeping everything on the home front in place; and to Laurie Bolach for her help and advice.

To the numerous adoptive families whose stories and experiences have enriched this book, especially Michelle Goff who inspired the title of this book, Madelyn Holmes, Albert and Karen Woods and Joann Vesper, a very generous thank you.

For their contributions, adoptive mothers Pegg Bournstein for clips on adoption, Amy Brown, Dawn Whitaker and Melody Dickey. Thank you to Attorney James Handy for reviewing the legal chapters; social worker Gerald Bowman for reviewing our international chapter; Melanie Billings for reviewing our special needs chapter; and to anyone I may have mistakenly left out, thank you.

To John J. Spina, Esq. for his article on "Recent Tax Law Changes 2003"; we appreciate being able to make it available for all those who have been touched by adoption.

To Carriage House Publishing editors, Lucille Carrillo, Paul Bagne, Jake Finch, and Rose Gander, and a special thank you to the editorial staff and assistants Eva Dacey, Kim Lopez, Josh Green, and Margaret Foard.

Thank you to Diane Covington for content review and coaching; Laine Latimere for believing in the project the moment she heard about it; Peri Poloni of Knockout Design who did an outstanding job designing the book interior; Doug Tocco, who designed the book cover; to Lauren Michelle Banister, Ainsley Bournstein, Julissa Garcia, Jazlyn Brown, the

Sgrignoli, Uhl, and Byerrum families, whose pictures grace the front of this book; and to the many people that have gone out of their way to spread the word about our adoption work, including Anne McDermott from CNN who spent her valuable time in sharing our story with the world, I thank you. Thank you to copy editor Gail Kearns and indexer Ken DellaPenta for their assistance and lastly, a special thank you to Louann Carroll whose dream of "Who Will Help the Children?" came true. I have a deep gratitude to the readers and others who provided insight, feedback and time in reading this manuscript.

Words can never express my appreciation. Thank you all for your kindness and help. I am grateful and exhilarated that this book is now available to help others in the adoption process.

*A percentage of all book sales will be donated to
charitable adoption organizations.*

# Preface

It is natural for me to want to help others interested in adopting. All my life, the one thing I wanted most was to be a mother and have a house full of children. I grew up the oldest of five, so helping and caring for children was a way of life for me as long as I can remember. I have always been in awe of women who were expecting; they just seemed to glow.

Now, through my profession and my own life experience, I have been blessed to be able to see the same glow on an adoptive mother's face as she gazes at her child for the first time. At that moment, an adoptive mother could never be more beautiful. I have seen exhausted soon-to-be mothers, after spending days on an airplane, hair tussled, eyes droopy and blank, suddenly light up with that same glow the moment their eyes alight on their child. They become different beings with their new babies in their arms.

As for the adoptive father, the true daddy comes out when he knows this child is his. There seems to be an immediate letting down of his guard and then a slight rising of his guard until he is sure everything will turn out right. Most men are doing what comes naturally—protecting and wanting the best for their families and emotionally protecting their spouses.

Many adoptive parents have gone through a great deal of challenges with infertility. This can strengthen a marriage or it can tear it apart. I have seen husbands and wives distance themselves during the infertility years, unable to speak to each other about their hopes and fears. Many times, only in the privacy of my office, have I seen their true feelings of sadness, grief and loss surface. Working with couples to build their families during the adoption process can bring out the best and the worst in a relationship.

It is my fervent wish that this book will assist you during your adoption process. With the power and the knowledge of the Internet, a long and difficult journey can be made easier for you and your soon-to-be family. With all sincerity, I say, "May God bless you all."

# Introduction

## About This Book

This book is designed to give readers a safe guide to finding the resources needed to be successful in adoption. Education and knowledge are the beginning, along with a desire and openness to parent and love a child who is not biologically yours. I believe for every family wanting to adopt there is a special child for them, one conceived in their heart, rather than in their body.

So, welcome to the world of Internet adoption. With a little bit of homework, the Internet will be able to assist you in planning for your new family. The length of time involved in adopting is becoming shorter and shorter with the advent of worldwide information. This book was written with that express purpose in mind, to help you find the family you were meant to have.

That said, you must note that the Internet changes daily as new sites are added and deleted. We have worked hard to provide you with the most up-to-date information available. The main purpose of this book is to help you get started and to guide you to the help you need both on and off the Internet in the search for your child.

We have included sites we felt were helpful and omitted some sites with poor reputations or that have outdated information. In saying this, new sites will inevitably spring up that are not listed in this edition, but would be helpful in future updates. If you find a site you feel we should consider in future editions, please e-mail us at **info@carriagehousepublishing.com.** Thank you, and welcome to AdoptingOnline.com.

# 1

# Are You Ready?

A few years ago I was caring for a baby who was going to be adopted. I had him in my arms and was standing outside my church after services when Grace, a woman I knew, came up to me. She was spry and cheerful at the age of 82 and she looked at the child with shining eyes.

"Babies are so wonderful," she said. She was quiet for a time. "I wish I had known you when I was younger. I would have asked you to find a baby for me to adopt." It turned out she and her husband were unable to have children of their own.

Grace was a loving person who was always around children, so I had assumed she was a mother. But on that Sunday morning, I learned she had lived her whole life without the joy of sharing her love with a son or daughter.

It was so sad watching Grace look in wonder at the baby, while she seemed to reflect back on her life with regret; it brought tears to my eyes. She had never adopted because she was afraid to.

"We didn't know what to do or where to begin," she said. "So we never did have a baby." If only someone long ago had helped her get started on the road to adoption, she would have had her little one.

If, like Grace, you are unable to have a biological child or have always wanted to adopt and with all your heart you want to love, nurture and bring up a child, then you should set out to find yours. Fifty-five years ago there was a child out there who was meant for Grace and today there is a child waiting, or yet to be born, who is meant for you.

## The New Era of Adoption

As a facilitator of private adoptions, I have devoted 17 years of my life to bringing together prospective parents seeking a child to adopt with birth parents or guardians needing to place one. Within the past several years, I have seen the advent of the Internet and the World Wide Web transform the world of adoption.

Computers and e-mail reduce from weeks to hours the time required to prepare and transfer documents. Prospective parents go online to read the stories of waiting children and to view their photographs. Birth parents seeking a home for their child go to dozens of websites to see profiles of parents wanting to adopt.

Day and night the Internet hums with the activity of thousands of people engaged in adopting. They meet online to ask questions, discuss issues and share their hopes and fears. They network with adoption professionals such as attorneys, facilitators and social workers.

The Internet will not replace face-to-face meetings between birth mothers and adoptive parents, appointments with lawyers to sign papers, or travel to pick up your adopted child and bring him home. Nor will it replace the adoption professional at a "brick and mortar" facility who screens birth mothers, alerts you to potential fraud, prepares you for the social worker visit to your home and is with you in a moment of crisis.

But the Internet is a marvelous tool that will help you in ways you can hardly imagine. This book contains the resources and proven techniques to make the best use of this tool, to optimize your skills to realize a safe, timely and successful adoption.

## MARDIE'S STORY

# Answered Prayers

As the oldest of five children, I had one sister and three brothers in my family. I loved and helped care for them starting when I was quite young. Mothering seemed to come naturally to me and by the age of eleven, I knew that when I grew up, more than anything else, I wanted to be a mother. I collected clothes and quilted a baby blanket that I kept in a hope chest for the child I would have one day.

I fell in love with a man who also wanted to have children. Bill especially wanted to have a son he could teach to fish, ride a bicycle and play baseball. From the first days after our wedding, we set out to have a family.

The months went by, then two years passed, but no baby came. Couples all around us seemed to get pregnant without even trying. I must have gone to a dozen baby showers during those early years of our marriage. I laughed with my friends as the expectant mothers opened their gifts, but I was crying inside.

We decided to go see specialists and we discovered that we both had fertility problems. I remember the months starting in the spring of 1985 as a blur of tests and fertility drugs, another ovulation on the temperature chart, more poking and prodding, the start of one more menstrual cycle.

I came to dread holiday gatherings because of the humiliating questions. Getting dressed before one New Year's Eve party, Bill and I took bets on how many insults we'd hear that night. He said ten and that was

*(continued on next page)*

about right. The topper was when my Grandpa asked at the dinner table, "Haven't you figured out how to *do* it yet?"

"We lost that page of the manual," I said with a smile, though his words had pierced me to the bone.

Some friends I had confided in offered remedies they said had worked for people they knew. We were supposed to eat fish twice a day, make love on the night of a full moon and I was to lie on a propped up board that stood me on my head.

I started to avoid those friends and even my business associates, fearing that someone would ask when we were going to have children or if I was pregnant yet. Bill and I continued to see a specialist who was growing less hopeful. As the months passed, life did not seem so bright.

As the owner of a medium-sized manufacturing company, I had come to believe that if you wanted something bad enough, worked hard and smart enough, you could have it. But that didn't seem to help with pregnancy. As the CEO, I came to expect that, when I needed something, I could pick up the phone and have it delivered. But I could not order a baby.

In my spiritual life, I came to wonder, since I was sure that God wanted us to have children, why He had not blessed us with a family. Was I doing something wrong? I prayed for an answer and prayed for a baby.

An avid reader, I bought books on infertility and human reproduction, on infant care and early childhood development. I hoped that somehow a baby might pop up out of a book as a result of all my study.

I went to the library almost every day (there was no Internet yet) and the librarian became my friend. One morning she gave me a book on adoption. I took it over to a table and set it down. I sat in the chair and looked at its cover, but I could not bring myself to open it. I pushed it away and got on with my research into getting pregnant.

When I left the library, I set the adoption book next to me in the passenger seat of my car and took it home. Finally that night, I opened it and started to read. It was scary, because it was about 15 years out of date and written about the old ways of adopting, which seemed cold, secretive and formal. Then I read another book about modern adoption, which seemed warm, honest and comfortable.

After some really bad news from our doctor, Bill and I lay in bed one night talking. I saw that the door to adoption was opening, just as the door to making our own baby seemed to be closing shut.

Within days we decided to adopt. Right away it seemed like there was light shining into our lives again. We were excited about our future with children. Adoption was the answer to my question and to my prayers. ꩜

## Infertility

One out of every six couples in America is unable to conceive a child after trying for a year. Some will go on to have a biological child, others will not. And each year some 60,000 couples, from all walks of life, will adopt because they share a belief that their lives will not be complete without a child.

In 40 percent of couples who can't have babies, the quality of the husband's sperm is the cause. Some women have had surgery to remove reproductive organs; others have trouble carrying a baby to term. And since fertility declines with age and so many women are pursuing careers, trouble conceiving is common among those who wait to start families.

Some infertile couples will try to become pregnant by utilizing home tests to detect ovulation, by taking fertility drugs, or by going to a clinic where the husband's sperm is injected into his wife's cervix. Others will pursue more advanced treatments that use high technology to combine sperm and eggs.

The most proven method is in vitro fertilization (IVF) where eggs are drawn from the ovaries and fertilized in a lab dish with concentrated sperm. Grown for three days into tiny embryos, several are placed in the uterus. If attempted for five cycles, this will make a baby in three out of nine patients. The cost? About $15,000 per cycle.

Driven by a seemingly desperate need, some patients have spent over $150,000 on the procedure. And with the financial toll comes an emotional one as well. When embryos fail to implant or when one finally does but then, eight weeks later, an ultrasound shows that the fetus has died, it can be utterly devastating. After one such tragic IVF procedure, one woman shared in an online chat room that it was like the death of a child. "We cried and mourned the loss and I don't know if I'm over it yet. Since we couldn't afford to try again, we had to find a new dream."

## Resolving Fertility Issues

Sometimes I see people rush into adoption without taking the time to grieve the loss of the biological child they did not have. They risk sabotaging an adoption or, worse, treating an adopted child as second-best to the son or daughter they might have had.

Before you can adopt with success, you must come to terms with your infertility. For some couples this may take years. Move at your own pace but realize that you are not getting any younger and the longer you wait, the more you delay the precious time you could have with your child.

For me, coming to terms with infertility meant accepting that there was a reason for everything. I don't know why I was unable to have babies, but were it not for my infertility, I would not have adopted my wonderful son. I would not have opened an adoption center which has brought hundreds of children and parents together, changing their lives.

I have known many couples who have faced infertility and moved on quite naturally to adoption. I have known others who have edged toward it uneasily, because their dream of having a biological child meant so much to them.

Before you are ready to adopt, you have to know the answer to this question: Do you want to be a parent or do you want to have a biological child?

Without resolving this issue, you run the risk that you will back out and break the heart of a birth mother. You may *settle* for adoption, but this you cannot do, because the child deserves to have parents who love and cherish him as the most precious thing on earth.

We recommend at our center that if you have unresolved issues about infertility you should seek counseling before you adopt. You may choose to put adoption aside and press on with treatment until you have exhausted all medical options. Then, when you return to take up adoption, you may find, as many people do, that the adoption process is less stressful than conceiving through medical technology.

If you are not sure that you can accept a child who will not inherit your genes, it may help you to talk with other adoptive parents or a counselor. We are still amazed by the traits and characteristics that parents pass on to their adopted children. Will science ever explain what we have seen? Like the adopted daughter whose hair and skin color change so she looks just like her mother. Or the son who has the same walk as his adoptive father, the same crinkling of his eyes when he laughs.

Families created through adoption are true families. After adoption you are a parent and your child will depend on you for his needs, both physical and emotional. All the joys and heartaches any parent experiences will be yours. You will be Mom and Dad.

## MARDIE'S STORY

# A Mother's Nose

Russ and Julie Connor were in their mid-forties and looked much older than the first time I saw them, two years before, when they first came to our center to inquire about adopting.

Now they were ready, Russ told me, after spending $60,000 on infertility treatments, trying but failing to conceive. The greatest cost, it occurred to me, was to their relationship. They had seemed so loving before and now they seemed edgy with each other.

Within months we located a beautiful birth mother named Sarah who chose them to adopt her unborn child. The Connors met with her several times and they really got along. Sarah thought they were just perfect for her baby.

Late one afternoon, as I was setting my desk straight and preparing to go home, Julie showed up. She seemed anxious. There was something she wanted to say.

We talked for a little while about how healthy Sarah looked and how happy she was. "She's a great person," said Julie. "Very engaging and all."

"I knew you'd like each other."

"Yes," she hesitated. "But we're declining her offer."

This is a decision that adoptive parents, once matched and after bonding with a birth mother, cannot take lightly. A birth mother is having a tough enough time. She finds the parents she wants and is so relieved, then comes this, like a bolt from the blue.

I asked Julie to explain, but she was evasive.

"Come on," I said at last. "What's really going on here?"

"Well," she answered. "It's her nose."

"Her nose?"

"That's right," she said. "We don't like Sarah's nose."

I was incredulous. I'd seen her nose. She had a cute little nose. I didn't know what to say.

Julie sat down in a chair. "Seeing Sarah pregnant like that, I don't know, it stirred up some feelings. I always wanted to be pregnant. Russ and I always wanted to have our own baby."

She looked away and choked back tears. "I want to be pregnant, Mardie. We're going back to Dr. Lewis and try again."

I went straight to Sarah's house. She cried when I told her. She loved the Connors and they had broken her heart.

From home I called the wife of another couple. They had three sons and wanted to adopt a daughter. After a miscarriage, she had become pregnant again, only to carry the baby for eight months before it died. She had known for a week that she'd have to deliver a still born girl.

I knew for certain that this couple had resolved their fertility issues. When I told the new adoptive mother about Sarah and her baby, who we knew was a girl, she was thrilled.

It took time for Sarah to get over the Connors but she did. In the hospital, just before going into labor, she said, "This new family we found was just made in heaven." ☜☞

## Infertility Treatment While Adopting

Many agencies will accept prospective adoptive parents into their programs while they are trying to get pregnant through infertility treatments, though some will ask that you discontinue it. In independent adoptions, those generally handled by attorneys and facilitators, you can usually pursue medical treatment while you are adopting.

At our center, we provide prospective parents with the opportunity to "freeze" their contract for up to nine months in case of emergency or for personal reasons in some cases. This means, for example, that they can change their minds about adopting and return to infertility treatments. Then, they can come back to adopt without additional charges. Some couples have frozen contracts because they became pregnant. After having the baby, they have gone on to adopt a sibling for their biological child.

If you wish to start an adoption plan and still try to have a baby through medical treatment, find an adoption professional who will allow you to put your contract on hold if you conceive.

## Fear of Adopting

If you have tried to adopt before and something went wrong, remember that it was not an indication that something was wrong with you, with the birth mother or with your adoption professional. Adoption is a complex process fraught with emotion. Sometimes circumstances spin out of control.

Learn what you can from your experience and keep looking for the child who is uniquely yours. If you stop your search because of a setback, you may miss out forever on the joy and love of your child. The bottom line is: Never give up.

I have had a few birth mothers who, during the pregnancy or after the birth, have decided not to place a child. But the prospective parents did not give up and it didn't take long for me to match them with another birth mother.

At my urging they tried not to project their fears of what happened before onto the next adoption. But some couldn't help themselves. If they didn't hear from the birth mother after a week or so, they'd say, "Oh my God, she's changed her mind."

In a few cases it became a self-fulfilling prophecy. One adoptive mother, Barbara, was so afraid that her birth mother Christie would disappear that she moved her into an apartment near her house and came to check on her at least once a day.

Christie e-mailed me. "This chick is too weird," she said. "I'm outta here."

If you have had a bad experience, which you haven't resolved, you should discuss this with your adoption professional until you realize that this particular case of failed adoption is isolated and you can move on to the next one with confidence.

In Barbara's case, I was able to explain that after screening and counseling her new birth mother, we were certain from years of experience that any risk of a reclaim was minimal. Barbara's fears diminished, she relaxed and the adoption was successful.

## Love Is the Reason

Some parents who have already raised children still have an abundance of love and energy to give. Conception is possible, though not likely, and it could be risky to the mother or the child, so they choose to adopt.

Some people adopt because they wish to give homes to children with special needs. Whatever the apparent reason people choose to adopt, underlying it is a deep, heartfelt wish to be parents, to share their home, their family and their lives with children.

# How to Succeed

- Learn all you can from books and the Internet about adoption and parenting. You may never again do something so important.

- Write out a clear and logical adoption plan: Decide which type of adoption is best. Review and revise your plan as you pursue your goal of adopting a child.

- Don't become obsessed: Shut down your Internet computer at a reasonable hour. Get your rest, eat well and take time to appreciate your life.

- Be realistic and honest when you evaluate your finances and work out your adoption budget.

- Be diligent in taking care of each job your adoption professional asks you to do.

- Be calm each time you face another stack of paperwork.

- Assess your emotional readiness, and that of your family, to adopt.

- This can be a stressful time for your children. They need their mom and dad. Tuck them in at night; tell them how much you love them.

- Be patient, remembering that it takes nine months to have a baby the old-fashioned way and your adoptive child may not even be conceived for months.

- Be prepared for the process to take several years if your specific requirements for a child limit the number who will become available to you.

- Get involved, online and in real life, with other adopting families for emotional support, to enhance your parenting skills and the quality of your adoption experience.

- Use the Internet to network with people who can help you in a big way.

- To relieve stress, visualize holding your child in your arms, knowing that when you actually do, your fears and anxiety will drift away.

- Know that adopting is like being pregnant. A wife may experience hormonal changes and both partners may experience fears and sleepless nights.

- Lean on each other and share the vision of your child out there. Your love will grow as you work together to realize your dream.

- Pray.

- You wouldn't stop searching for a child lost in the forest, so do not give up on finding your adopted child. ෨෨

# 2

# Adopting Online

The Internet has changed the way adoptions are done and the way people communicate and move information across the country and even across town. An adoption professional without a presence on the Internet will, most likely, be online soon. More and more people are becoming reliant on the computer as an information highway and soon, more people than ever will have a computer in their home.

In the past several years I have seen the adoption community develop a substantial presence on the Internet. It has connected adoptive parents to agencies and facilitators, lawyers and social workers. It has created a thriving online community of adoption professionals and enthusiasts. Without the Internet, many thousands of families would not have found the children who have made each of their lives wonderfully complete.

You can use the Internet to navigate through the process of adoption, to find resources and to connect with people who will become involved in your adoption. With a click of your mouse, you can access a thousand sites offering a wealth of information. Non-profit groups use the Internet to educate the public about adoption. Agencies and other adoption professionals use it to publicize the services they provide. In online chat rooms and forums, prospective adoptive parents freely discuss their frustrations while parents who have successfully adopted share their knowledge.

# Things to Do on the Web

- Scroll through photos of waiting children at **http://www.adopt.org**

- Visit a chat group to see what the members with infertility concerns are saying at **http://www.fertilethoughts.com**

- Point your browser to **http://www.adopting.com** to see some of the lawyers, facilitators, agencies and social workers who can help you.

- Subscribe to an adoption newsletter at **http://www.lifetimeadoption.com/newsletter/lta.html**

- View birth mothers discussing matters such as the kind of adoptive parents they are seeking at **http://www.abcadoptions.com**

- Locate a real-life adoption support group in your area on a website like **http://www.adoptivefamilies.com/support_group.php**

- Get information about placing a child for adoption on websites like **http://www.openadoption.com**

- See profiles of adoptive parents as presented by a facilitator at **http://www.adoptiontree.com**

- Read *Dear Birth Mother* letters from adoptive families who have created their own websites; enter the words and characters "dear birth mother" into the **http://www.google.com** search engine to find more.

- See how to book flights, reserve rental cars and hotel rooms at **http://www.hotwire.com, http://www.federaltravel.com** or **http://www.trip.com** for your trip to bring home your adopted child.

Internet zone

## Faster, Better, Less Costly

In the old days, before the Internet, I helped adoptive parents compose what we call a profile. It includes photographs, telling potential birth mothers why they would make great parents, small paragraphs describing their home, their hobbies and even their pets. We had the profiles printed up, then mailed them out to prospective birth parents, doctors and counselors or others who might know of a birth parent placing a child for adoption.

Some adopting families still prepare their own two-page profiles and *Dear Birth Mother* letters the old way. They pay for printing, postage, mailing lists, labels and envelopes. They spend hours assembling, folding, stuffing and affixing. Finally mailed, the profiles slowly progress, and, once arriving at their destination, most get tossed in the trash.

On occasion, the mailing works because it takes just one birth mother to respond and get matched with an adoptive family. But most of the time it generates a few leads that go nowhere. The cost? About $4,000.

At our center, we advise clients to save this money for their adopted child's college fund. Our staff helps write the profiles and we have a designer prepare them on the computer. Then we upload these Dear Birth Mother letters to our website at **http://www.lifetimeadoption.com** for thousands of birth mothers to see. Doing it the Internet way gets more responses than we ever saw from a postal service mailing and it costs thousands less.

## The Information Highway

The Internet, as studied by the Pew Research Center in Washington, D.C., has been embraced faster than any other technology and was evolving by the year 2001 into a standard household appliance like the telephone. By June of 2002, in equal numbers of men and women, more than 104 million Americans had access to the Internet.

> ### Internet Quick Start
> • Find an Internet service provider such as AOL, MSN, Earthlink, etc.
> • Get instructions from your service provider and install your Internet connection.
> • Go online and set up your adoption homepage.
> • Become familiar with your search engines. You can use Yahoo, Google, Ask Jeeves, or MSN.
> • Begin to search using familiar adoption terms.

At the time of this writing, more than 60 million Americans are logging on each day. Eight of ten users say they connect with people in groups who share their concerns. Women in particular say they use e-mail to cultivate relationships with friends and family. A Pew survey in 2002 found that 78 percent of users go to the Net for medical information and most of them said their research had influenced family medical decisions.

## Raised on the Internet

Younger members of Generation X and virtually all those in Generation Y are online. These are people who were born, according to demographers, between 1978 and 1994. At this writing, that's 60 million young people between the ages of 9 and 25 who are surfing the web. They chat with friends at http://www.neonteen.com, research school papers using the http://www.dogpile.com search engine and buy prom dresses at http://www.go-girl.com.

When faced with a crisis, like an unplanned pregnancy, a teenager often turns first to the Internet. She visits with others in her circumstance at a website like http://web.icq.com/channels/lifestyles/events/pregnancy and if she chooses to place her child for adoption, she can visit hundreds of sites like http://www.adoptiontree.com or http://www.resource4women.com to find profiles and photographs of couples seeking birth mothers.

---

email

To:
Cc:

# What Can I Do with E-mail?

- Quickly transfer papers and documents.

- Receive newsletters and other writings on adopting.

- View the photograph of a waiting child sent within minutes from your agency, facilitator or attorney.

- Correspond with the network of helpful people you meet online.

- Expedite the transfer of forms and legal documents with electronic signatures.

- Use encrypted email to correspond in confidence with a birth mother.

- Take your new child's picture with a digital camera and send it in minutes to family and friends nearby or far away.

*(continued on next page)*

**What Can I Do with E-mail? (cont.)**

• Get confirmations of rental car, airline and hotel reservations.

• Dispatch updates with one click of your mouse to a group list of friends and family back home when traveling to pick up your new child! ☯

## Your Competitive Edge

According to market analysts, the population of Internet surfers is growing at the rate of 2.6 million new users each month. Still, many who are setting out to adopt are not yet online. They will each find their child, but those who skillfully use the Internet will likely find theirs sooner. Using the Internet with the strategies and resources of this book will give you more leverage and opportunity than other adoptive parents have yet discovered the old fashioned way.

## The Internet Whirlwind

People today don't want to wait four or five years to adopt. Most families are on budgets, some large, others modest, and the methods of traditional adoption use up a lot of time and money. With the Internet you can acquire knowledge and can network with other people more efficiently and for far less money.

But beware of this irony: it's easy to get caught up and spun around in the whirlwind of technology. At the speed of streaming electrons, the

Internet can connect you to resources throughout the world. While you sit in your chair at home it can bring you together with people who share your special interests and concerns. It gives you access to a database of information so massive that not even science fiction writers can imagine it all. And it can be a bit overwhelming.

## The Greatest Database on Earth

Enter a string of precise words like "adoption parental relinquishment rights Wyoming" into a search engine, because, let's say, you have found a potential birth mother in that state. Your search will turn up a hundred or so Web pages, including one with an article explaining how many hours the mother has after the birth to change her mind.

If you do a search and many hundreds or thousands of pages come up, do it again, using more and more precise terms until your results are manageable.

Also, study the tips for better searching at the website of the engine you prefer. You'll find a list with direct links to many search engines at **http://www.thefrontpage.com/search**. With practice and patience you'll find the jewels of information you seek and you'll be astounded at the power of your fingertips on the keyboard. ෨

## Internet Strategy

Before using the Internet to adopt, spend some valuable time thinking about what will get the results you want in your unique search for a child.

## Top Ten Search Engines

The editors at http://www.
12c4.com/hotcool/search.htm
selected and ranked each search
engine by testing its speed, ease
of navigation, the clarity of its
interface and the depth of
results. They only chose websites that are widely used, have
longevity online and retain
adequate staff to keep them
running well.

1. http://www.altavista.com
2. http://www.teoma.com
3. http://www.askjeeves.com
4. http://www.alltheweb.com
5. http://www.dogpile.com
6. http://www.google.com
7. http://www.looksmart.com
8. http://www.MSN.com
9. http://www.yahoo.com
10. http://www.lycos.com

Take time to carefully consider the hundreds of options that appear on your
computer screen. Be prepared to stop
and turn back if you sense that you've
invested too much effort in following links
on a detour or to a place where you really didn't want to go.

Your success in using the Internet as a
tool for adopting will depend on the quality and consistency of your efforts and on
your willingness to make changes as you
go along.

I can tell you with certainty, after participating in hundreds of online adoptions,
that one key is networking: finding people
who can help you and cultivating your
relationships with them, by email at first,
later by telephone and letters. By using
the Net effectively, some families will be
able to adopt within months! For some it
will take two years (about half the time of
the old way) because you can't always
rush to find the child meant for you.

# Scenes from a Chat Room

The Internet was born when Department of Defense researchers linked computers at six universities in 1969, sending out the message, "Are you receiving this?" As more research centers connected up, the scientists were soon e-mailing each other about personal matters. Among them was a group of science fiction buffs who wrote software that sent the messages to a mailing list. They formed SF-LOVERS, the first *virtual community*.

Today, at thousands of web forums and chat rooms, people with common interests gather. They study the Bible, debate politics, talk about new treatments for male infertility and more. What a fantastic development this is! Before the Internet, a woman might not find a support group to help her cope with infertility. Today, she can go online to share her feelings. In the Adoption Hotlinks *(See Adoption Hotlinks)* section at the back of this book are dozens of websites where people discuss issues related to adoption. Here's a sample of the support you will find online.

Carol: I've been having doubts lately. Not about the adoption itself. We love children and can't wait, but doubts about, I don't know. I'm not sure what I'm feeling. Maybe it's hormonal or because I'm about to turn 40. On most days I'm so excited and it feels right. Other days, I'm not sure. Sometimes I think we're already blessed with what we have, and maybe we should leave things the way they are, especially when seeing friends who are divorced with kids.

*(continued on next page)*

Internet zone

## Scenes from a Chat Room (cont.)

Terri: We were older when we adopted. I'm 43 now and my husband is 52 and our adopted child is two. Our oldest daughter, who I had before my hysterectomy, is in second grade and our age doesn't matter to her at all. Maybe it helps that I have friends who had kids late in life and my own mother was 42 with my dad six years older. I was a teenager at the time and, thinking back on it, the age of our parents was not something we kids thought about. I can't imagine what it would be like, just me and my husband, without our adopted daughter. I think what you are feeling is normal; like part of the waiting, the anxiety that comes from waiting.

Jennifer: When it got closer to the due date for our birth mother and the day our baby Matthew would come to live with us, I was so nervous that I almost called it off. It's scary. It's something that changes your life forever. It didn't help that I was getting real tired of the adoption thing. I was so afraid the birth mother would change her mind and take him back. Then, after he finally did come home, I had post-adoption depression for about two months! We had waited so long and then I was like, okay, now what? I agree with Terri. These are emotions everybody seems to go through. It was like the feelings I had with infertility, of not letting myself get totally excited for fear it wasn't going to work out.

Sherri: We've been waiting for eight months and I have days when I think it will never happen. I just keep busy, because I don't want to focus on the waiting; I have our dogs to take care of; we have church activities and have people over for dinner. I'm even taking lessons to learn how to play the harp. Sometimes I wonder, *What will I do when*

## Scenes from a Chat Room (cont.)

*I don't have to wait? How will I like giving up these activities I've made the center of my life? My priority must be the baby. That's when I think, I can't do this!*

Valerie: I knew we were ready to adopt because we were confident and relaxed about parenting. My husband had a daughter from his first marriage we were raising. Of course I never had to deal with poopy diapers and late night feedings, but I even like that part of it. I don't mean to say that I had it all together. We went through two years of infertility treatments and that was making me depressed. At one point we were thinking, oh, well, we'll be fine without a baby. But we knew we wouldn't be. And when we decided on adoption, I was less stressed-out than I was with all the tests and procedures. So, anyway, I'm a mommy now. We just celebrated Brittany's adoption day. Don't give up now! ∞

Internet zone

## MARDIE'S STORY

# Julie's Choice

Julie had to get out of Coldwater, Kansas, before the townsfolk found out she was pregnant.

Her fiancé, Daniel, who helped get her into her predicament, had told her that he would marry her right away and help raise their first

*(continued on next page)*

child if she decided to keep the baby. "Whatever choice you make," he said, "I'll be there with you."

Daniel was a comfort to have around because Julie had rarely felt calm since the first days after she missed her period and from the morning the dot in her home pregnancy test turned pink. When she looked in the mirror she didn't see a glow, that's for sure, only worry and stress on her face.

Her best friend and roommate in the apartment they shared while attending junior college had pressured her to get an abortion. For days and through some tearful hours, Julie and Dan considered this option. But they could not abort the little person growing inside of her.

Julie kept her secret even from her mother though she hated having to lie. To see a doctor, she had to sneak away and drive 75 miles to Dodge City since her aunt was the office nurse for the only obstetrician in town. Now Julie was starting to show. She knew that somebody would notice and then the gossip would start.

"What am I going to do?" she asked, sobbing.

She was on the phone with me and crying hysterically. She had seen our website and had called our 800 number. She had contracted with our center to find an adoptive family for her unborn baby. I had talked with her several times.

"Let's keep looking for a family," I said. "Then maybe things will work out and you'll feel better."

She wanted a Christian couple with at least one child so her baby would have a sibling. She was on her computer in her apartment in Coldwater while, on her second line, she spoke with me by phone in California.

As we talked, we were both viewing the same website where prospective adoptive parents had posted their profiles.

"I don't really like this mother," said Julie. "She looks, I don't know, kind of, too stern or something."

"Okay," I answered. "Click down and over to the next family, Peg and Dale."

She took a look. "Oh, they're really cute," she said. "Their daughter is precious and look what a cute little dog."

Later that day, Daniel came over to Julie's apartment. Sitting with him at the computer, they went back to the website together to read the *Dear Birth Mother* letter from Peg and Dale. They were one of several couples Julie wanted to interview, and, as it turned out, the one she chose. Soon a match was made.

By e-mail, we sent Julie the required paperwork. She printed it out and went over it with an attorney in Dodge City. She sent us a medical release and proof of pregnancy. She faxed these documents and the signed papers to our office.

We advised her to utilize counseling to deal with the emotions of placing her baby because we sensed it might be difficult for her. But she couldn't risk seeing a counselor in her hometown. So we arranged for one to talk with her by phone.

In the era of open adoption and the Internet, for every case like Julie's, we have ten where the pregnancy of an unwed woman is not cloaked in secrecy or shame. Far from it. Young expecting women go online with their mothers, boyfriends or just plain friends looking for adoptive parents. They e-mail profiles to grandparents asking, "How do you like this family?" The birth and the adoption are well planned events.

*(continued on next page)*

For Julie, we found a family in a state where laws allow certain reimbursements to birth mothers. Peg and Dale agreed to help keep the pregnancy secret from the folks in Coldwater. They flew Julie to their city and found her an apartment near doctors and close to the hospital where she would give birth. Julie told her mother, family and friends that she was accepting an internship as part of her college studies.

Daniel shipped Julie her computer. Each day, she logged onto the distance learning center at the college, reading lectures, taking tests online and e-mailing in research papers. She didn't lose a single credit and kept up her grades.

Once the baby was born and she saw him settled in with the adoptive family, she moved back to Coldwater without regrets and went on with her life.

Only a few short years ago, a woman in her shoes was limited to placing her child through agencies located in her county and the baby was, more than likely, placed with a family that lived nearby. The whole town would learn of her pregnancy and as the birth mother's privacy was shattered, any wishes she might have for her baby were ignored. Now, with the help of the Internet and open adoptions all of this has changed. ೧

# 3

# Frequently Asked Questions

The weather was blustery and cold. Rain was coming down in sheets as my husband Bill and I hurried across the dark street to an old brick building downtown.

It was early in January 1985. After months of hesitating, we had committed to adopting and I was scared to death. I didn't know where to start, who to see or what to ask. I just wanted a baby to hold in my arms.

I had looked in the yellow pages under adoption (as there was no Internet yet) and, on this Wednesday night, we ended up at an adoption agency for an orientation meeting.

We entered the conference room and settled into chairs around tables that faced each other. I pushed wet hair away from my face and looked around. I counted at least 30 people who had come out on this stormy night. *Are there really this many couples in our town wanting to adopt?* I wondered.

The others, with notebooks in hand, seemed as anxious as we were, except for one really attractive couple. *They'll probably get chosen right away,* I thought. *They seem so much younger than we do.* I was going on 30 at the time and my husband was 39.

But the oldest person in the room was the woman who stood up to give the presentation. She had the look of someone who had lived a stressful life and an attitude that clearly told us that she did not want to be there.

She spoke without a hint of compassion in her voice. "The children available now are older and in foster care," she informed us. "If you want a Caucasian newborn, you'll have to wait four to seven years."

But we wanted a *baby* and so did others; I could tell by the murmur in the room and the shifting of chairs. Some people asked questions that challenged the woman's assertions, but she was unmoved.

"This is the only way you can adopt from us," she said. "Are you interested or not?"

*What?* I thought. *No discussion, no options? No creative ways to work something out?*

"Four to seven years for a newborn," she repeated.

Then she looked coldly at Bill and me.

"By then, some of you will be too old to adopt an infant. You should really consider an older child."

My heart sank and I looked away from her. I don't remember much about the meeting after that and soon it was over. We went back out into the rain to our car and drove home in silence. Inside the house, I threw the agency application packet on the living room table, then went upstairs to bed and cried myself to sleep.

The next morning at breakfast, Bill and I decided that we would not give up. By the weekend we had started *networking*, talking to and connecting with anyone with adoption experiences, in church and at work, in the grocery store and at the bank. Wherever we went, we talked about our hope to adopt a newborn baby.

Soon we had organized a support group of people who were just getting started with adoption. Some, like us, had been turned down by an agency because they were too old, had been married before or failed to meet other strict requirements.

At one of our meetings, a member of our group told us she'd met a professional in town called a facilitator who helped prospective parents find birth mothers, women who are pregnant and choosing adoption for their children. "Denise is skilled in the new ways of adopting," she said.

The next day, Bill and I went to her office in the suburbs. We found Denise to be a warm and caring person and an adoptive mother herself. She believed that the mother who gave birth to the child we would adopt should have some say in choosing the parents. She looked at us and smiled. "Most of these mothers won't think you're too old," she said. "They'll think you're just right."

She helped us write a *Dear Birth Mother* letter, our profile that told all about us and how much we would love the child we hoped to adopt. We attached our photograph to each of these profiles, and then Bill and I started handing them out to anyone who might know of a pregnant young woman wanting to place a baby for adoption.

Within three months, several birth mothers asked if they could meet with us. We especially liked Karen and she liked us. Thoughtful and kind, she was a single mom with a young child; given her circumstances, she felt it would be unfair to the child if she tried to raise another one. She wanted a father in the home and adoptive parents who could give the baby the good life and Christian upbringing she hoped for. Before long Karen gave birth to our wonderful son Cory, the child meant for us.

I decided to devote my life to bringing birth mothers and adoptive parents together, and, in 1986, I founded an adoption organization, later incorporated as the Lifetime Adoption Center. Using what I had learned through personal experience, and as I facilitated one adoption after another, I developed plans and methods for open adoption which increased the likelihood of success.

In 1993 a software engineer in Santa Clara, California, showed me a new computer program called Mosaic. He called it a *browser* and he used it to navigate a new and evolving system on the Internet known as the World Wide Web.

On the screen was the page of a document he'd downloaded from a computer at Stanford University. In the text were some words underlined in blue, *hypertext links* to related documents. He clicked on one of these and it took us to the page in the file of a computer at Carnegie Mellon University. On the screen I saw a photograph appearing.

*Photographs*, I marveled, *from a computer in Pittsburgh.* It dawned on me: *We could post pictures of prospective families for potential birth mothers anywhere in the country to see!*

In 1997, I put up our first website and birth mothers started to find us. They called on our hotline or e-mailed asking how to contact prospective adoptive families whose photographs and profiles they had seen online.

Because of our early presence on the Web and the large number of people visiting our site daily, the center grew at a rapid clip. By 2003 our team had grown to 15 employees. In 17 years we had completed over 1,000 adoptions.

Thousands of people considering adoption visited our site. Many of them e-mailed our staff asking how to get started and what to expect. I made a list of the most frequently asked questions and present them here, along with the answers of course.

# E-mail Questions and Answers

*Why them and not us? My wife and I have been waiting to adopt a newborn for almost three years now. Meanwhile, two of the couples in our support group have already found a baby, one after only six months.*

From across the room I can spot couples who will be matched with a birth mother sooner rather than later. They have absolutely resolved any infertility issues and they have made adoption the focus of their life. They are not remodeling or shopping for a new car. They are diligently searching for their child. They are organized and resourceful; they are proactive.

I remember one such couple, Dave and Leslie. They showed up at our new prospective parents meeting with the photographs for their profiles already taken. Dave asked what they should do next. I started going down the list. The writing of their profile was done, ready for posting on the website, and they had already seen their attorney. So I suggested they do the paperwork to get ready for their home study.

"Oh, that's finished," said Leslie. So I advised them to go ahead and contact a social worker to do their home study. Leslie looked at me matter-of-factly. "She's coming over to the house on Tuesday," she said.

Dave and Leslie were several months ahead of the others, and that much closer to finding their baby.

### How long will it take us to adopt?

It depends on your circumstances, the type of adoption you choose and the effort you make. Normally it takes less time to adopt an older waiting child, a biracial or special needs infant than to adopt a healthy baby. Rarely will you find a healthy newborn in a public agency, unless you are fortunate enough to find one through a fost-adopt program. The swiftest way to adopt a healthy baby is through an independent adoption and to work alongside an adoption attorney or facilitator in your search for a birth mother, doing additional advertising (if allowed in your state) and networking on your own. By doing so, you should expect in most cases, to adopt a child within four months to two years.

### What is closed adoption?

Around 1950, when laws in every state sealed the records of adoption, including the child's birth certificate, nearly all adoptions in this country were closed. The birth mother had no contact with the child. The adopting parents typically pretended the child was biologically their own. Psychologists advised parents not to tell the child he or she was adopted. There's more about this at **http://www.openadoption.com/history.html**.

The worst aspects of the old ways, like the deceit, are mostly gone. Though even today, closed adoptions are still practiced by some agencies. The birth mother relinquishes to the agency her rights to the child. Agency social workers choose the adoptive parents and little or no information is exchanged.

### What is open adoption?

This is where the birth mother meets the adoptive parents and participates in the placement of the child. The birth mother relinquishes all legal rights to the child, of course, but she retains the right to have some future contact. It can be as minimal as an exchange of Christmas cards or as extensive as phone calls or even visits with the child and adoptive family. As a general rule, open adoption is better for the birth mother, for the child and for the adoptive family. See articles on the origin and purpose of open adoption at **http://www.openadoption.com**.

### Why is open adoption good for adoptive parents?

Knowledge about the birth mother, when the child is old enough to ask about her, is better for the child's emotional well-being. Moreover, contact with the birth mother provides you with medical information.

Five years ago we completed an adoption where the adoptive parents agreed to exchange letters and photographs with the birth mother but never made any effort to stay in touch with her. Their adopted son needed a bone marrow transplant and the doctors were searching for a match. Their best hope was the biological mother but she had moved and the adoptive parents couldn't find her. If that birth mother had known that this child needed her, she would have come on the next plane. To see the sort of contact adoptive parents have agreed to, visit http://www.americanadoptionlaw.com.

### Will the Internet end closed adoptions?

In the Internet era, a young pregnant woman goes online when trying to decide between abortion, parenting the baby or choosing adoption. She finds a website with profiles of prospective parents seeking newborns. She sees one family living in upstate New York on a horse ranch and she says, "Hey, I'm into horses and I want parents who can teach the child to ride."

And the one agency in town tells her she can't choose the family?

Not anymore. She has options now. She goes to the Web and finds another agency, an attorney or a facilitator who will match her with the adoptive parents she wants.

### What is the percentage of adoptions that go wrong?

Producers at the Hallmark channel once called the attorney who does legal work for our center and asked him if he had adoption stories they could use. They wanted conflict, trouble and drama. "I don't have any like that," he said. "Do you want to tell one of our usual heartwarming stories?"

They weren't interested.

Instead of reporting on the vast majority of adoptions that succeed every year, the media reports sensational cases. For a while I researched the failed adoption cases that were in the newspapers and on television. In each case, red flags were flying, which adoption professionals or adoptive parents failed to see, like matching a family to an emotionally unstable birth mother who was asking for a great deal of money. In the cases I reviewed, some of the parties did not have all the facts, some were dishonest and others were outright fraudulent.

But these cases, and those dramatized by the scriptwriters, are extremely rare. Better than 90 percent of adoptions are finalized quietly and happily without difficulty.

### Will my birth mother want her child back?

I hear this all the time. I am amazed that so many people think the birth mother can come back during the child's life and reclaim the child. This is not true. If the adoption is legal (no fraud and no duress), then it is irrevocable.

However, for a period of time after the birth, as set by state law, the biological mother may decline to sign papers relinquishing parental rights to her child, an act known as *reclaim*. In Washington State she has 48 hours, in California, 30 days, and in some states, six months.

So reclaim is a possibility, but it doesn't happen as often as it's presented, or rather, as it's *sensationalized* by the media. It is very unlikely to happen if the birth mother has emotional support from her family, the adoptive parents, an adoption professional or a counselor. It rarely happens when a birth mother is confident in her decision to give her child, through adoption, the promise of a better life.

### Can you do anything to prevent reclaims?

Adoption professionals watch for red flags indicating that a birth mother is at risk of reclaim. Our vigilance starts with the screening of potential birth mothers. We can often spot one who fits the profile of a woman who will be unable to relinquish her child. We also know the questions to ask so we can really find out what a birth mother wants in adoptive parents. A good match and a good relationship between them reduces the risk.

The rate of reclaim varies and precise numbers are hard to come by. Some sources report rates as low as 3 percent, others as high as 15 percent. A qualified professional who properly screens, monitors and provides counseling for birth mothers should have a reclaim rate of around 6 percent.

We know how hard it is on adoptive parents when a birth mother has this change of heart and reclaims. We work hard to prevent it but we cannot predict all outcomes. Sometimes we see a red flag prior to the placement and it goes through. Other times we are surprised by a reclaim. If it happens to you, take some time off until you are ready to start again. Visit one of the support groups at **http://www.abcadoptions.com/boards.htm**. If you don't give up, you will find your child because nine out of ten adoptions do succeed.

# Birth Mother E-mail

To: Lifetime Adoption
From: Birth Mothers
Subject: Considering Adoption

Mardie:

I am 17 years old and have decided on giving my two-week-old daughter, Kelsey, up for adoption. I love her so much, with all my heart, but I am too financially unstable to give her the kind of care she deserves. I don't have a phone at all, so I'm hoping we could communicate with each other via e-mail. Thank you. —Ashley

Hi Mardie!

My name is Emily. I am like three months pregnant and considering adoption. I am 14 so it would be kind of difficult to raise a baby at the moment. I make A's and B's in school. I have blonde hair and brown eyes. The father of my baby has brown hair and blue eyes. He is 17 years old. We have known each other for three years and have been boyfriend/girlfriend for almost a year.

We are very truthful with each other. He knows about me being pregnant and he supports me in whatever I decide to do. We don't do drugs or drink alcohol. He is the only one I have ever had sex with and I am the only one that he has ever had sex with. I have told you a bit about me and I am very interested in hearing from you. I check my e-mail like every day so I will write you as soon as I get an e-mail from you. Feel free to ask me anything you are curious about. I don't mind at all. —Emily

## Birth Mother E-mail (cont.)

Dear Mardie,

I am not quite ready to give my phone number. I am very nervous. I am 27 with blonde hair and blue eyes, in very good physical condition, very conscious of nutrition. I've never used drugs or tobacco. I am a single mother of two beautiful, healthy boys, age three and six. I am also three months pregnant.

The birth father and I lived together for five months until he violated his parole when he assaulted my children. He is once again incarcerated. Being together again will never happen because my children and I are scared of him.

I live in a small, low-income apartment, work full time and go to school. I am almost finished with my AA degree and my dream is to have a Masters in psychology. I am working hard at just caring for the children I have and am afraid that a baby would be impossible for me now.

I would want this child to grow up with strong Christian values. I hardly make much money but am sending my two children to a Christian school. I would love to have any sort of contact with this child in the years ahead. Although no longer mine, I want to offer the connection of love so this child never questions why he or she was given to adoption.

I cried when I read the profile of Ken and Patricia on your website. I thought of the life that I cannot give this child. I thought of the opportunities I never had growing up.

I want the best for the children that I have and for the one who has not been born yet. I would love to see my child have such wonderful opportunities as a couple like Ken and Patricia could give. Please e-mail me back. I am due in June. —Sandra ❧

*Should birth mothers have counseling?*

A qualified and caring professional should offer this service. Their staff members will establish and maintain a relationship with the birth mother throughout her pregnancy. They will monitor her prenatal care, her emotional state and provide her with counseling if she is open to it.

At our center we consider a birth mother's social, emotional and medical needs:

- **Does she have someone to support her—a friend, family member, husband or boyfriend?**
- **Is she emotionally prepared for the separation from the child?**
- **Is she healthy and keeping appointments with her doctor?**

For insight into the birth mother's emotional needs, see **http://www. resource4women.com** and just imagine her feelings at the time of the birth. For months this child has been growing under her heart. Then she gives birth and the baby is no longer a part of her. She is not doing what comes naturally, not nursing and holding the baby who has gone off with the adoptive parents. This is a difficult time for her. At such a moment she may desperately need support and counseling.

*What do birth mothers look for in adoptive parents?*

It depends. It might be someone with pets, a mother who can stay at home, a parent with a college degree. Birth mothers want to know what's in the heart of an adopting parent. Most want a loving, stable family life for the child, parents in a good marriage and a secure relationship. They look for a safe home and parents who can live a full and active life with the child. Some want an extended family, grandparents and aunts and uncles who will accept the child with open arms.

## MARDIE'S STORY

# The Cookie Mom

Mona and Dan lived in the High Desert of Nevada with their son Jake who was four years old. They had adopted him through a state agency two years before and wanted to adopt again, so they called me.

Full-figured with her strawberry blonde hair cut short, Mona was outgoing and had a great smile. Dan was slender and handsome but, unlike his wife, was quiet and shy. Both were in their early thirties, neither had finished high school. Don worked as a mechanic, Mona as a stay-at-home Mom.

Our center started working on their profile. One photograph for the Web page was of them standing with their son Jake in front of their neat double-wide modular home surrounded by sand, sagebrush and cactus.

I got to know them pretty well. They lived a simple and unhurried life centered on their home and family. They rarely went on vacation trips and their extended family consisted of some friends who lived hundreds of miles away.

Mona and Dan worried that their profile wouldn't stack up to those they'd seen of other adopting parents who had college degrees, a lot of money, big houses and lawns, grandparents nearby and Hawaiian vacations planned.

I asked Dan if there was anything special about Mona.

"There is one thing," he said.

"What's that?"

"Well, she's famous for her chocolate chip cookies. They're made from a secret recipe."

*(continued on next page)*

Mona blushed and waved her hand in the air.

"Oh those old things," she laughed.

In the profile we wrote that her cookies were the best around those parts. One month later Mona and Dan were chosen by a pregnant birth mother named Sarah who told me that the cookies were the thing that had first appealed to her.

She imagined her child coming home from school to chocolate chip cookies fresh from the oven, then climbing into Mona's soft lap to cuddle. Four other birth mothers, attracted by Mona's warm smile and motherly appearance, asked about placing their children with the family living in the High Desert.

Around the office, Mona is remembered as our Chocolate Chip Cookie Mom. And I've got to tell you, hers were the best cookies I ever tasted, though she never would give me the recipe. ◉◉

### How important is the faith of an adoptive parent?

To some birth mothers, your commitment to raise a child in the faith of her choice is one of the most important aspects of her selection. A number of agencies exist to place children within families of their faith. Bethany Christian Services, **http://www.bethany.org** will only work with Christian families.

Not all agencies with a religious name require that you be of their faith. Jewish Family and Children's Services at **http://jfcsphil.org/adopt.htm** and Catholic Charities, as listed by state in Adoption Hotlinks in the back of the book, provide services to adoptive parents of varied religious backgrounds. Visit **http://www.christianadoptiononline.com** for resources.

*What does an agency, attorney and/or facilitator do?*

Their roles vary, as described at http://www.adoptionquestions.com and their expertise is essential to your success. Which professional you select will depend on several factors, including how much of the work you want to do yourself, the type of child you seek and the method of adoption you use.

If you plan to adopt a newborn through an open, independent adoption, in most states you can choose a full service facilitator who will locate and match you with a birth mother and connect you to and work closely with a qualified attorney.

A facilitator will also help you fill out the required stack of paperwork and refer you to a social worker who will help you prepare for the home study process. Their staff will help you write and design your adoptive parent profile, post it on the Web and send it out by mail. See the chapter on creating your profile and visit http://www.adoptiontree.com.

An adoption agency can help with the entire process, or depending on laws in your state, can provide a stand-alone home study, as does http://www.adoptionoklahoma.com. Some agencies will allow you to find your own birth mother, help you prepare for the home study and will complete the adoption for you, including finalization.

---

### So Many Questions

Whether you are eager to adopt, or not sure if it's right for you, there is much to ponder about a process that can sometimes seem overwhelming.

- **Do you wish to adopt a child from the United States or from another country like China or Russia?**

- **Do you prefer to raise an older child, a toddler or to bring up a newborn?**

- **Do you hope to find a child who looks like you? Or a baby of another race?**

- **Will you use an agency, attorney or facilitator?**

- **Do you want to do much of the leg work yourself or let the professionals do most of it?**

You will want to use a private or public agency if you decide to adopt an older child, usually defined as over the age of five. This child may have psychological or physical challenges. See http://www.spaulding.org.

An attorney who specializes in adoption will handle the legal work, which has to be perfect, assuring, for example, that all paperwork is in order and crucial documents are signed and filed with the court allowing the birth parents to legally relinquish their rights to the child. Some attorneys also facilitate adoptions or work hand-in-hand with agencies or facilitators.

Most adoption professionals will be able to acquire medical records on the birth mother and child. They should also provide you and your birth parents with support throughout the adoption process. Go to http://www.adoptionprofessionals.com for a directory.

### Is it difficult to qualify for an adoption?

You will need to be mentally stable, of course, and healthy enough to engage in activities with your children. You can't have a disease that will shorten your life span and leave a child without a mother or father. If you have had cancer and it's in remission or if you have a chronic condition such as diabetes that is under control, you'll need your doctor to verify this.

You need a house or apartment with enough space for a child. You need indoor plumbing and a clean, safe home. If married, you need to show stability in your relationship.

At our center we advise prospective parents to have health and life insurance and to consider the serious issues that arise from the responsibility of raising a child. How would you pay for medical care to treat a serious illness? Who would care for your child if you died in a car accident?

## What is a home study?

In most states a social worker will evaluate your fitness to parent during what's known as a home study. It's really a study of the adopting parents. Requirements in each state differ, but it usually includes a home inspection, physical examinations by a doctor, an audit of your finances, references from friends and coworkers, a search of motor vehicle and court records and, most of the time, an FBI background check.

Nearly all people who apply to adopt do qualify and most prospective parents worry way too much about the home study. Its intent is to screen out people with mental illness, drug or alcohol dependency, a criminal record of child abuse or those with so little income that an adopted child would be placed into poverty.

If your home life is stable, if you are in reasonably good health, if you have enough income to raise a child, if you are a loving and responsible person with a heartfelt desire to parent a child for life, you can usually adopt.

> ### Adoption Myths
>
> "They can't adopt because ..."
>
> - They've only been married two years.
> - Already have biological children.
> - Already have an adopted child.
> - They're over forty.
> - He has a physical disability.
> - Both parents work full-time.
> - They've been married before.
> - They don't make enough money.
> - They don't own a home.
> - She's a single woman.

## Do you need to be wealthy to adopt?

You don't have to own your own home or reach a certain income level to be eligible with most organizations. You must show that you can afford to provide for your family and for your new child on the income you currently have. The government recently estimated that it costs a middle class family $160,000 to raise a child from birth to 18 years. That's about $9,000 per year, enough to frighten people into raising parakeets instead. But you can't put a price on the joy a child brings. Without children, life just isn't as rich and it certainly isn't as much fun.

### How much does it cost to adopt?

Costs vary wildly by state and by the type of adoption, so the national average of $12,000 to $18,000 may not apply to your adoption. On the East Coast an adoption of a healthy newborn can cost from $20,000 to $30,000 or more. In most western and plains states it costs half as much. A public agency adoption of an older child may cost $2,500 or be cost free, as detailed at **http://www.adoptionfamilycenter.org/resources/adoption/costofadoption.htm**. The range of fees for an international adoption is $9,000 to $25,000 and up.

Some adoptive parents turn over all the work to an agency and then wait for their child. This can be expensive. Others save by doing some of the work themselves. With independent adoption, if allowed by your state laws, adoptive parents pay for services "a la carte"; for example, an attorney for legal work, a private social worker for the home study and a facilitator to locate birth mothers.

As a general rule, facilitators charge less than agencies to find and screen birth mothers. Some agencies have sliding fees based on income or will allow you to save by finding your own birth parents. Home study fees average $2,000 across the country but are higher in certain states; for example, Massachusetts can run as high as $20,000. In some states you can save thousands by using an independent social worker instead of one attached to an agency. Legal fees vary. Some attorneys charge from $125 to $375 or more per hour; others charge a flat fee of, perhaps, $5,000 for an adoption.

On the positive side, there are substantial tax benefits allowed by the IRS, which, depending on your situation, can amount to $10,000. There are subsidies for adopting children with special needs, as described in the chapter on this topic and at **http://www.nacac.org/adoptionsubsidy.html**.

If your adoption is going to cost you more than $18,000 you need to ask why. Always compare the prices and services of at least three professionals and ask how much you will save by finding the child yourself. Go to **http://www.adoptionwishes.org/cost.htm** for a concise accounting of costs and see the chapter on adoption finance.

### How old can you be and still adopt?

In the past, you could be no more than 40 years older than the child you wished to adopt. Today this rule is not hard and fast. In fact, we have birth mothers looking for older, more mature couples.

A large number of baby boomers in their forties have waited to start families, and are now adopting because they are unable to conceive. Many of them are as healthy and active as people 10 to 15 years younger and they have caused the adoption system to ease up on age restrictions.

At our center, we've seen people well into their fifties adopt successfully. In one situation, the husband was 62 and, because his wife was 15 years younger, they were able to adopt. If you are an older couple, you can usually adopt internationally with less trouble, provided that you are both in good health.

Ask yourself this question: When the child is in his early twenties will he still have parents around who are in pretty good shape?

### What about second marriages and adoption?

In domestic independent adoptions, the birth mother makes most of the choices about who will parent the child. She often has no problem with a couple where the husband or wife has been married before. Some domestic agencies and some foreign countries do not allow adoption for anyone who has divorced.

Many agencies look at the stability of the current marriage and will consider couples who have been divorced. If you are going on your fifth or sixth marriage, this indicates to birth mothers and to adoption professionals alike that your present marriage may be short-lived and you may not be able to adopt.

### How long must we be married before adopting?

Some private and public agencies require that a couple be married for a period of time, usually from one to five years. In private, independent adoptions, the birth mother decides. At our center we have facilitated adoptions for couples who have been married for only 12 months and for as long as 25 years. Many state agencies have relaxed the rules on the longevity of marriage so more parents can adopt waiting children in foster care.

### We already have children. Can we still adopt?

Since the adopted child will have siblings, it's considered an asset to many birth mothers and adoption professionals, though some may prefer a couple without children.

### Can single people adopt?

Yes. If you know in your heart that you can provide a child with a balanced life, devote the time required to raise him or her right, and if you have male and female friends and family to help. You'll also need a professional experienced in single-parent adoptions. The joy and challenge of single parenting is discussed at **http://www.singleparentcentral.com** and **http://www.members.aol.com/onemomfor2**. Single parents are not usually matched as quickly as married couples. Most birth mothers choose married couples, though some request a single parent because, as one told me, "the mother would pay more attention to the child if she isn't distracted by her spouse." Some birth mothers feel they are helping someone who otherwise might not be able to adopt. In your profile, let birth mothers know how committed you are to raising a child. One single mother was chosen because she had taken parenting classes.

### Do overweight people have trouble adopting?

On occasion, they've been turned down by both private and public agencies, based on their risk of health problems, a potential lower life expectancy or because of prejudice. Independent, open adoptions are usually easier for overweight people. The National Association to Advance Fat Acceptance, **http://www.naafa.org**, is working to see that heavy people have equal access to adoption services.

### Can someone with past criminal behavior adopt?

If you were convicted for theft when you were young and doing stupid things, you might still be able to adopt. If you were arrested for drunk driving a week before your home study, you'll have trouble. If you abused alcohol or used illicit drugs in the past, you must provide proof that you have been clean and sober for a period of years. Some past felonies can be excused, others cannot. If they are child-related, you cannot adopt. Be up-front about problems in your life as they will likely be discovered and your dishonesty alone may jeopardize your adoption.

*When should we tell our family that we are adopting?*

Start right away by telling them that you are thinking about adoption. Some in your family circle may only know about the darker days of adoption in years gone by and you'll need to inform them about the way adoptions are done today.

Go to http://www.comeunity.com/adoption/realmoms to sign up for the upbeat Real Mom's Adoption Newsletter. You can either e-mail it or print it out for doubting kin. At http://www.adoptivefamilies.com, you can order a magazine for them, which celebrates adoption. At the websites in Adoption Hotlinks, you'll find information to allay their specific concerns. Before long, they will come around!

From what I have observed over the years, I can assure you that most members of your family will be thrilled about the prospect of adoption and the new child in your life and theirs.

# Ask Yourself These Ten Questions

1) Have you resolved infertility issues and come to peace with building your family through adoption?

2) Can you accept that adopting the child meant for you can happen quickly or take as long as several years?

3) Do you have confidence in your adoption plan and will you project this to others around you?

4) Can you afford the cost of adopting?

5) Can you afford the cost of raising a child?

6) Can you cope with filling out a ream of paperwork?

7)  Will your other children and your relatives love a child who is not biologically yours?

8)  Are you prepared, if you choose open adoption, to keep in touch with the birth mother of your child?

9)  Will you be honest and never secretive about how your child came into your family?

10) Will you, for a lifetime, raise, love, nurture and support a child conceived in your heart, not in your body? ☜☞

If you have answered yes to these questions, your chances of success are much greater. Congratulations! If you are still struggling with a few questions, don't give up, keep learning and read on.

# 4

# Legal Information

## Adoption Law on the Internet

Web pages brimming with good information on adoption law number in the hundreds of thousands. Using a search engine, in a matter of seconds, you can scan every one of these pages, seeking answers to your questions. If a birth father, previously unknown, comes into the picture, you can find papers by law professors about his burden in claiming any parental rights. If you are adopting a child of another race, you can read the very law that prohibits agencies from discriminating against you. If you are matched with a birth mother in Alabama and she is about to deliver, you can check the rules in her state to see how long you'll be staying at the Holiday Inn, Tuscaloosa, before you can bring your baby home.

In the Internet era, lawyers often go online to research aspects of a case. If you practice precise web searching and learn to discern clear and accurate pages from those that are confused and inaccurate, you too can make use of a collection of writings more diverse than that of the best law library or of the finest medical library for that matter. And, in medicine as in law, the informed client or patient can help with his or her case. But, just as you wouldn't do your own brain surgery, you should not do

53

your own legal work. For an adoption that is safe and secure, you need experienced counsel.

In the course of adopting, you may find that matters of law come in shades of gray. Your attorney may present you with several courses of action, putting you in the position of knowing enough to make a good choice. If the going gets complicated, the adoptive parent who better understands the law is less edgy and more rational. Attorneys appreciate clients who do research on their own, if only to make their meetings with you more efficient. You must understand that your attorney knows the legal intricacies of adoption and you must rely on him or her for handling your specific adoption situation.

## When Federal Laws Matter

In adoption, federal laws apply in certain areas. To free more children from foster care, for example, the Safe Families Act **http://www.cwla.org/advoca-cy/asfa.htm** increased financial incentives, streamlined court procedures and encouraged more assertive terminations of the rights of unfit birth parents. As a result, many more prospective parents are adopting special needs children, most notably in Illinois, Iowa, Texas and Wyoming.

The Multi-ethnic Placement Act is concerned with the large numbers of minority children in foster care waiting for loving homes. It prohibits public agencies from using race, color or national origin of prospective parents or children to deny or delay placements.

When adopting a foreign-born child, the laws of his or her country apply, as do federal law. Rules of the Immigration and Naturalization Service (INS) require, for example, that you submit a favorable home study report before you can bring your adopted child into the country. To adopt a Native American child, federal law also applies. It requires, for instance, that parents obtain consent to adopt a child, not only from birth parents, but also from the respective tribes themselves if the child should fall under the act. See **http://www.ptla.org/wabanaki/icwa.htm**.

For more about adoption special needs and foreign born children, see chapters 9 and 10.

## State Adoption Laws

In virtually all other areas of adoption, state legislatures create the laws, and state agencies write the regulations. The state courts finalize adoptions, settle disputes and set precedents, except in cases involving constitutional rights, such as those of birth fathers.

Even in matters addressed by federal law, states have their say. In response to the Multi-ethnic Act, for example, some have their own statutes prohibiting discrimination in the placement of ethnic children. When an international adoption is approved by another government and by the INS, the laws of the states still pertain. For example, several require that you provide written consent of the birth mother before your child can enter the state.

While federal regulations do not always require you to re-adopt a foreign-born child in your state of residence, the laws there may require this. To be safe and sure the adoption conforms to state laws, many attorneys advise such re-adoptions. See **http://www.orphans.com/faq/g.htm#1**.

The laws of the various states commonly seek to protect children, to balance the rights of birth parents with the needs of adoptive parents and to prevent fraud and forbid baby selling. But on essential points, in the diverse ever-changing statutes, we confront a jumble of rules and procedures.

Some states make adoption easier, as do Alabama, Illinois, Kansas, Oklahoma, Louisiana, Texas, Washington and now California. In such adoption-friendly states, prospective parents who are nonresidents can often finalize their adoptions, provided the birth parents live there. Nearly all states make it much simpler for stepparents and other family members to adopt. Some states give preferences to parents who adopt children with special needs.

Some states have residency requirements. Several impose the number of months parents must live in the state before they can adopt. A few stipulate that adoptive parents be older by a certain number of years than the adoptee. Some require adoptive parents to provide a separate attorney to represent the birth parents. Always check with a local attorney to learn more about the laws of your state.

## Types of Adoption

The laws recognize two basic types of adoption which differ by how birth parents consent to the adoption. With an agency adoption, birth parents relinquish parental rights to an agency that knows the legal rights of the child. Through independent adoptions, birth parents give consent directly to the adoptive parents they have chosen. Go to **http://www.theadoptionadvisor.com** click on <independent> link, and you will see that all rights remain until the adoption is final or they have their parental rights terminated by the court. Every state provides for agency adoptions. In any agency adoption, the parental rights are either voluntarily surrendered or have been terminated by the court; in cases of neglect or abuse, for example.

Public agencies are usually operated by social service departments and place children with special needs. Private agencies, licensed or supervised by the states, are for-profit or non-profit and tend to specialize in foreign born, special needs or minority children and sometimes in infants.

Colorado, Connecticut, Delaware, Wisconsin, Florida and Massachusetts do not allow independent adoptions. All other states provide for birth parents and adoptive parents to find each other and agree privately to the adoption. When the birth parents relinquish rights directly to adoptive parents, the laws call it direct placement. Some state laws are virtually silent on this practice, while others regulate it closely. Most states provide that an intermediary, such as a lawyer, clergyman, doctor or facilitator can help arrange independent adoptions. If you reside in New York or Kentucky, you can only pay for services that locate a placing birth parent to an in-state agency.

As the Internet made it feasible for finding adoptive parents, more and more birth mothers chose to adopt independently and to abandon the agencies which had decided for them who would parent their child. In response, agencies began offering birth and adoptive parents the option to contract with them to complete an adoption, while going out on their own to find one another. Many states now permit this melding of the two basic adoption types in what is called designated or identified adoption. See **http://www.adoptionnavigators.com/types.htm**. Where state laws allow, an intermediary like an attorney or facilitator can help connect birth and adoptive parents. Once they are matched, the agency does the home study, qualifies the adoptive parents, counsels the birth mother and so on. The birth parents relinquish parental and legal rights to the agency, which then consents to the adoption.

# Top Law Links

State adoption laws change often and websites do not always keep up. Never act on what you learn about laws on the Internet without consulting your attorney.

- **http://calib.com/naic/laws**: State and federal laws, collection of writings which explain aspects, areas and themes of adoption law.

*(continued on next page)*

- http://www.webcom.com/kmc/adoption/adoption.html: Information on reforms; state codes, international adoption laws, search engines and legal links.

- http://lawyers.findlaw.com: Lawyer locator by state and city.

- http://www.adoptionlawyer.com: Browse major search engines to locate legal resources and attorneys.

- http://www.law.freeadvice.com: Easy to navigate; state laws and information; attorney locator.

- http://www.americanadoptionlaw.com: A guide to finding attorneys and legal assistance on adoption issues and ebooks on state adoption laws.

- http://www.uscis.gov/graphics: Immigration laws and news related to international adoption.

- http://www.nolo.com/lawcenter/ency/index.cfm: Encyclopedia and dictionary on adoption; frequently asked questions about court procedures and legal proceedings.

- http://www.theadoptionguide.com: Assistance in finding a facilitator, agency or attorney in the field of adoption. ෧෨

# Just the Facts

- In an estimated 130,000 to 150,000 domestic adoptions each year, 30,000 to 40,000 involve babies or newborns.

- Of all domestic newborn and infant placements, one-half to two-thirds are through independent adoptions.

- About one-half of all domestic adoptions are by stepparents or other relatives of the child. ∞

# Handy Guide to Interstate Adoption
*by Jim Handy*

As a California attorney who assists in locating birth mothers and birth fathers for prospective adoptive families and facilitates adoptions, I specialize in interstate adoptions and have worked with birth mothers in over 40 states.

As more adoptive parents and birth parents use the Internet to find each other, lawyers are doing more interstate adoptions. In a legal process fraught with potential pitfalls, I must apply the laws of two states, the one where the adoptive parents reside, known as the receiving state and the one where the birth parents live, known as the sending state.

Generally, the laws of the receiving state control the adoption, though, in most cases, certain laws of the sending state will prevail. The Interstate Compact on Placement of Children (ICPC) requires an administrator in each state to review my papers and documents to ensure that I comply with both sets of state laws, see **http://www.adoptioninstitute.org/policy/inters2.html**.

*(continued on next page)*

In the direct placement of a newborn, my role is to orchestrate the adoption with you, ultimately through the court, but initially through the Compact administrators and the birth parents, usually the birth mother. I contact her as soon as you are matched and stay in touch throughout the adoption.

As an adoptive father, I can understand what you are going through physically, mentally and emotionally, so I know what you should expect of your attorney. On the road to securing the approval of two administrators, both with their own changes in laws, both with their own rules, we may encounter a few bumps along the way. A good lawyer will smooth them out so that you hardly notice.

Doing the paperwork is tedious and sometimes irksome to attorneys and adoptive parents alike. To acquire just the medical history of the birth mother, for instance, I must contact doctors and other health providers, secure forms and get releases signed. But it's worth the hassle, as in the end, you will obtain valuable information.

When my wife and I adopted our daughter, we learned from her medical reports that ovarian cancer runs in her family. Informed of this, our doctor said she is at risk for the disease and should be watched, so, if it occurs in her, it is detected early when curable.

At or near the time of the baby's birth, you will travel to the state where the birth mother delivers. Once the baby arrives, there is a time period that the birth mother must wait before she can sign the adoption consents, most commonly 3 days or 72 hours, but it can be longer or shorter depending upon the state. Once the adoption consents are signed, all the paperwork is sent by overnight mail to me for review. If all the paperwork meets the requirements, I then forward the paperwork, again by overnight mail, to the sending state's administrator.

Once the sending state's administrator has approved all the paperwork, it is then sent to the receiving state's administrator. Upon approval of the adoption documents by the receiving state's administrator, it is now permissible for the adoptive parents and child to return home. During your stay in the sending state with the baby, you can travel anywhere in the state you like, you just cannot cross state lines. The whole process from birth to approval generally takes 10 to 14 days.

I encourage you to make this a wonderful time. You will have your new child with you in your hotel room. Take this opportunity to bond with and marvel at the infant in your arms. Remember that you are adopting this child for the rest of your lives. When you get home, it's likely that friends and relatives will be dropping by. Soon you will be looking back fondly on those quiet days away from home with your new baby. ෙ

## What Is Consent?

Consent is the agreement of the birth parents to terminate all rights to a child and to place this child for adoption. With older and special needs children, another person or entity usually acts in place of the birth parents because a court has terminated their rights due to abandonment, abuse or neglect, for example.

A mother who is under age has the same parental rights as someone of age and can consent to adoption without her parent's approval, unless she is very young, that is, under the age of 13, in many states. The birth father must also consent, though in most cases, with notable exceptions where the father asserts his rights and is even at times the placing parent, he does not participate because he either waives his rights or has failed to protect them through his neglect of the mother or child. See http://www.calib.com/naic/laws/putative.cfm.

## Advising the Birth Mother

Many states require that a licensed social worker serve as an advocate for the birth parents to advise them of their rights and obligations, to explain legal matters and to assure that no person has coerced them into placing the child. This worker also provides counseling to help the mother cope with feelings of grief and loss. See http://www.resourcesfor-women.com.

By engaging the birth mother in the adoption process and by helping her understand the law and attending to her needs, she is less likely to change her mind. And for the adoptive parents, because issues which could give rise to a contested adoption are faced head-on, they gain confidence in knowing that once the adoption is final, the child will be with them always.

The social worker, in one crucial meeting for the advisement of rights, will make sure the birth parents understand that they intend to legally give up the baby for good. This will happen again when they sign a document in which they give their consent.

## Waiting for Consent

Placing a newborn child for adoption is an event that taxes the birth mother's thinking and emotions. She is drained physically, has just been through labor and is usually exhausted. Her baby has been born, her milk is coming in and her hormones are imbalanced, all making her emotional and vulnerable.

For this reason, most laws provide a period of time for the birth mother to pause and reflect. This is especially true in a direct placement, that is, when the baby goes directly to the adoptive parents from birth.

Usually, after the advisement of rights and after giving birth to the child, the birth mother must wait to sign the consent document. It is 24 hours in Utah, 48 hours in Missouri, 72 hours in most other states, though as long as 12 days in Kansas and 15 days in Virginia. During this time, until consent, an adoptive parent from another state must remain in the state, although they can usually have the baby with them in their hotel room and travel freely throughout the state.

## What Is Reclaim?

An adoption is meant to create a permanent home for the child and consent is irrevocable in about 6 states. In 19 states, the birth mother can revoke consent, commonly known as reclaim of the child, only when there is clear evidence of fraud or duress.

In Connecticut and Wisconsin, birth parents can revoke consent for a period of 60 days, if a court finds that it's in the best interest of the child. In a few states, the adopting family and the birth parents must mutually agree to a reclaim.

In many states a birth mother may revoke her consent for any reason for a period of time: 5 days in Alabama, 10 days in Minnesota, 21 days in Vermont and 30 days in California. In some states the birth mother may waive waiting periods to make the adoption irrevocable sooner.

At **http://www.abcadoptions.com/consent2.htm**, you will find excerpts from the statutes, listed by state, which pertain specifically to consent: who must consent, how and when it is executed, if and how it can be revoked.

## Who Is the "Birth Father"?

Many birth mothers are unwed and some get pregnant while living with a boyfriend or by having relations with someone they hardly know. One father may not know that he even got a woman pregnant, another may find out and leave town, some have taken in a child not related to them. So in adoption law, the father goes by different names, such as presumed, alleged, custodial, biological, natural or legal. Who must consent, and under what conditions, depends on the diverse rules of each state.

In some states, a presumed or legal father is one whose child was conceived during marriage, or within 300 days of being married. In a few states he qualifies if conception occurred within 300 days of trying to marry the mother or if he has taken the child into his home and acted like a parent. These fathers have parental rights. Your attorney should try hard to reach the birth father and secure his cooperation, or failing that, to show the court that he has abandoned or neglected the child or is not the biological father, hence his consent is not required.

In many cases where birth mothers have conceived out of wedlock, in the eyes of adoption law in most states, the biological father is only the alleged father and he must earn his parental rights. See **http://www.adoptionplan.com/putativefathers.htm**. State laws commonly require that he support and care for the mother during pregnancy, acknowledge his infant through an act like attending prenatal appointments, signing the birth certificate, or by behaving like a father. If he does not do such things prior to adoption proceedings, in most states, he may not claim or exert his rights. If he has not visited, communicated with, or supported the child for one year or for six months in some states, his consent is not required.

During the past decade, in several celebrated cases, putative or biological fathers emerged late, pleading ignorance of their child's birth. They went to court and set aside or prevented some adoptions. Some states responded by limiting the rights of putative fathers. In Utah, Oregon and a few other states men are on notice to start protecting their rights soon after sexual relations with the mother. About one-half of the states responded by setting up registries for putative fathers. See **http://www.adoptionsolutions.com/general/father_register.htm**.

The birth fathers, after recording their name, address and identity of the birth mother into the registry, requires the court to notify them of any legal proceedings related to the child.

But the rules are unclear as to when he must sign up; soon after intercourse, within a period of time preceding or following the birth, or even soon after adoption. Open to interpretation, at a time when more unwed fathers want to raise their children, even if the mothers don't want them to, these confusing laws increase the risk of a jeopardized adoption. Both your attorney and yourself should keep a watchful eye on the birth father and his rights.

## Patchwork of Rights

These fathers have rights, and, generally, must consent to placing their offspring for adoption:

- The biological father in Hawaii who has shown a reasonable degree of interest in the child.

- The Missouri man who acts to establish paternity and registers with the state.

- A legal guardian in Montana.

- The acknowledged father in New Mexico.

- The presumed natural father in North Dakota.

- The Ohio man who establishes paternity.

- A father who has had a relationship with and provided support to the child has rights.

- Putative fathers have a right to notice of adoption proceedings if they have registered with the state.

- No rights accrue to fathers who have not provided support or registered.

# The Precise Legal Search

For a big subject like adoption law, there is no "one stop" website to visit. The best way to find something is to use one of the meta-search engines listed in Adoption Hotlinks, found in the back of this book, and to gradually narrow your search until you find pertinent Web pages.

Let's say that you live in Tyler, Texas, and your birth mother Melinda lives in Altoona, Pennsylvania. Melinda is separated from her husband Rodney and has filed for divorce. Late Friday night he shows up at her door. She calls you.

"He knows about the baby," she says nervously.

Melinda tells you that Rodney was mad, stomping around and shouting at her. So she shouted back, "It's not your baby!"

"So, okay, so it's not," he answered. "But I'm still your husband and guess what? I've got rights. Nobody's gonna take this kid."

Melinda is crying now. "Rod's not the father," she says. "You know who the father is and he wants you to have the baby."

Melinda is due in ten days, and you are making travel plans to attend the birth. Her phone call hits you like a bolt of lightening and makes you terribly anxious. It's the weekend so you can't reach your attorney, but you need to know something, anything, tonight.

You go to your computer and into the **http://www.google.com** search engine you enter the string of terms <consent adoption Pennsylvania>. But that brings up a list of 45,600 pages. You try again with <consent adoption Pennsylvania "putative father"> and this hits on 260 pages, about 100 too many.

The next time you add <husband> to the search terms and the list of hits seems workable, as, with Google, the best sites usually rise to the top. Scrolling through, glancing at the first ten records, you spot one that looks promising. ☜☞

# Advanced Search Preferences

## Language Tools Search Tips

Searched the web for consent adoption Pennsylvania "putative father" husband. Results 1-10 of about 116. Search took 0.17 seconds.

## Petition for Adoption

Pennsylvania Consolidated Statutes. DOMESTIC RELATIONS TITLE 23. ADOPTION. CHAPTER 27. PETITION FOR ADOPTION....Consent of the husband shall not...members.aol.com /StatutesPA/23.Cp.27.html

*©2003 Google*

You click on the link that takes you to one single paragraph of the Pennsylvania statues, the one you want to see: "The consent of the husband of the mother shall not be necessary if, after notice to the husband, it is proved to the satisfaction of the court by evidence, including testimony of the natural mother, that the husband of the natural mother is not the natural father of the child."

You intend to call your attorney on Monday to see what he thinks. But for now, you feel pretty good. Rodney can make a fuss to get back at Melinda for filing the divorce papers and you're pretty sure it won't matter. It looks like you will be bringing your new baby home soon. You go to bed with some peace. ໑໑

Internet zone

## Birth Mother Expenses

Most states impose criminal penalties for the act of selling a baby. Yet many states allow payment of reasonable fees for adoption services, though most laws require that the court review and approve the expenses. The rules vary by state, but adoptive parents can usually pay for legal services, costs of facilitators, agency fees and, sometimes, birth mother's living costs and medical care.

## Advertising

Out of fear that such a practice would give rise to a black market for babies, laws in a few states prohibit any party to an adoption from advertising. See **http://adoption.about.com/cs/statelaws/**. In California, for example, adoptive parents seeking a baby cannot place a want ad in the personals of their local newspaper. Some states permit advertising only by licensed agencies, and others variously allow it for adoptive and birth parents or their intermediaries. Always hazy, these laws are made murkier still by the Internet where the parties to adoption, from the computers on their desktops, can post profiles and build Web pages or tell about the baby's ultrasound in adoption forums for millions of Web users to see.

## Adoption Day

Once the consent or court order terminating parental rights is in hand, your attorney will file the petition in the court where the adoptive parents, or sometimes, where the birth parents live. A request to approve the adoption, the petition notes why the birth parents surrendered their rights. It explains the relationship of the adoptive parents to the child and why the adoption is in the child's best interest. A request to change the child's name is often made in this filing.

The child has already been placed with you, and in some states, post-placement begins, which sometimes includes the home study. The home study is most often done before placement, but in a few states it is done afterwards. Laws usually require this examination. Commonly done by a social worker, it assures that nothing in your home or background will endanger the child. Many states and also the INS, in intercountry adoptions, require a fingerprint check to clear you of child abuse or similar convictions. The home study, in most states, must be completed before the adoption is finalized.

Once the report is in hand, your attorney will schedule a hearing to finalize the adoption. Prior to this date, by some 20 or 30 days, your attorney will mail or serve a notice of hearing on persons required to consent. A birth father may have waived his right to be notified; a party who cannot be found is, in some states, given notice in the newspaper.

Judges who approve adoption are usually seeing family law cases, i.e., divorce, child custody and other rather ugly proceedings. So they love to do adoptions! When the judge issues the final decree of adoption, the child is legally yours, as though born to you. Have a great time on this wonderful day, and, for the years to come, you may wish, as many families do, to celebrate Adoption Day with parties and presents.

# 5

## Birth Mothers and You

It was in late spring of 1996 when I received a phone call from Jim Handy, a prospective father at the time. Jim and his wife Deb had been trying to conceive for many months and had finally gone to her gynecologist just before Mother's Day. It was on that day they discovered that Deb's fallopian tubes were hopelessly blocked. "We were standing in the exam room when the nurse came in," said Jim. "She was as cold as ice. She said we would never conceive naturally."

I invited the couple to visit my home to discuss adoption. Sitting in my living room over a cup of coffee, Jim said the two of them had met in Texas, fell in love and married eight years before. Jim, who had gone back to school to study law, struck me as feisty and detailed. He got right down to business. "We want a Caucasian newborn and it has to be a girl," he said.

Uh, oh, I thought. After years of facilitating adoptions, I had learned that clients with predetermined expectations are likely to give me grief. *Can I work with this guy?* I wondered.

"I know you find some of your birth mothers in the south," he said. "As for ours, definitely not one from Texas." He winked. "I've got enough Texans running around the house!"

Deb whacked him on the arm and we laughed. I realized then that what I'd observed in Jim was a dry sense of humor. He was actually a kind and caring man.

But he was serious about wanting a daughter. We counsel most clients against this, as it tends to upset and discourage potential birth mothers. But we had succeeded with some gender specific adoptions; for clients who were willing, as the Handys said they were, to wait patiently while the search takes place.

I started to search for a birth mother and considered a few situations, but they didn't seem right. After nine months, I received a call from a young woman, Kelly, who asked me to find a family for her unborn baby girl. She lived nearby and I invited her over for iced tea and to chat. I like to meet in person, when possible, with the parties to an adoption.

When Kelly arrived at the door, I saw that she looked just like Deb, the same hair and skin tone and the same clear blue eyes. They looked like sisters. I told her about the Handys. Since I'd been spending a lot of time with Jim and Deb, I felt I knew them well. They had become more like friends than clients.

I introduced Kelly to Jim and Deb and they quickly learned they were from the same area. Soon I knew that they were a good match. As Kelly was leaving, I gave her two maternity outfits.

When the Handys met her, they fell in love. I know that sounds corny, but I hear it often. It means there's a good match. A few months later baby Savannah was born. She was a wonderful blend of her birth family and her adoptive parents.

Feeling so good about his adoption success and intrigued by the process, Jim decided that after he passed the Bar in June of 1997, he would devote his practice to adoption. Since that time, as a facilitator of adoptions and as an attorney, Jim has finalized hundreds of adoptions.

The adoption coordinators at our center work with Jim's office on over 60 adoptions each year. We have a good relationship with his assistant, Laurie Leiser, who manages the office and sometimes goes to the hospital in the middle of the night to help a birth mother in an adoption placement.

In October of 2002, I asked Jim and Laurie to come to my home in Nevada City, California. We sat around the dining room table and talked about our experiences with birth mothers.

## Saving a Baby

**Jim:** A birth mother's decision to place a child for adoption is the answer to the question "Should I get an abortion?" There can be no more important decision for a person. This is about whether or not a child lives and if so, what kind of life the child will have.

I carry in my wallet a picture of my adopted daughter as she walked up the sidewalk to her kindergarten class on the first day and I think: What if she wasn't here? What if her birth mother had aborted her?

## Respect for Birth Mothers

**Laurie:** Some adoptive parents disrespect birth mothers because they don't live in the same world as they do. I think we have figured out that the typical birth mother is in her mid-twenties and may already have a couple of kids. She may be pregnant without a husband. She may be homeless and on public assistance or she may just be needy and hard to deal with. But we have to understand that placing her child is an act of love. She deserves our respect.

## Birth Mothers Deserve Honesty

**Mardie:** We had matched a birth mother, Rachel, with an adoptive couple from Texas who said, "Rachel wants to have some contact, and we agreed." But, the adoptive family continued, "We really don't want that and we're under no legal obligation." I went to see Rachel and told her the situation was not a good one and she selected another couple.

In the meantime we matched the original couple with another woman who wanted no contact afterwards. But, after very strenuous labor, she chose not to consent to the adoption. The couple was extremely upset with her even to the point of using foul language. A few days later, this birth mother decided to place the child after all. Of course she chose another family. I don't think that first couple ever did adopt. They only needed to have compassion and empathy for the birth mother and they would have had their baby.

## Birth Mothers in Trouble

**Jim:** Sometimes an adoptive parent will ask, "How can she be giving up this baby?" And I say, thank God she is. Without her we wouldn't have adoption and we wouldn't have children going from a bad situation to the promise of a good life.

The child is not responsible for the circumstances of his biological parents. The decisions made are very difficult for the birth mother and we have to feel for her, protect her and help her along the way. Sometimes she's in a bad situation.

We had one recent birth mother from the East Coast who called us from a phone booth at a truck stop in New Mexico. Her boyfriend had dumped her off when he found out she was pregnant. Somehow she found the strength to place her child, hoping to give it a better life than she could have. This takes courage. That's what we need to know about the birth mother. It is not for us to judge the life she has lived.

## The Match

**Mardie:** The adoptive parents don't have to approve of the birth mother's lifestyle to be matched. In open adoption, the birth mother is the one who is moving the adoption forward, choosing the parents. I ask what's foremost in her mind. Does she want a stay-at-home mom, outdoor type parents, a specific faith or perhaps siblings for the baby? I look for a connection, common interests, someone she can bond with. Sometimes it's as simple as the state where the prospective parents live or the adoptive father's occupation.

The sense of a good match comes in some measure from a gut feeling. Like saying to a friend, "You should meet Claire. I know you'll hit it off." After she meets the prospective adoptive families, I listen to her words. If she says, "Well, they're nice" or "I'm not sure," then I present her with other families.

If she says, "They're perfect!" they probably are. She has to feel that she can release her child to these parents, knowing they will love and care for him or her as their own. Without this confidence, the birth mother may decide not to place the child or may, in the future, come to regret the adoption.

## Why Things Happen

**Laurie:** Sometimes we just don't know why things happen as they do, why this birth mother picks a particular family. Sometimes I send out a profile to a birth mother and everything seems to match up. And we send her another profile and I'm thinking, there's no way, but that's the one she picks. You wonder; what is it about that one? And in a lot of ways you don't know. And maybe you don't want to know.

We sometimes see situations that fall through and we go, "Oh, the child is going to end up in a life that's difficult." But we just don't know. Maybe it's for the best. We need to have faith in what we are doing. We can't always wonder: Is there something we should have done or didn't do? But we can't keep going back and go crazy over it. Whoever is making this decision, God's decision, we can't know for sure why it's made but it is.

## MARDIE'S STORY

# "I Don't Want to See Them!"

Late in the morning one Sunday in June, I was on call for our 24-hour birth mother hotline. The phone rang. It was a 22-year-old named Melissa. She was on the pay phone in the maternity ward at the tiny hospital in Oakdale, California.

"If you don't find me a good, loving couple," she said. "Social Services is going to take my baby away."

"I understand," I said. "I can help you."

"Can you send them before three o'clock this afternoon?"

"Sure I can ... of course," I answered, wondering how I was going to pull this off. Oakdale was four hours away.

"I want a family with a nice house and a yard," she said. "But I don't want to, I mean, I just can't see them."

"That's up to you...."

"I want to sign the papers," she said tearfully. "Say goodbye to my baby and just go."

I phoned the social worker at the hospital. She said the baby had been examined. A healthy boy with lots of hair, he weighed seven pounds, eight ounces. There were good medical records on Melissa from the state funded medical program.

On Friday, when Melissa was admitted to the hospital, she had told a counselor that she wanted to keep her baby, that somehow she would manage, even though she'd been evicted from her apartment, had no job or money and the father had disappeared.

On Saturday, after giving birth, Melissa had changed her mind. She wanted a better life for her baby, she decided, and when she was discharged the next day, she intended to leave her baby with the nurses.

I called Daniel and Mary Bryant right away. Just six months before, they had come to our center to adopt. Then Mary got pregnant, so we put her contract on hold. I too was pregnant at the time and since we both had trouble carrying babies, we looked to each other for emotional support. I miscarried, and later, Mary delivered a premature baby who died after two days.

Mary had come to my house, grieving her loss. She was crying and I remember her saying, "I want a baby so bad." This happened just weeks before Melissa called.

So on that Sunday morning I called Mary. I told her about the birth mother, the healthy baby boy and the urgent matter at hand. "Grab your credit cards and your cell phone," I said. "Get in your car and start driving. I'll walk you through the procedure on your way down."

I started making numerous calls from the office in my home. I called our lawyer to get the legal work started. He arranged to use the hospital fax machine to transfer documents that Melissa would sign to relinquish

*(continued on next page)*

her rights to her child. I called the social worker. She agreed to be our coordinator at the hospital. An adoption service provider was located and met with Melissa at the hospital to take her signature.

Mary and Daniel got held up in traffic on Route 99 north of Modesto, less than 20 minutes from the hospital.

"The accident is just ahead," reported Dan. "It's starting to clear. So we might make it yet."

Melissa called. She wanted to know more about the family I was sending. She was having doubts about the family showing up on time.

The attorney was on the other line.

Then my cell phone rang.

It was Mary Bryant from the hospital.

I put Melissa on hold.

"There's nobody on the floor except for a young woman on the pay phone," Mary told me. They were looking down a long corridor. "I'm sure it's the mother," Mary added. "She has long blonde hair."

"That's her," I said. "She's talking to me on the other line. Don't let her see you!" They moved down the hallway, around a corner.

"We need to see her," said Mary, whispering. "We want to thank her." She pleaded, "Ask if she'd meet us for just one minute."

I put down the cell phone and asked Melissa.

"I don't want to see them," she answered firmly.

I spoke to Mary. "She doesn't want to meet the adoptive parents," I said sadly. "That's the way she feels about it."

I reassured Melissa that the adoption would provide a good life for her child. She signed the papers in her room and left. She never saw the Bryants.

Mary and Dan named their new baby Joshua. He developed into a precocious and active toddler. Several times the Bryants tried, but failed, to locate Melissa.

When they came back to our center a few years later to adopt a second child, Mary said they regretted not having contact with the birth mother. Though they were grateful for the miracle of having Joshua, she asked us to find a birth mother who wanted to stay in touch for their next adoption. ☜☞

## What Is My Birth Mother Like?

In my own domestic adoption, I know very little about my son Cory's birth mother. I don't even have medical records. We have a few photos and cards and a letter with her signature on it. For some months after the adoption we were in contact, but she soon stopped writing. I wish I could find her to see if she is okay and to let her know that Cory is doing well. But this is my need, not his or hers.

Cory has said he has no desire to meet his birth mother now that he has grown up into a teenager and is attending high school. He knows that she loves him very much because I have always told him that it was an act of love for her to place him with our family for the promise of a better life for him.

Cory has asked questions over the years, as any child would, and I have answered them lovingly and to the best of my ability. When he was six, we were driving to church when he said the dreaded words that all adoptive parents know they are going to hear, but don't know when.

"You're not my real mom," he said. "She's nicer than you, she wouldn't have grounded me!"

I thought about my response. "Yes, she is a nice lady," I said. "Maybe she wouldn't have grounded you."

Later, sitting beside me in church, he snuggled up-close, slipping his little hand into mine. I knew I had been forgiven and had faced the dreaded words and handled them well.

Some months later we were driving to school when the radio announced the news of a terrible storm in Maryland where he was born. He looked out the window. "Gee, I hope my birth mother is okay," he said, then quickly moved on to another subject.

This made my heart swell with gratitude. My son had learned to not only love me, but to care and sympathize with the birth mother he hardly knew. This was confirmation to me that I had done my job well.

# Birth Mothers Talk Profiles

**Laura:** I must have looked at two hundred profiles online and just started weeding them out. I didn't want the Brady Bunch, just a regular family. It didn't matter if they had the most expensive car or the biggest house. And I didn't want a family with a frou-frou dog. If there was a picture of their dog with a bow in his ear, they didn't make my list of finalists. I knew they wouldn't let my kid play in the mud.

**Erica:** I liked it when adoptive parents seemed down to earth and honest. I was looking for a family with at least one young child to be a brother or sister for the baby. The adoptive parents I picked had a little girl named Cassie. She was in almost every picture in the online profile and I thought, *Their daughter is at the center of their lives, they're proud of her and they love her.* Another big thing for me was when they wrote about how they were willing to have an open adoption and that I'd be getting letters and pictures and could even visit! ☯

## What's Next?

Now that you've seen some examples of getting to know your birth mother it's time to ask yourself one of the most important questions of all. Do you want an open, semi-open or a closed adoption? Which option will fit best with your family? Which option is the right one for the newest member of your family, your adopted child? These are hard questions to answer and deserve all the thought you can give them.

# 6

# Open, Semi-open or Closed Adoption

In the past, adoption was that of secrets, pain and shame for many birth parents. Women (and men) had little say in what happened to their children. Well meaning hospital staff very often would not allow the birth mother to see her baby. The birth parents of yesteryear faced silence and denial. *Don't feel, don't talk and it will all be better soon* was the advice of many. Social workers coldly told birth mothers, "You need to get on with your life."

As we now know, many of these women experienced years of pain, struggling with unanswered questions and shame. Dark secrets ate at their hearts on each anniversary of their child's birth and years of silent Mother's Days would bring not flowers and cards, but revisits of the shame and anguish.

Today, birth parents have many choices with open adoption. Open adoption is seen as a viable practice in adoption and is growing in popularity. There are not only practical reasons to have an open adoption, but real benefits for the child too. Families must understand and believe in open adoption before they can proceed, or they will find they may struggle with the concept for years to come.

A number of websites are devoted to open adoption while others are filled with stories of birth parents reliving the horror stories of their closed adoptions. With an open adoption, many birth parents have the opportunity to select the family that will parent their child.

The adoptive parents and birth parents may only meet once before the birth; then afterwards communicate only by mail or by sending pictures and photos. For families online it is common to share e-mails and scanned photos of each other and as the birth mother progresses in her pregnancy she can send photos of ultra sounds and often additional photos throughout the pregnancy.

Even though the ultimate decision regarding the future of their child is up to the birth mother and father, many birth grandparents are being included in choosing the adoptive parents who will raise and nurture their grandchild. Some birth grandparents even have an option to remain in contact after the birth, again through photographs and letters, though a few might request an occasional meeting, if the adoptive parents agree. Some birth families and adoptive families have become so close they vacation together and celebrate holidays as one big family, with the child receiving double doses of love and attention!

The choice is up to both families to consider what is best for the child. As an adoptive mother and an adoption professional, I have seen a variety of scenarios that work out beautifully. There are many open adoption online communities where visitors gather to talk and exchange ideas about open adoption, many of which include both ordinary and challenging experiences.

## MARDIE'S STORY

When I first started my adoption journey, I wanted a white stork to just drop the baby off on my doorstep. I wanted to see him or her in a Victorian wicker basket swaddled in a pastel pink or blue blanket. I imagined opening the door, gazing down on my precious heir and with one fell swoop parenthood would begin.

After years dealing with infertility and several pregnancy losses, I desperately wanted a break, something easy that would bring me into parenthood. As usual, I discovered that adoption is not always easy, however, the rewards are great for the informed and caring. After speaking to other adoptive parents and reading some informative books on open adoption, I had a new awareness of the value of openness.

We eventually adopted a beautiful little boy at five weeks, after a long, drawn out and difficult adoption. But, even after the heartache and pain, I still believed that my son deserved to know about his birth parents and that his adoption was to be celebrated. For without my son's beloved birth mother, I would not be a mother myself.

We both deeply loved the same child and wanted the best for his life. The love and courage his birth mother had to give my son and I allowed me to feel some of the pain of loss and heartbreak that she and most birth mothers quite naturally experience. ☜☞

## Closed and Semi-closed Adoptions

Traditional closed adoptions still exist and are requested by some families who fear the birth parent might *come back to reclaim the child.* But, as you know from reading the chapter on adoption law, once finalized and provided there is no fraud or coercion, an adoption is irrevocable.

Most adoption professionals know from personal experience and from research that it's a disservice to an adopted child if his parents do not have adequate information to share about his birth parents and why he was placed for adoption. When he asks a simple question about his heritage, for the sake of his emotional health, you cannot respond with secrecy, lies or blank stares.

Even in an adoption where there is little contact with the birth mother called a *semi-open* adoption, you can, in a domestic adoption, garner enough information so you can answer such questions. In adopting a foreign-born child you will learn very little about the birth parents but you can usually discover enough about the village he came from or the circumstance that brought him to the orphanage, so you can be honest in telling the child his story. Children who grow up knowing that they are adopted by honest, trustworthy and supportive parents will grow up healthy.

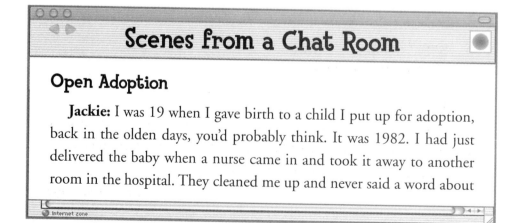

# Scenes from a Chat Room

## Open Adoption

**Jackie:** I was 19 when I gave birth to a child I put up for adoption, back in the olden days, you'd probably think. It was 1982. I had just delivered the baby when a nurse came in and took it away to another room in the hospital. They cleaned me up and never said a word about

Internet zone

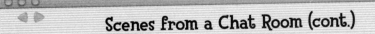

## Scenes from a Chat Room (cont.)

the baby. I asked the nurse, "Is it a boy or a girl?" and "How much does it weigh?" Nobody told me a thing. I was sad lots of times because I never knew what became of the baby. I'd go to the mall and see a child and wonder if it was mine.

**Rachel:** I couldn't have done that. I know the adoptive parents of my baby really well. They live in another town not far away. We went to lunch like four times. I talked with the mom on the phone. She asked me if I liked the name Sophia and I probably wouldn't have even thought of that name and I loved it! They came to the hospital when I was admitted for the delivery. Knowing them made me feel good; I mean giving up the baby was still hard, but knowing that Sophia was going to be raised by this great couple, that made me feel good. ∞

*Internet zone*

---

## Nervous about Open Adoption

To: Mardie Caldwell
From: Mary
Subject: Open Adoption

Dear Mardie,
We are very nervous about open adoption and I heard you on your Internet radio talk show **www.LetsTalkAdoption.com** say that open adoption is better. Why do you say that?

*(continued on next page)*

---

To:
Cc:

## Nervous about Open Adoption (cont.)

Dear Mary:

Closed adoptions are rare and mostly occur at the request of the birth parents. If you want a closed adoption, you most likely will have to wait longer until you can find a birth mother who wants a closed adoption. Many parents often start out thinking they want a closed adoption; then many decide on an open adoption with varying amounts of contact, after reading stories at **http://www.abcadoptions.com** and research sites at **http://www.openadopt.com**.

They discover why so many adoptees experience a deep void that can only be filled by knowing the reason they were placed and in discovering something, anything, about their birth parents. After participating in hundreds of adoptions and observing adopted children as they grow, I know that open adoption is usually best for the child. You can chat about this with other parents online at **http://www.fertile-thoughts.com**.

Most adoptive parents come to feel relieved when they can be honest with their child. They find that peace comes in knowing they have prevented hurt and emotional struggles over the secrecy and sense of abandonment their child might feel from not knowing. ๑๑

## Hear the Children of Closed adoption

Many agencies that have not listened to birth mothers and have declined to embrace open adoption have had to shut their doors because, in the Internet era, the birth mother has the option of choosing the adoptive parents and adoption professionals she will work with across the nation.

If you search the Internet for "closed adoption" you will find websites like **http://www.geocities.com/CapitolHill/2991/affects.html** operated by people opposed to the practice of closed adoption. Visitors to the various sites are often searching, sometimes desperately, for a way to connect with their heritage, their birth parents and the circumstances of their adoptions.

Before you consider adopting a child through a closed adoption, you may want to visit some of these sites and read through the postings to see how the practice has hurt some adoptees, even 20 and 30 years down the road of life.

Closed adoptions will continue, though less than 1 in 10 adoptions are closed today. Some birth parents and adoptive families feel that it's best for their situation. Time will tell if it truly is.

We always counsel a birth mother, especially when she is young, not to close off her options to find out about her child. How a young pregnant woman at the age of 14 feels now and what she

### Adoption Facts & Stats

Out of 1,000 California placements studied in 1987, 60 percent of the adoptive parents had met the birth parents. Today, in our center, over 90 percent of adoptions have some degree of openness.

An estimated 80 percent of adoptions are open nationwide.

Most birth mothers want to meet the adoptive parents and later receive cards and photographs without any additional contact.

wants in 10 years will be different. We ask all families to be open to at least letters and photos if the birth mother asks for them.

## Open Adoption Supports Emotional Health

Sometimes a birth mother requests a closed adoption. She'll say, "I just want to get it over with and go on with my life." This is probably not good for her emotional health because there is no closure and there will always be uncertainty about what became of her child.

This fear of open adoption typically grows out of her low self-esteem and her impending sense of loss. Lifetime will provide a network of past birth mothers to speak with those women considering placing their children. Afterwards, the new birth mother feels reassured and generally will agree to an open adoption. By knowing the child is going to a family who can offer her/him the good parenting and loving home she wants, the healing can begin.

## Being Open to Open Adoption

At our center, perhaps several times a month, adoptive parents will contact us, asking that we choose a birth mother for them in an adoption that is essentially closed. In other words, they do not want to meet the birth mother or to have any contact with her and little information is exchanged. They are motivated by fear of meeting the birth mother and the fear that she will one day come to take back the child.

Many prospective adoptive parents shun the idea of any type of open adoption because they don't understand what this means or that there are varying degrees of openness. Usually after some discussion, they are willing to consider at least a semi-open adoption and meet once with the birth mother prior to placement.

Open adoption is healthier for the adoptive family and for the birth parents. The birth parents will be satisfied that they made a correct choice, and the adoptive parents will have access to the medical information necessary to raise their child. That's what adoption is all about: raising a child in the best atmosphere possible. This can mean putting your emotions aside until you grow used to the situation, but it's worth it. The benefits far outweigh any risk.

In any case, our center will release to the adoptive parents any and all information allowed by the birth mother. In almost every adoption done today, most agencies, attorneys or facilitators, will provide to the adoptive parents any medical records available as long as the birth parents sign a waiver of confidentiality allowing its release.

## Open Adoption Quick Study

Virtually all adoptive parents and birth parents in domestic adoptions can learn each other's identities whether they decide on having contact or not. Until the late 1970s, agencies generally selected adoptive families for children without consulting birth parents.

Today, in many agency adoptions and in virtually all independent adoptions, birth parents are actively involved in selecting the adoptive families for their children. It is increasingly common for birth and adoptive families to have some form of contact before and after placement.

The degree of openness can vary significantly. Birth and adoptive parents may meet before the adoption is finalized and have no further contact, or the families may maintain some level of contact throughout the child's life. It may be the exchanging of photos and letters or having more direct contact such as telephone calls, or, in some cases, getting together on occasion. It is really up to both parties.

# Birth Parent Contact Agreement

Though not recognized as a legal document in most states, adoptive and birth parents often write out an agreement that describes the contact they intend to have over the next five years.

At our center, we often have the parties to the adoption sign a *contact afterwards* form. It provides a checklist of the kind of contact they want: cards and letters, telephone calls or in some adoptions visits on holidays etc. After that, it is up to the adoptive family and birth parents to maintain the agreement to each other.

## Birth Parent On-Going Contact Preferences

Birth Parents

Name:_____

Adoptive Family:_____

I am aware that my contact preferences are that of my own wishes and this form is not legally binding.

### THE FIRST YEAR

**Letters and Pictures**

I would like letters and pictures: Yes:_____ No:_____ How Often?_____

I would prefer not to receive letters and pictures _____

**Telephone Calls:**

I would like telephone calls: Yes:_____ No:_____ How Often?_____
I would prefer not to receive telephone calls _____

**Videotapes**

I would like videotapes: Yes:_____ No:_____ How Often?_____

I would prefer not to receive videotapes _____

**E-Mails:**

I would like e-mails: Yes:_____ No:_____ How Often?_____

I would prefer not to receive e-mails: _____

**Visitation**

I would like visits: Yes:_____ No:_____ How Often?_____

I would prefer not to have visits _____

## THE SECOND YEAR

**Letters and Pictures**

I would like letters and pictures: Yes:_____ No:_____ How Often?_____

I would prefer not to receive letters and pictures _____

**Telephone Calls:**

I would like telephone calls: Yes:_____ No:_____ How Often?_____

I would prefer not to receive telephone calls _____

**Videotapes**

I would like videotapes: Yes:_____ No:_____ How Often?_____

I would prefer not to receive videotapes _____

**E-Mails:**

I would like e-mails: Yes:_____ No:_____ How Often?_____

I would prefer not to receive e-mails: _____

*(continued on next page)*

**Visitation**

I would like visits: Yes:_____ No:_____ How Often?_____

I would prefer not to have visits _____

## THE THIRD YEAR AND BEYOND

**Letters and Pictures**

I would like letters and pictures: Yes:_____ No:_____ How Often?_____

I would prefer not to receive letters and pictures _____

**Telephone Calls:**

I would like telephone calls: Yes:_____ No:_____ How Often?_____

I would prefer not to receive telephone calls _____

**Videotapes**

I would like videotapes: Yes:_____ No:_____ How Often?_____

I would prefer not to receive videotapes _____

**E-Mails:**

I would like e-mails: Yes:_____ No:_____ How Often?_____

I would prefer not to receive e-mails: _____

**Visitation**

I would like visits: Yes:_____ No:_____ How Often?_____

I would prefer not to have visits _____

Additional comments about the amount of contact you desire:

_____

_____

_____

## After the Agreement

When a birth mother allows herself to place another individual's life above her own, that is when maturity and growth begin in her life. For many of these parents it is the first unselfish step they may have ever taken. They also feel empowered knowing the choice was theirs to make and they made it not for themselves, but for their child. In turn, the child will always have the knowledge and reassurance that his/her birth parents wanted the best for them. A sacrifice and a dream of a better life was made by their biological parents and a promise and a plan by their adoptive parents.

I ask many of the adoptive parents coming to us for help in building their families to do a simple yet effective exercise, helping to clarify their thoughts and feelings toward open adoption.

Picture this scenario: You have two wonderful young children and have just found out you have an incurable disease. Your life expectancy is one to six months, but within one month you will be incapacitated.

Your dilemma is that you have no family or friends who can adopt your children or help you. All your life you have struggled on your own to care for yourself and your children and you have been successful, at least up until this point.

Now, you sit in your living room, watching your children play. Time is passing swiftly; you realize that you must find a loving home for the most precious people in your world, all within one month. You will have to depend on total strangers to help you find permanent homes for your loved ones. What information would you want to have about the people who will adopt your children? Who will adopt your children? Would you want to know what they look like? What about their lifestyle and religious beliefs? Would you want to receive photographs, letters and updates on their progress for as long as possible? On the other hand, would you feel more comfortable just saying good-bye?

Many times, we ask others to do what would be impossible for us to even consider doing. I have found, when I look through the eyes of the birth mothers I work with, I see a completely different view. With love, compassion and knowledge about what a birth parent is faced with, only then can we have a deeper understanding of the true gift she or he is giving their child and the adoptive family. How can we deny the birth parents the peace of mind of knowing that their choice was the right one and their child is thriving in a loving home that they chose for him?

Open adoption is now a loving choice made possible. Even if the birth parents make the choice not to continue contact, it was their choice. They will know that the first gift they gave their child was the breath of life and a chosen family for a lifetime. By visiting birth parent posting sites dedicated to birth parents, you can read about the struggle many go through to provide what they feel is the best choice for their child.

In my opinion, there is a great need for education regarding open adoption. It is making its way into many conferences and is the topic of many books. You'll find a number of sites on the Internet with information on open and semi-open adoption. Don't be afraid to research this option, explore it and become comfortable with it before deciding if it is for you. For in open adoption, much of the fear can be alleviated, questions can be answered, leaving your child opportunities to move upward in their lives without secrets. See **http://www.openadoption.com/**.

# 7

# Dear Birth Mother Letter

Your *Dear Birth Mother* letter is your *adoptive parent profile*. It is your own personal story told intimately. It might tell about an event in childhood that helped make you who you are. It might tell about the love you have for your niece and how she loves to come and see you because she gets to look through your telescope at the planets and the stars. It might tell of your views about discipline as an act of love in parenting.

So it's an important document, which, from the very first sentence and the first photograph, has to capture the interest of a potential birth mother. It has to sketch an intriguing and truthful portrait of who you are and the kind of parent you will be. And remember, you've got competition. Other parents are out there trying to attract a birth mother, so your profile has to stand out.

## Telling Birth Mothers about You

You know yourself, your hopes and your dreams. You have always known that you would have a child in your life to love and cherish, to make safe, secure and happy. Late into the night you have talked about your son or your daughter and the day you might see him or her go off to college. You know that you'd be great parents.

Now, imagine having to tell all of this to a complete stranger. Your birth mother is probably a young woman who is pregnant out of wedlock. She is seeking to place her unborn baby with parents who can provide the life for her child that she wishes she could give.

In the Internet era, when nine out of ten adoptions are open, the birth mother usually chooses the adoptive parents. She will go through a process that is not unlike reading resumes when there's a job opening. She will put them in two stacks, one group to consider, one stack of rejects.

# Advertising and Your State Law

Laws change all the time. Always check with the state you are going to advertise your *Dear Birth Mother* letter in before doing so. As of the time of this writing, the laws of these states allow you to advertise for birth parents by posting a *Dear Birth Mother* letter online. We have families on our site from virtually every state and there has never been a concern. But, because you may want to advertise on your own or in a newspaper we have listed the states below that allow it.

| | | |
|---|---|---|
| Alaska | Louisiana | Rhode Island |
| Alabama | Maryland | South Carolina |
| Arizona | Mississippi | South Dakota |
| Arkansas | Missouri | Tennessee |
| California | Montana | Texas |
| Colorado | Nevada | Utah |
| Connecticut | New Hampshire | Vermont |
| District of Columbia | New Jersey | Virginia |
| Hawaii | New Mexico | West Virginia |
| Illinois | New York | Wisconsin |
| Indiana | Oregon | Wyoming |
| Iowa | Pennsylvania | |

# Sample Profile: Todd and Susan

Susan has always dreamed of being a mother.

"I watch Todd play and cuddle with Olivia," says Susan, "and it warms my heart."

A summer cookout and stargazing party with marshmallow roast.

Dear Birth Parent,

We are Todd and Susan, an energetic and loving couple with a tremendous love for children. We fell in love in high school and dreamed of having a family. After ten years of marriage and seven years of trying to have babies through infertility treatments, we knew God had a different plan for us.

We had a nephew Christopher who was adopted, and, in seeing the joy he brought to Susan's sister and their family, we decided to adopt. In June of 1999, our beautiful daughter Olivia came into our lives. Now we want to adopt a brother or sister for her.

Todd has nine siblings and Susan has two. Our families live nearby and we are fortunate to see them often. Our parents are thrilled about having a new grandchild!

## About Our Home and Interests

We have a spacious three-bedroom colonial house. Our backyard is filled with flowers, a sandbox, a playhouse and a beautiful wooden swing set.

One of the swings, in the shape of an airplane, was Todd's as a child. We live near the beach, the zoo and other recreational facilities.

*(continued on next page)*

Internet zone

## Sample Profile: Todd and Susan (cont.)

We have three adorable cats: Callie, Willow and Dewey. They love sunning themselves on the deck, pouncing on unsuspecting leaves or cuddling with us on the couch.

We gather in the summer with our neighborhood friends and their children for cookouts and stargazing parties with our traditional marshmallow roasts. This past summer, we stayed at a cozy family resort in the mountains. Olivia loved feeding the ducks in the pond, learning about nature and, of course, swimming in the pool!

### Todd Tells about Susan

She's the love of my life! Because of her passion for children, Sue works part-time as a pediatric nurse at a community hospital. The children like her because of her patience and sense of humor. Active in the community, she volunteers at vaccination clinics and teaches a babysitting class to young teens.

For as long as I've known Sue, she has wanted to be a mother. Adopting Olivia was a dream come true for her. I see her with Olivia and know that she was meant to be a mother. One of her most wonderful traits is the respect she has for the feelings of others, for each of the adults and children in her life.

### Susan Writes about Todd

He's a committed husband and a wonderful listener. If I could use only one word to describe him, I'd say he's sensitive. He'll do anything for a friend who needs him and is always ready to help someone less fortunate than he is. He runs his own successful tile business and works out of our home. As a little league coach, he always has words of encouragement for his players, especially when they lose a game.

## Sample Profile: Todd and Susan (cont.)

It warms my heart to see him play and cuddle with Olivia. He has settled easily into being a daddy. Creative and artistic, he plays the guitar, writes music and poetry. Olivia and I especially enjoy it when he sings off key!

### We Love Olivia

What a happy little girl we have. An outgoing and energetic toddler, she can't wait to be a big sister! Her favorite things are piggyback rides, singing, playing in the leaves, making snow angels and helping Mommy make chocolate chip cookies. She named her favorite doll *Sara*.

### Our Thanks to You!

Together, we share a loving relationship built on trust, mutual respect and commitment to our family. We were both raised with a strong faith in God and believe that a child should have a solid spiritual foundation. We value education and will provide our children with every opportunity we possibly can to live meaningful and fulfilling lives.

We admire your devotion to finding a secure, loving home for your baby. If you choose us as adoptive parents we are willing to keep you updated, if you wish, through letters and pictures. Please know that there will never be a moment when your child will doubt that he or she is cherished and loved unconditionally.

Warmest regards,

*Todd and Susan*

Thank you for taking the time to read about us.
Please call 1-800-923-6784 for more information.

## Getting Started on Your Profile

Gather friends and family around to brainstorm. Ask them what it is about you that they appreciate most and what they think are the qualities that would make you a great parent.

Write down their ideas; note the details of anecdotes, the stories they like to tell about you. Then gather together your photographs, the special ones you have framed or the ones in your albums and shoe boxes. Sit down with your spouse and go through the pictures. Reminisce; add ideas and stories to your notes. This is how you start shaping the *treasure-trove* of things you'd like a birth mother to know about you.

## "We'll Be Great Parents!"

Next, start working on your *profile,* which in storybook or scrapbook form will tell about you and who you are to an audience of one, your birth mother. Think of its working title as *Our Lives Preparing to Be Good Parents.*

Tell the birth mother what you like to do, who you like to be around, what it's like to live in your home and some of the adventures and fun you've had. Tell her what it will be like, living with you in a stable, loving home with the kind of people she can trust to parent her child.

## How to Write Your Profile

Before you put pencil to paper, do what professional writers do first: picture your reader in your mind; ask yourself: *what does my birth parent want to know?*

Well, she's a birth mother! She wants to know what kind of parents you will be. She wants to imagine her baby growing up in your house where it's safe, having fun and getting help with homework. Be yourself and don't exaggerate or make up anything.

Look to your treasure-trove to find what a journalist might call your *lead story:* the anecdote that will draw your reader in because it tells why you are the perfect parents for the child she is carrying. Hopefully your lead story is funny or pithy or even dramatic too. Let your outline grow out of your treasure-trove of material.

There's another way to do this, the wrong way: many people will start with a *straightjacket* outline; they might decide, *let's start at the beginning* and their first heading might be: *Growing Up in a Small Town.* This approach will result in a profile that is difficult and boring to read. Odds are birth mothers will put it into their reject pile.

As you reach into your treasure-trove, you will pull out some gems, like building a tree house with your dad or finding a porcelain doll in the attic of your grandma's house. Give titles to these top stories and put them under a heading such as *Growing Up.*

As you start roughing out the text, think again (and always) of your reader. When you tell about your childhood, she wants to know what you learned that made you into the person you are, the parent you will be: the morning you saved the life of a sparrow fallen from its nest; or the time after school when you broke your mother's favorite cookie-jar and your mother responded not with anger, but with love and a kiss.

You want to cover essential topics: life in your home, the people in your family, your pets, the fun things you do and your ideas about parenting. Share yourself with your birth mother. She will appreciate it.

## Dear Birth Mother

Now you can start the draft of your *Dear Birth Mother* letter. This is the most important part of your profile.

Its tone is intimate. You are speaking from your heart. Be honest and brief. In its pages you will put some highlights that shine through to the core of your lifestyle. The letter also serves as a sort of introduction, touching on the major points you make in your profile.

While editing and polishing your letter, seek advice from loved ones and from your adoption professional. Once you've finished the letter, leave it alone. Don't get stuck trying to make it perfect or you might lose the sentiment that touches the hearts of birth mothers.

## Picture Perfect

Edit the photographs you'll want to include. Look for the top ten or so that you will use in the profile to illustrate your interests, your traditions and your lifestyle. Include some photos where you are celebrating a birthday or holiday with the special people in your life. Include a picture showing you pursuing a passion in life, like coaching a little league team, or you with a child as a volunteer for your niece's school or another volunteer program. If you have a favorite picture but it's blurry or underexposed, it can't go into your final profile. Include only the best quality photos you have. Originals are best when possible.

From your scrapbook photos, your birth mother will get a glimpse of you in the past. Now it's time to show her photographs of you in the present because within a few months or so she may be placing her child with you.

Make some calls and find a professional photographer who will come to your home to take casual portraits of you, first as a couple and then as a family. Tell the photographer why you need the photos and allow him to use his expertise to help you set up the poses you need.

Ask family members or your best friends to come and be a part of your pictures. Your birth mother will want to see the people her child will be sharing his or her life with. Take some photos of you with children: the prospective adoptive father pushing his nephew on the swing in your backyard, you and a friend laughing together, a prospective mother brushing her niece's hair. Show family pets if appropriate.

## Putting It Together

Now that you've written your *Dear Birth Mother* letter and have your profile, choosing only the best of your photographs, it's time to put it all together. To get an idea of what you want your profile to look like, ask your adoption professional to provide you with samples of some of the best profiles of successful adoptive families that he/she has. Then take a look at profiles on websites like **http://www.open-adoption-services.com** or others listed in Adoption Hotlinks in the back of this book.

You'll need to have the profile designed on a computer. Your adoption professional could do this job or you could ask a friend or go to your local print shop or copy center. To show your designer what you want, you can use the *cut and paste* method to make a *dummy* of the layout.

Get some glue and scissors. Print out your text and gather your photos, make color copied photos for your dummy layout. Cut the text into sections. Stick them to blank sheets of paper along with the photos you'll use to illustrate the words. Under the photos, write out captions by hand.

With the sample in hand, sit down with your designer. Create the long version of your profile first, the one you will have printed and bound. She/he will design the text around your photos, which are scanned into the computer. This will look like your dummy sample only more professional, like a magazine layout.

Take a copy of your paper profile home and start making some edits because your online version may be more compact. Back at the print shop, your designer will make changes in an electronic file and your online version will be ready to upload to the Internet for thousands of birth mothers to see. Finally, *you're ready to go!*

# Mardie's Top Twenty Profile Tips

1) Imagine yourself as a birth mother. Put yourself in her shoes. What would you want to know about prospective adoptive parents?

2) Share with her your genuine feelings, written personally. This will touch her heart and set you apart from other *Dear Birth Mother* letters.

3) Tell her that you will love her child unconditionally.

4) Most women are looking first and foremost for a family they can trust.

5) Don't make your profile too good to be true. The birth mother will sense that you're trying to manipulate her to get her baby. She won't trust your words.

6) Don't misrepresent yourself or try to impress by stretching the truth. Be yourself.

7) Tell stories; they move readers and are the most natural way to communicate.

8) Have several friends and relatives review the draft of your profile and make suggestions.

9) When you write about your life in areas such as *Around the House, Holidays, Work, Your Passions,* tell about the unique things that make you who you are.

10) Phrase your profile in a way that will not offend anyone. For example, don't write: *I can provide your child a home you never could;* instead say: *I can provide a loving and safe home for your child.*

11) Your faith may be important to birth mothers, but be brief when writing about it.

12) Don't preach or sound like you're trying to convert or rescue a birth mother. She'll sense that you're judging her for her lifestyle.

13) If you have a passion, for example, about basketball, don't bring it up in every paragraph. A birth mother wants adoptive parents with balance in their lives.

14) Don't whine about your infertility or the birth mother will believe you have unresolved infertility issues.

15) Briefly mention that you've tried to conceive, that doctors did all they could and that now you're thrilled to bring a child into your lives through adoption, if this is in fact what you did.

16) Your profile and the website where it's posted are the first images a birth family will see to judge you as prospective parents. Make the best first impression you can!

17) Few birth mothers respond to profiles on websites that are cluttered and poorly designed. So find a well-designed site for yours.

18) The number one reason that Web users click the stop button is slow downloading. If your profile doesn't load fast, put it on another site with a faster server or reduce the size of your images.

19) Be there when the birth mother calls. Be sure there's a live person to talk with her—i.e., your adoption professional, a friend or relative or answering service personnel; it certainly should not be a machine or voice mail.

20) Have fun creating your profile and it will show you are really happy about adopting! ☺☺

For more information on creating wonderful profiles see
**http://www.lifetimeadoption.com/forbirthmothers/profiles.html.**

## Your Profile Online

Most professional adoption agencies provide profile preparation services. They will edit and design your online profile, place it on the Internet and promote it through their website and through search engines. One site that draws thousands of birth mothers is the one we have set up for the clients of our center. Take a look at some samples then decide what you want your profile to look like online. Point your browser to http://www.adoptiontree.com.

You may also want to post your profile on another website or on several. Some sites will charge you a monthly fee and some a set-up fee to post your profile. Go to sites devoted to posting profiles, such as http://www.hopetoadopt.com or http://linkadoption.com. You'll see that some of them are simple and effective. Others are stylish. Look for sites that are easy to navigate and pleasing to view.

In this new era of adoption, it is your profile and most likely the one you post online that will connect you with the birth mother of the child meant for you.

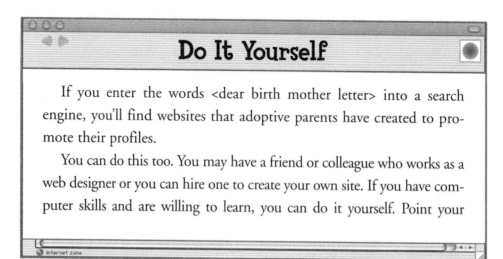

## Do It Yourself

If you enter the words <dear birth mother letter> into a search engine, you'll find websites that adoptive parents have created to promote their profiles.

You can do this too. You may have a friend or colleague who works as a web designer or you can hire one to create your own site. If you have computer skills and are willing to learn, you can do it yourself. Point your

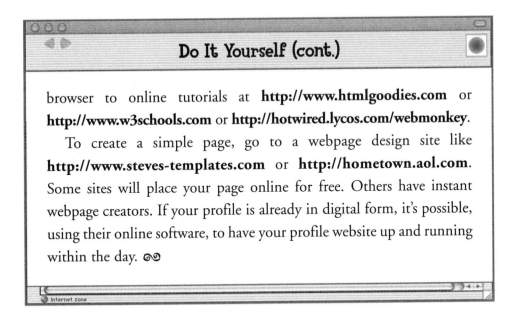

**Do It Yourself (cont.)**

browser to online tutorials at **http://www.htmlgoodies.com** or **http://www.w3schools.com** or **http://hotwired.lycos.com/webmonkey**.

To create a simple page, go to a webpage design site like **http://www.steves-templates.com** or **http://hometown.aol.com**. Some sites will place your page online for free. Others have instant webpage creators. If your profile is already in digital form, it's possible, using their online software, to have your profile website up and running within the day. ꙮ

## Fine Tuning Your Profile

If you go to a number of *Dear Birth Mother* sites, you'll see some nice looking profiles and others where the photos are poor in quality or where the husband or wife looks gloomy. These couples will be waiting a long time for a match. Sometimes all it takes is a small change in your profile to make it effective, a change that will result in a lot of birth mother interest in you.

If your adoption professional asks you to make changes, like taking a better photograph, or changing your text, don't take offense, *do it!* We want one thing, lots of birth mothers reading your profile and wanting you to adopt the baby they're seeking a family for.

## MARDIE'S STORY

# Larry's Scary Beard

"Why are we not getting even a nibble?" asked Renee Groves. She had come by my office wondering why five other couples who were adopting through our center had been matched, while not one birth mother had expressed an interest in her and her husband's profile. Our coordinators had presented their paper resume to some 50 birth mothers.

I looked straight at Renee. "Would Larry shave off his beard if you asked him to?"

Renee glanced at me with surprise.

"He's had that beard since I've known him and that's been over 15 years," she said, wondering what I was thinking.

I gathered myself to speak boldly. If I remained silent, I knew they might never get their baby.

"One of the birth mothers said Larry looked like an ax murderer!" I blurted out.

I showed Renee the picture. Larry's full beard, badly in need of a trim, hid his face and his smile. All you could see were his eyes looking menacingly at the camera. He was one of many prospective fathers I've worked with who needed a shave before a birth mother would consider them.

Renee was still holding the resume in her hand, looking at the photograph. She set it on my desk.

"I'll tell him to shave it," she said.

A few days later I opened a Federal Express envelope. Inside I found the portrait of a clean-shaven man who looked kind and loving, holding hands with his lovely wife Renee.

We sent the new profiles out and soon several birth mothers wanted to talk with the Groves. Unlike the previous birth mothers who saw someone looking sinister, the women who saw the new photo saw Larry's true nature with a nice warm smile that had been hidden beneath a beard. They weren't put off by a first bad impression and took the time to read through the profile and learn why he and Renee would make good parents.

We soon matched them with a birth mother who fell in love with the Groves while talking with them over the phone. When they finally met in person, Larry had grown his beard back and that was okay. By then the birth mother had gotten to know the person inside. ☺☺

# Little Things Mean a Lot

Something you might consider trivial could be the deciding factor for a birth mother. Go for those things that make you unique. Some tidbits that are a big hit with birth mothers are:

- We built a beautiful home in a quiet neighborhood on half an acre. It's a bit too large for us now, but we are anxious to grow into it.

- Our home is the meeting place for almost all our family gatherings. It was designed to entertain and we fill it with lots of family, friends and fun, every chance we get.

*(continued on next page)*

• Traditions are a big part of what ties our family together. We particularly enjoy Christmas Eve dinner by candlelight, Thanksgiving Day parades, autumn pumpkin festivals and Easter sunrise breakfast.

• We promise that our child will know from day one that s/he was loved and cherished by you and that we will love and cherish your child as well. Together we can create a loving bond that will surround our child for life.

• Greg will be a great father, devoted to helping a baby feel welcome and secure in God's world.

• We enjoy our small-town living and the quiet, safe environment it gives us. We enjoy knowing most of the people in our community and the closeness it provides.

• We will provide for a quality education and give your child the support to become whatever he or she desires to be.

• We have two loving dogs, Gus and Rufus. They are wonderful companions and love children.

• Together we have over 30 nieces and nephews, consisting of both adopted and biological children. ☺

# "I Wanted to Ask You..."

Just as adoptive parents go online for help and advice, so do birth parents. For them, there are suggested questions to ask of you! This list, compiled from several websites, will help you write your profile by answering the questions birth parents want answered and it will help you prepare to speak with prospective birth mothers.

- Why do you want to adopt?
- How do you feel about adopting?
- How long have you been married?
- Do you have children already?
- Do you have experience with children?
- What kind of recreation or hobbies do you enjoy?
- Do you have strong religious beliefs?
- How old are you?
- Do you both work or will one parent be home with the baby?
- What are your views on child discipline?
- Do you have extended family or relatives living nearby?
- What do your family and relatives think about you adopting a baby?
- Will you tell the child he is adopted? When and how?
- What will you tell the child about his birth mother? About his birth father?
- What do you hope for the child's education?
- Are you willing to maintain contact with the birth mother as your child grows up?
- What type of contact would you like to have with the birth mother? ☺☺

Once you have answered all the questions and you're comfortable with your answers, your profile is almost complete and ready to go. Hopefully, you've taken the time to wisely choose the right adoption professional to represent you, but you've got one last thing to consider.... At the moment you're stressed, tired and anxious, wanting desperately to be a parent. What happens next? What will it be like when a birth mother calls? What if you're not home? What if you're on vacation? What if you went out for a quick dinner? What then?

## Are You There for Birth Mother Calls?

Birth mothers tell me they don't feel comfortable calling collect and most of them can't afford to pay for a long distance call to you. Consequently, you'll need a toll-free number where they can reach you.

Many adoption professionals have an 800 number for birth mothers to call. To make sure we don't miss a call at our center, it is open 24 hours a day, 7 days a week. You'd be surprised how many birth mothers call at 3:00 in the morning.

Your professional is a buffer between you and birth mothers. In your profile you should clearly state, "If you'd like to speak with us, and we'd love to hear from you, please call this organization at this toll-free number."

A birth mother will call and say, "I saw Sally and Tom's profile on the website and I'd like to speak with them."

Your professional will determine if the birth mother is legitimate, consider her circumstances, decide if she's serious about placing her child, verify her pregnancy, assess her situation as it relates to yours and only then present her to you.

If you decide to set up your own 800 number, and toll free numbers are more affordable than ever before, you need the capability to forward the line to a friend or family member who can take the call when you're not home. If a birth mother calls and gets no answer, or is greeted by a machine, she may never call back. Whoever answers must be prepared to ask her the appropriate questions without scaring her away.

If you put your personal home phone number on the Internet or in the newspaper for anyone to see that you are seeking a birth mother, be very careful. It is always better to get an 800 number from your long distance company or even a remote call-forwarded number that attaches to your main line at home or the office.

So, now you've chosen what method you'll use for your birth mother to contact you. No matter what happens or where you are, someone somewhere will answer the phone. Your profile is now complete and posted online. Hopefully, your adoption professional will also have a binder where your profile will be featured along with other waiting families. Often, profiles are distributed to physicians, clinics and counselors. Now that you're done and it's out of your hands, the waiting begins. You wonder, *When will she call? Will she call? How long will it take? What will I say?*

# 8

# A Child for You

At our center, once a birth mother has contacted us, we mail her a packet of information for her to fill out, including prenatal care and medical history, desired ongoing contact with the adoptive family and more. All concerns, if any, are noted as well.

Then, once a birth mother has picked your profile, your adoption professional will discuss with you the information received from the birth mother to make sure this might be a match. Next, the birth mother is given your toll-free number and a time is set up for both of you to speak or meet in person.

Remember that the birth mother will have already seen pictures of your home, your pets, your other children, the baby's room and whatever else you have posted. She will know a little bit about your background, your hopes and desires. In turn, we will inform you of the birth mother's circumstances including any ongoing concerns.

Each of you will know a little bit about the other, but be prepared—generally birth mothers will contact more than one family, so the choice is not usually made immediately.

Many adoption professionals encourage both the adoptive family and the birth mother to seek counseling before the conversation takes place.

Your professional should assist you on what questions to ask and/or any actions to take.

Some birth mothers have been known to choose families from the pictures alone before the initial phone call. We had one birth mother that selected a couple because the adoptive mother looked just like her aunt. That small distinction allowed the family to stand out enough for her to choose them to parent her child.

## Finally, a Birth Mother on the Line!

When you finally receive that long-awaited phone call, you may be nervous or scared to death. So is the birth mother! Take a deep breath, relax and talk as you would with a newfound friend.

Be concerned about her. Ask how she's feeling. Ask about her situation, not as a prospective parent, but as a caring person. Encourage her to express her fears and anxieties. The more you let her talk and the more you listen, the more comfortable you will both feel. She will mirror your tone. She may carry the conversation or be quiet and shy. Let her converse at her own pace, you've got plenty of time.

Share information with ease, adding a question here and there. Be prepared for her to ask questions that strike you as blunt: *Why didn't you have your own children? How old are you? Have you ever been divorced?*

Answer graciously.

Don't tape the conversation. By law you can't legally record a call without asking and if you do ask, she may hang up. Don't use a speakerphone. It is too impersonal.

We ask birth mothers to call and share their first conversation. "They were very nice and all," they sometimes say. "But they didn't seem excited. I want to talk with a family that's excited!" So let your positive emotions show through. If you are thrilled that she called, tell her. Share with her your feelings of excitement and joy.

## Hard Questions

Be careful how you ask about the father of the baby. Some birth mothers don't know who the father is. If she tells you she's not sure who it was because she slept with several men at the time of the month she was fertile, don't act shocked or surprised and do not judge her.

Many prospective parents stammer their way into asking about the child's ethnicity. You can ease into this by telling the birth mother what you and your husband look like, that you are Hispanic, say, with olive skin and your husband is white with brown hair and hazel eyes. Then you might ask her what the birth father looks like.

A birth mother may not know the word Caucasian or use politically correct words. She may describe herself as white, black or Mexican. She may say the unborn child is mixed and this usually means with some African heritage, though some mothers consider their child mixed when the father is Latino and she's Caucasian. You can clarify this without her taking offense.

### Questions to Ask a Birth Mother

- Where do you live?
- Are you working?
- Do you go to school?
- Do you have other children?
- How old are they?
- Are you staying home to take care of your other children?
- Does your family know you are pregnant?
- Do you have others to support you throughout the pregnancy and the adoption?
- Do they visit you?
- If so, what are they feeling?
- Do they know you are considering adoption?
- Do they support your plans?
- Are you close to your mother?
- Your father?
- How much contact do you want before the adoption and after?
- Would you like us to be with you at the hospital for the delivery?

You can avoid having to ask the tough questions: leave that to your adoption professional, who talks every day with birth mothers about touchy subjects and, as your buffer, and with her permission, will pass the information on to you. That way, when you talk with her, you can concentrate on matters that will help the two of you befriend each other and bond.

# Ten Tips on How to Speak with a Birth Mother

1) On your first call, take the time to get to know her. This is someone who may play a big part in the rest of your life.

2) Treat her as the equal partner she is in adoption. You are trying to decide if your lifestyle is what she wants for her child.

3) Do not pressure her to commit to you.

4) If you pepper her with questions or try to interrogate her, she'll take offense and hang up.

5) Use words she understands. Don't talk down to her.

6) If she shares something about herself that doesn't fit with your moral code, don't act shocked but respond with unconditional caring.

7) Don't judge, preach or try to be her parent.

8) Give her room to consider whether adoption is the right choice for her and the child.

9) Don't push to get her phone number on the first call.

10) Leave the conversation with her wanting to call you again. ◌◌

*Any questions you might think to ask after hanging up can be asked by your adoption professional, or by you on your next call or e-mail.*

## There Will Be Other Birth Mothers

The first call you receive could be the birth mother with whom you feel so comfortable that you may want to make an immediate commitment. On the other hand, you may feel a sense of reluctance or feel uncomfortable. When closing the conversation, tell her how much you enjoyed talking with her. If you feel good about the situation, ask if she'd like to meet and would it be okay if your adoption professional called her.

Be aware that some birth mothers will never call you back. She may select other prospective parents or she may change her mind and choose not to place her child. As hard as this is for us as adoptive parents, remember that it's not unusual for a couple to talk with four or five birth mothers before the perfect match is made with the birth mother of the child meant for you. Hold fast onto hope, for tomorrow is always another day.

### Are There Less Caucasian Newborns?

- Before 1973, 19.3 percent of children born to never-married white women were placed for adoption. Between 1989 and 1995, this number fell to 1.7 percent.

- The number of adoptions by Caucasian adults not related to the child peaked at 89,200 in 1970 and declined to 47,700 in 1975, because, concluded the researchers, fewer U.S. white infants were available, all this due to Roe vs. Wade.

- There are still numerous Caucasian infants to adopt contrary to what the public believes.

## Caucasian Newborns and Infants

It is true that for every couple that adopts a healthy Caucasian newborn, there are many others waiting to adopt one. More single women are deciding to raise their children, birth control is widely used and abortion is legal. As a result, fewer white newborns are available for adoption.

So it may take a little longer to find yours, but for you it may be worth the wait.

There are newborns available out there. And because of the Internet, you will be exposed to thousands of birth mothers pregnant with Caucasian children all across the land. If you have taken time with your adoption profile and have an effective presence on the Web, you will find your newborn. At our center, it usually takes from 4 to 12 months to locate a Caucasian newborn for our adoptive parents.

Most Internet adoptions of newborns result from the contact you make with a birth mother. She is usually pregnant and looking to place her baby before it's born. Sometimes she is a college student ready to accept responsibility and place her child. Many times she, occasionally along with the birth father, will try and provide a good home during the early months of the baby's life. Often they will come to realize they can't handle the responsibility or the cost of raising a child and will begin an adoption plan.

## A Match Is Made

Once a match is made between the birth mother and the adoptive family, they continue to stay in touch with each other throughout the pregnancy. Together they will build a relationship, learning about each other and sharing with each other. The adoptive family and birth mother have discussed and agreed upon the type of contact they both want. Generally, the birth mother will have already shared with the adoptive family how much or how little contact she would like at the hospital.

# Four Weeks Prior to Your Due Date

- Prepare to take a leave of absence at your job and tie up loose ends.

- If in a state that requires birth mother counseling, speak to your birth parent and set up an appointment with your ASP (Adoption Service Provider) to meet with your birth mother for her advisement of rights.

- Prepare the nursery (if you are comfortable doing this ahead of time). Some families set up a bassinet beforehand in their bedroom and a small drawer for baby items.

- Interview pediatricians. Ask other new parents for recommendations.

- Do as much as possible before your birth mother's due date.

- Pack bags for the hospital, one for you and one for the baby. Don't forget to remind the person coming with you to pack a bag as well. You don't want to find yourself short on time.

## When packing the adoptive family hospital bag bring:

- Your camera, extra film and batteries.

- Cash (change) in an envelope for phone calls and vending machines.

- Credit card/checkbook.

- Phone numbers.

- Adoption folder and travel release form for the doctor to sign allowing the baby to travel by air.

- Gift and card for the birth mother if allowed by state law.

- Cellular phone and charger.

*(continued on next page)*

- Video camera: Ask your birth mother about taping the birth. If she is not comfortable, you can videotape in the nursery after the birth.

- Small ice chest with snacks and drinks/juices (hospital cafeterias are often closed at night and vending machines are limited).

- Deodorant.

- Personal items (razor, hair brush, medications etc.).

- Tissue.

- Magazines to read while waiting.

- Book for Dad to read during delivery.

- Remember airport security! Pack any items not allowed on planes in your *checked* bags at the airport.

## Hospital bag for the baby:

- Diaper bag

- 1-3 outfits in different sizes for baby to travel home in, more if you are going to be staying longer in another state until released to go home by ICPC and your attorney.

- Newborn diapers (ask the hospital for a gift pack, they will give you one; samples for new parents vary, but are helpful and FREE–ask for yours!).

- Baby wipes and plastic bags, tissues.

- 1-2 receiving blankets–more if the weather demands it.

- Hat/bonnet (sun hat).

- Four cloth diapers or soft cloth for spit up.

- Car seat and instructions–if this is the first time you have used one.

- Bottles and liners–ask the hospital what formula the baby needs or has been on. Sometimes they will give you a free sample of formula. ☺☺

## The Day of Adoption

This day can be one of the most memorable days of your life, but it can also be one of the most stressful. Depending on the type of adoption you are involved with, the needs of the day will vary. We will cover a few suggestions to keep this day special and hopefully ease some of the tension.

## Important Hospital Tip

If you are adopting a newborn, do not leave the surrounding area if the baby is still in the hospital. If you had given birth to a child, you would be in the hospital with your child until the hospital released both of you. It is important to show the same care in your adoption as you would for a birth child.

Don't disappear for long lunches and unnecessary shopping trips. If you need to leave, try having one parent or grandparent stay in the hospital with the baby. This doesn't mean you can't go pick up necessary items for the baby, a car seat or to meet with your attorney, but some parents go back to work if they live nearby or decide to visit friends in the area.

I have had a number of adoptive parents make the mistake of leaving and going about their lives until the baby is released from the hospital, leaving the birth mother alone to wonder what happened to them and to ponder her decision on this family and their commitment to the child and parenting. Birth mothers often feel the baby has been left all alone in the hospital nursery and guilt sets in. It is important to spend as much time with the baby as possible.

Stay at a hotel near the hospital or see if the hospital can provide a room for you as adoptive parents. Many hospitals do this for the adoptive family at no charge, but remember it is not a rule, so you'll need to ask and not demand it. Your birth mother needs to know you care enough to want to stay and start bonding with your new son or daughter.

## Fearful Adoptive Parents

Often an adoptive mother and sometimes the adoptive father are so fearful that they will ask the birth mother repeatedly if this is really what she wants to do. It is fine to ask about her feelings but don't try to make yourself feel better by asking her what she wants to do more than once. Let your adoption professional assist if you feel there is a problem.

## Other Children

If you have other children, ask a friend or relative to watch them while you take the time to pick up their new brother or sister. Make your babysitting plans before you are matched or in advance of the birth if you have a due date. Remember, due dates can change; babies come early and sometimes late.

# Things to Do

## 1. While you're waiting at the hospital:

- Call your adoption professionals.
- Read.
- Play Cards.
- Order flowers for the birth mother.
- Take pictures.

- Drink liquids.
- Eat snacks.
- Take a change of clothes and toiletries (labor may be long or you may want or need to stay with the baby). And always wear clothes that are comfortable!
- Smile, hold hands.
- Pray!

## 2. Once the baby is born:

- During daytime hours call your adoption professionals.
- Call your family and friends.
- Take lots of photos.
- Spend time with the baby and your birth mother, as much as she feels comfortable with.
- Get a bite to eat. Ask your birth mother if she would like anything special. Many women would love a burger or something from a fast food restaurant.

## 3. When leaving the hospital:

- Say good-bye to your birth mother; most birth mothers like to leave before the baby does, others prefer to stay and be sure the baby's release has gone well. Say good-bye and thank the hospital staff.
- Exchange gifts (if allowed).
- Take pictures of you checking out with the baby; always ask the birth mother first if she is comfortable with your photographing her.
- Sign paperwork releases and ask the pediatrician at the hospital to sign the *permission to fly* form if traveling by plane.

*(continued on next page)*

• Bring your car to the front of the hospital (ask the nurse which entrance to come to). Be sure the car seat is securely in place before placing the baby in it. Do this in advance, not while the nurse is standing there with the baby or she'll make you nervous!

## 4. Picking the baby up from the hospital:

• Both parents should pick up the baby from the hospital. If you were giving birth would your husband stay home and have you drive yourself home? I hope not. If you are both excited about adopting, you both need to be at the hospital.

• If one of you has to work and can't take the week off for an out-of-state adoption, then ask one of your parents to accompany your spouse. It may be beneficial to have a caring grandparent come to the hospital.

• A word of caution: If the grandparents are not educated in open or semi-open adoption, you may be setting yourself up for more grief. Educate them on open adoption. Give them books to read on the subject so at the very least they will know what to say and what not to say.

## 5. Traveling home:

• If driving, you'll probably sit in the back seat with your baby or child while your spouse or a relative drives home. Keep some pillows handy for comfort as you may need to doze off if the wait has been a long one.

• If traveling by plane, board early when allowed. Ask for additional pillows to prop up under your arms when feeding and holding the baby.

• Take pictures as you prepare to leave and when you get home. This is a once in a lifetime trip to be added to your baby book.

- You may need a cloth diaper for spit ups and a bottle for feeding on your trip home.

- Use bottled water for the baby's formula. Test the bottle before giving it to the baby. Many new parents forget that and find that the bottle, warmed in the microwave oven, is so hot it could scald the baby's mouth.

- Relax, enjoy your trip home and your new baby. Live in the moment and don't miss this time by thinking about anything else.

## 6. When you arrive home:

- Ask relatives to wash their hands before holding the baby. As this can be awkward, some new parents put up a sign that says, *Please wash your hands before holding (baby's name). Thank you.* Little children and adults sometimes forget that a newborn is still new to this world and hasn't developed the needed defenses against germs yet.

- Have a friend or family member graciously remind guests when to leave if they stay too long. You need your time to rest. You won't be getting much sleep and any rest time is precious indeed.

- And, lastly, celebrate. Look at your child. Study him, his little toes, fingers and eyelashes. Take note of how small and delicate his nails are, how firm and round his little tummy is. Hold him, cuddle him, share him with your extended family and remember that this child was *meant for you!* ☺☺

# 9

# Special Needs and Foster Adoption

Perhaps you've decided not to adopt a newborn. There are many children lost in the foster care system that are desperate for homes. An older child adoption can sometimes be quicker than a newborn match. Sibling matches are also quicker because so few adoptive parents want two or more children at once. The fact of the matter is: Most hopeful parents want a newborn, leaving many children without parents to love and care for them.

## MARDIE'S STORY

### Annie's Story...Out of Foster Care

I remember Annie watching me shyly from behind the skirt of her foster mom. Seven years old, petite with dark hair and sparkling blue eyes, abandoned by her mother, she suffered from detachment disorder, the inability to trust or love.

One night in September 1989, when Annie was only four, her single mother Brittany, addicted to methamphetamine, left her rental house

*(continued on next page)*

in Grass Valley, California, to make a drug run to nearby Auburn. Sheriff Deputies later found her passed out and disoriented in a flophouse near downtown. They arrested her for drug possession and took her to the county jail.

She had left Annie home alone. A concerned neighbor, and her landlord next door, suspected as much. He watched anxiously for Brittany's return. Finally, one hour later he used his key to go inside and get the child. Removed from her mother's custody by child protective services, Annie was placed in the foster care system.

After serving 30 days in jail, Brittany was released on probation. She entered a residential drug treatment center and started to put her life back together. Social workers and the family court judge monitored her recovery and worked hard to reunify her with Annie.

Brittany was clean and sober for six months. Released from the treatment facility, she went to a rehabilitation center for 30 days, but then relapsed. She promised the judge that she would go back for treatment and he gave her a second chance.

But one night soon after, driven by the power of her addiction, Brittany slipped away from the treatment center. She hitchhiked to Auburn where she hooked up with an old drug contact and got high. This time she went to jail to serve her two-year sentence. The family court judge terminated her parental rights and Social Services set out to place Annie for adoption.

Annie waited and prayed anxiously that someday she would have a mother and father like the other children she knew at school. Over a period of three years, she lived in five different foster homes in the Grass Valley area. Each time she moved, she dutifully packed her meager possessions into one cloth suitcase and a big canvas duffle bag.

Nearby, in the tiny town of Rough and Ready, Steve and Linda Michaels were thinking about adoption. Their marriage was happy and solid. They were involved in community activities. Linda was a career mother and Steve an engineer. In their early forties, they already had three biological sons and wanted a little girl. Complications during the labor and delivery of their third son had left Linda with secondary infertility, meaning she was unable to conceive again.

At first, they wanted a newborn and got the word out that they wanted to adopt. A friend and social worker with the county told them about Annie. One day she brought them some photographs of her and they thought she was precious.

The Michaels came to me. I connected them with a support group of parents with special needs children and with a couple I knew who had adopted a little girl with attachment disorder.

I went with the Michaels to see the county psychiatrist who was treating Annie. For children like her, she said, the anxiety over abandonment can cause severe distress, such as episodes of panic. Sometimes they fear going to school or even leaving the house. They do not trust adults and are unable to sustain loving relationships.

The disorder is treated by parents who can provide love and attention for the rest of their childhood years and with counseling and medication. (Annie was taking medication for attention deficit disorder, one manifestation of her underlying condition). In Annie's case, the doctor advised, a full recovery was possible but not certain.

Over the next weeks, because their faith was strong and they were concerned about this tender, hurting child, the Michaels moved closer to a decision about adopting Annie.

But they were unsure.

"Can we handle this?" Linda asked me. She felt she was meant to adopt this child. "The emotional scars seem so deep," she said. "Will they heal?" Her voice was shaky. "What if she doesn't get better?"

(continued on next page)

Finally we went to see the foster mother, Laurie. "Annie's behavior is good," she said. "She's polite and smart, mostly she's withdrawn."

Laurie felt that Annie's experience with foster care had delayed her recovery. "Just when she started bonding with one set of parents, she was uprooted and sent to another."

She looked at Linda and spoke from her heart, "If someone would take her in permanently and love her, I think she'll be okay."

The Michaels chose to adopt Annie. They built an addition to their home so she'd have her own bedroom. They furnished it with white French provincial furniture. They put pretty things on her dresser and dolls on her hope chest.

When the Michaels came to get her at the foster home, Annie was sitting on her bed, the duffle bag by her feet.

She looked up at Laurie, her foster mother. "I'm going to miss you," she said. She thought she was moving on to one more foster home. When the Michaels lovingly explained that she was going to live with them forever, her eyes got wide.

"Really?" she said. "You mean you're going to be my mom and dad?"

It was a testament to Annie's resilience that, after the childhood she had endured up until then, she could still be optimistic.

Steve and Linda dedicated themselves to their child. They consulted with other parents and with specialists. They took parenting and child development courses at the community college. Their three biological sons accepted and loved Annie. After school they played together in the yard and the older brother watched out for her, their little sister.

Because of the love and caring she got from her adoptive family, along with the counseling and medical care she received, Annie improved. Over the next few years she put her fears behind and grew into an assertive and precocious little girl.

Soon, Annie was getting A's and B's on her report cards in the fifth grade and then she won the spelling bee. Now, Annie is an honor student in high school and she plans to go on to college and study child psychology. May God bless people like Steve and Linda. For without them, so many little children would be lost. ꩜

## A Child's Life

Most of us look back on our childhood with pleasure. Free of most worries and troubles, those days are among the most wonderful times of our lives. But, sadly, they can be the worst of times for some children in foster care. Foster care is a patchwork system of transitional homes where children with physical or emotional problems too difficult for their parents or whose safety is threatened by the very mothers and fathers who brought them into this world are placed.

Thinking about Annie's story, I am reminded how much of a blessing adoptive parents like Steve and Linda are. While many couples have in mind the image of the child they hope to adopt as a healthy newborn that looks like them (and this is wonderful too), the Michaels, out of love, adopted a troubled child they hoped to help. Imagine the patience they needed to understand Annie's view of the world, the advanced parenting skills they had to acquire and the level of the commitment they made to help provide a good life for her.

Shuffled from one foster home to another, thousands of children dream that maybe one day they will have a family to call their own. If they are adopted, tucked into their very own bed by a parent who has promised to keep and protect them, they experience a sense of permanency for the first time. This is their first step on a journey that is sometimes long and hard and more often than not, ends up being a life of happiness, which each child deserves.

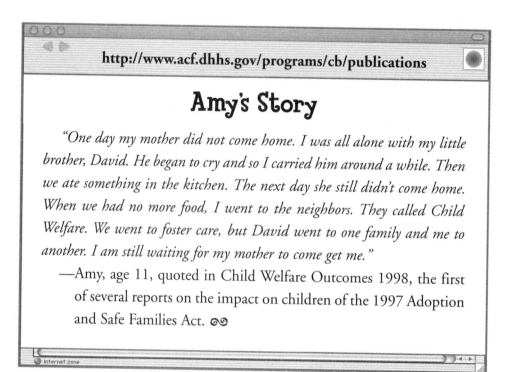

http://www.acf.dhhs.gov/programs/cb/publications

# Amy's Story

*"One day my mother did not come home. I was all alone with my little brother, David. He began to cry and so I carried him around a while. Then we ate something in the kitchen. The next day she still didn't come home. When we had no more food, I went to the neighbors. They called Child Welfare. We went to foster care, but David went to one family and me to another. I am still waiting for my mother to come get me."*

—Amy, age 11, quoted in Child Welfare Outcomes 1998, the first of several reports on the impact on children of the 1997 Adoption and Safe Families Act. ☙

# Just the Facts

- Nearly 60 percent of the 251,000 children who exited foster care in 1999 were reunited with their birth parents. About 20 percent were adopted or placed with a permanent guardian.

- Of special needs children adopted in 1999, 80 percent were placed with a foster parent or relative.

- The Adoption and Safe Families Act pays incentives of $6000 to state agencies, which increase, over the previous year, the number of special needs placements.

- As a result of the 1997 Act and state initiatives, 26 states doubled, while Wyoming and Delaware tripled, the number of adoptions from foster care between 1997 and 2001.

- In 1999, nearly 70 percent of waiting children had been in foster care for at least two years and 25 percent for five years or more.

- Of waiting children, 60 percent are at least six years old.

- Once a foster child is nine years old, his chances of placement in a permanent home are less than 50 percent.

- Of children in the child welfare system, an estimated 30 to 40 percent have physical health problems.

- Some (admittedly inadequate) studies estimate that 60 percent of children in foster care have moderate to severe mental health problems.

- Even with the recent increases in adoptions, for every 100 children adopted each year out of foster care, 250 still wait. ⊙⊚

## Children in Need

Each year, state child welfare workers investigate some four million cases where parents abuse, neglect or otherwise mistreat children or lack the skills or resources to cope with a child's medical conditions, emotional or psychological problems.

The workers remove some 580,000 of these children from their homes and place them for proper care and safety with foster parents or relatives, in institutions, group homes or residential treatment centers. There they will remain for two years on average and, not uncommonly, for five to seven years.

Difficult circumstances compel social workers to move many of the children from one temporary foster placement to another. Meanwhile they try to help the birth parents resolve problems like drug and alcohol abuse or domestic violence so they can prudently reunify them with their children. Failing that, they initiate legal action to terminate parental rights and seek permanent placement of the child outside the home.

## The Waiting Children

More than 125,000 of these children, more than half of them of minority descent, have an adoption plan, that is, an agency has prepared the paperwork to place them with an appropriate family, though most of them will remain in foster care through childhood. **See http://www.cap-book.org** for more information.

# One Waiting Child

Number: T47469

Grant, a soft-spoken and inquisitive child, is quick to flash a charming smile. He may appear shy upon first meeting, but is quite talkative once his trust is earned.

He enjoys playing outdoors, riding his bicycle and playing video games. Grant was significantly developmentally delayed when he entered care, but being a determined young man, he has made tremendous progress since being placed in therapeutic foster care.

He is academically delayed, but continues to make progress in small structured classrooms. He makes good grades and gets along well with his peers. Grant needs a family that is patient and willing to earn his trust.

His new family should also be prepared to continue to participate in his ongoing therapy, which addresses his many losses.

If you are interested please contact his social worker. ∞

## Special Needs Children

Special needs children usually have varying degrees of physical, mental or emotional challenges. They include school-age children who were neglected and have learning disabilities or adolescents who were traumatized by sexual abuse and have psychological disorders. Others have physical conditions like asthma, Down's syndrome or cerebral palsy. Some, born addicted to drugs their mothers were taking, are at risk of eventual physical and emotional difficulties.

Some are abandoned infants but most are over the age of 5 and under the age of 18 and are known in the field of adoption as *older children*. Many will struggle with the effects of maltreatment or physical ailments through childhood and often throughout their lives. They require adoptive parents who can provide them with stability and structure, special care and professional help, patience and love. Visit **http://www.adopt.org** for more information.

### Foster Care Statistics

#### Waiting Children

*(AFCARS 1999)—Note—This is the most current study available.*

The average age of children in foster care as of March 1999 was 9 years. The average (mean) length of time that children had been in foster care was 33 months.

As of March 1999, The United States Department of Health and Human Services estimates that as many as 117,000 children currently in foster care need adoptive families. The ethnic backgrounds of these children are as follows:

- 51% were African American
- 32% were White
- 11% were Hispanic
- 2% were Native American/Alaskan Native or Asian/Pacific Islander
- 5% were of unknown/unable to determine ethnic backgrounds

## MARDIE'S TOP TIPS

# When Adopting a Child with Special Needs...

- Do not jump in just because you hear of a child in need. Take time to decide if this is what you want for your life.

- Observe and talk with parents raising a child who is similar to the one you might adopt.

- Think about the severity of the disabilities and behavioral problems you can handle.

- Be prepared: Enroll in instructional parenting classes provided by your adoption professional. Read books recommended by your social worker.

- Visit Internet forums to read about adoptive parents whose lives are filled with purpose and joy, and also to hear from those who are struggling.

- Seek guidance by e-mailing and relating to parents you meet online who've *been there and done that*.

- Make sure you apply for the Adoption Assistance Program.

- Always finalize a special needs adoption through an agency even if an attorney or facilitator has located a child for you.

- Search the net for information about your child's condition, new treatment methods and advice in the writing of experts. See http://www.webmd.com.

- Use the Web to find medical resources, equipment and supplies.

- Commit yourself to providing the quality of life, the patience, understanding and unconditional love your child deserves.

- If your agency requires counseling for your family to adopt a special needs child, accept it graciously and don't be offended, because it will help you.

- Stay in touch with social workers for guidance and to help you adjust to your new reality.

- Learn new skills to meet the child's needs and be prepared to make a lifelong commitment. ෧෨

## What Is Foster Adoption?

Through foster adoption, also known as fost-adopt, children who are wards of the state and cannot be reunified with their birth parents for their safety, or other reasons, are placed in permanent homes with foster parents, relatives, or with prospective parents with no prior relationship to them. The adoptions are arranged by state child welfare agencies or through private adoption agencies under contract.

Trying desperately to place special needs children, social service departments have turned to the Internet to tell people of their plight, and to connect them with adoptive families. Beware, not all fost-adopt programs work out. Do your homework. To see photographs and read the stories of special needs children, go to **http://www.adoptuskids.org** or **http://www.adopt.org**. In Adoption Hotlinks, you'll find sites for special needs children listed by state.

# The Adoption and Safe Families Act

Congress passed legislation in 1997 to encourage the adoption of special needs children and it worked! Foster care adoptions increased 78 percent from 1996 to 2000.

The Act provided federal funds for states taking action to:

• Limit the months that children can stay in foster care.

• Offer more postadoption services to special needs children and adoptive families.

• Streamline court procedures for terminating parental rights.

• Place children before terminating parental rights.

• Hire more social workers to reduce caseloads.

• Bring in adoption specialists to work in social service agencies.

• Pay for health coverage of special needs children.

• Get the word out that thousands of children are waiting and it's not too late for them to have a good life through adoption.

# And the Survey Said...

University of Nevada researchers surveyed 249 parents who had adopted 373 children with special needs. The full report is located at **http://kidscount.unlv.edu/2001/specialneeds.pdf**.

• 77% said their relationship with the child was good to excellent.

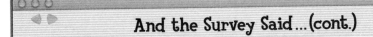

## And the Survey Said...(cont.)

- 66% said the adoption's impact on their family was positive.

- 49% said the impact on their marriage was positive.

- 10% said the impact on their marriage was negative.

- 32% viewed their child's behavior problems as severe.

- 27% regarded their child's physical disabilities as profound.

- 58% said they did not receive enough information about the child before adopting.

- 37% believed the child's problems were more serious than they were told prior to adopting.

- Social workers at the Iowa Human Services Department questioned 533 parents of adopted special needs children. For the 44-page study, go to **http://www.cfpciowa.org** and click on the <publications> link.

- 61% said their adoptees were minority children.

- 81% who adopted sibling groups were satisfied with the adoption.

- 89% were satisfied with their adoption when the child had one physical disability.

- 84% were satisfied when the child had one behavioral problem.

- 76% were satisfied when the child had a combination of three medical and behavioral conditions.

- Satisfaction decreased with the number of years gone by since the adoption was finalized, indicating that parental challenges may increase as the child gets older. ☺☺

Internet zone

## Desperate to Adopt

Dear Mardie:

My husband Trevor and I are in our mid-thirties and have been married for two years. I have early onset of menopause and we desperately want a family.

Our home study is done and we are waiting to adopt a newborn. Every morning for the past 12 months I have awakened hopeful, but, so far, no baby. It is the waiting, I think, that is causing the problems we are having. Lately we have been arguing and fighting.

The social worker at our agency said she could have a baby with special needs for us within a few months! We are ready to jump at this. What do you think?

Dear Christine,

You cannot make this decision on the spur of the moment, like standing in front of K-Mart and gathering up a puppy from a cardboard box.

Adopting a special needs child is a reality check on what you want for your life. How would you feel, for example, about getting up at night to feed your new baby every two hours for the next few years?

As for me, I love children and have always climbed out of bed at night with a joyful heart to the crying of my own children or a baby under my care. But I would not have the patience to look after a child who needs a feeding tube.

We are blessed that some parents are in their element when caring for children with physical challenges. They see it as their mission in life and you may too. If so, then in time, you should consider adopting such a child.

---

**email**

To:
Cc:

## Desperate to Adopt (cont.)

But first you should ask: What time will I have to take away from my spouse to care for this child? More than one marriage has ended when the husband felt that his wife was neglecting his needs. To hold together against the long-term stress of raising a child with disabilities, first make sure your marriage is strong. ☺☺

---

## A Special Gift

God has blessed some people with the gift of loving patience to adopt older and special needs children. Not everyone has this gift. Beware that some prospective parents, driven by emotions like compassion or pressured by social workers, will adopt a special needs child when they are not capable of making it work.

Depending on the nature and severity of an older child's behavioral problems, some children will need extra nurturing while others require strict discipline. Some parents, like those with a background in teaching, psychology or the military, for example, or mothers who can stay at home to supervise, may have the tools to help these children. Others may not.

Visit forums like **http://www.ilovejesus.com/missions/adopt/re-source_fams.html** to connect with couples who are struggling to make such adoptions work and those whose lives are filled with purpose and joy.

# 10

# International Adoption

## Orphans of the World

The images are heartbreaking of children starving in poor countries, living in run down orphanages or on the streets. There are literally millions of children living in desperate conditions in the world and adoption can save only a precious few every year. Yet it is the only realistic chance they have of escaping their life of despair.

Responding to the needs of orphans and motivated by the desire to find healthy infants, American couples began adopting foreign-born children in the late 1940's. This trend has continued and increased through the years.

Between 1948 and 1953, American parents adopted children who were orphaned by the Second World War—6,000 from Europe and some 2,500 from Asia, mostly Japan. A few years later, when the demand for newborns exceeded the supply, they turned to children orphaned by the Korean War. In the early 1970's, American couples turned to South and Central America and by the 1990's some 2,500 of these Hispanic children were being adopted each year.

## International Adoption Facts

· · · · · · · · · · · · · · · · · · · · ·

Intercountry adoptions by American parents numbered 6,536 in 1992, climbed to 13,620 in 1997, and reached 18,539 in 2000. The children came from 50 countries, but more than half were from Russia and China. Korea was third in numbers, followed in descending order by Guatemala, Romania, Vietnam, India, Colombia and the Philippines. Two-thirds of the children were girls and one-third were boys. Nearly 100 percent of the Chinese adoptees were girls.

Half of foreign-born adoptees coming to the U.S. are under one year of age while 40 percent are between one and four. After any natural disaster abroad, we receive numerous e-mails and calls about how to adopt from the region. Thousands of Americans rush to adopt orphans whose parents are killed, but the children must be placed through standard procedures and, often, it takes years.

Starting in the 1990's and continuing today, due in some measure to personal desire or a perceived shortage of domestic infants, the number of children adopted from other countries in what's known as international or intercountry adoption has increased dramatically and has reached all-time highs.

U.S. couples are, for the first time since the early 1950s, adopting large numbers of white infants and children from Europe. The economic collapse and political upheaval from the fall of Communism has created large numbers of orphans, first in Romania then in Albania, Bulgaria, Poland, Russia and countries of the former Yugoslavia.

If you have decided to adopt internationally, you almost certainly want to use a well-known reputable agency and you'll find many listed in Adoption Hotlinks. You will want one that specializes in intercountry adoptions because of their complex nature, the changing rules and the yards of red tape involved.

Some countries have become hostile to sending their children away to America and, in some instances, prohibit adoption by foreigners. Some countries build legal barriers that make adoption unduly complex and expensive. U.S. immigration laws can make some foreign adoptions difficult.

But it can all be worth it! Ninety percent of these adoptions are successful and the children, research shows, remain proud of their ethnic, racial and national origins, happy in their adoptive families and proud of themselves.

---

**http://www.hometown.aol.com/romriter**

# One Special Russian Child

Linda's Adoption & Parenting Page

*By Linda Morelli*

## My Children

She was 3-1/2 years-old, living in a Russian orphanage, when the adoption agency showed me her photo. She was one of hundreds, yet I couldn't put her photo down. Her smile and the mischievous twinkle in her eyes stole my heart. I knew immediately that she was the daughter I longed for, the *dream* I had hoped would one day become a reality. My husband and I traveled across the world to get her. I can't begin to tell you the thrill of holding her trembling body in my arms for the first time, of hearing her say *Mama* in her soft, tremulous voice, or her face when I answered, in the Russian I had learned especially for that moment, "Yes. I'm your Mama. And I love you."

Our daughter is now eight and we have adopted another child, a little brother from Kazakhstan. Since our return in September 2000, our son has adjusted extremely well to his new sister, his family and his country. He's thrilled and amazed by everything he sees and the happiness in his eyes shines constantly. Needless to say, laughter (and sometimes a wee bit of fighting) echoes throughout our home. Our children are the joy of our lives. ☺☺

# 8 Keys to Success

1) Respect your child's country and culture.

2) Know that your values are not superior to your child's.

3) Foster your child's curiosity about her birth parents life and history.

4) Keep alive your child's knowledge of his original culture.

5) Acknowledge your child's need to identify with others from her country.

6) Embrace your culture and that of your child.

7) Surround yourself with people who will honor his cultural roots.

8) Address this challenge to become multicultural before you adopt a foreign-born child. ∞

# 5 Tips for International Adoptions

1) Use books, travel magazines, and videos to learn about the countries from which you hope to adopt your child.

2) Work with qualified professionals with experience in adopting children from those countries.

3) Get involved with online intercountry adoption support and parenting forums, and find yourself an adoption e-mail pal.

4) Learn about the country's adoption system through the experience of others and through your online research.

5) Find local support groups for people who have adopted from your child's country. For example, Hand in Hand supports families built through adoptions from China. ∞

# Tips for Smoothing the Way Home!

Here are some ways you'll help your child adjust to his or her new home:

- Invest in books, dolls and toys from your child's country.
- Plan play days with other families that have adopted from the same country as your child.
- Play cassette tapes or CD's of music from his/her country. This is great for nap time and bedtime.
- Learn to prepare ethnic dishes from your child's country.
- If your child is used to sleeping on a mat on the floor, prepare both a traditional bed and a mat, allowing him or her to make the choice.
- Hang pictures or artwork from the country and region your child is from.
- As a family, you might all want to sleep on mats once a week as a treat; this will often help your child to bond with you.
- Attend cultural festivals in other towns and *participate!*
- Purchase musical instruments found and used in your child's native country. ☺☺

---

email

# Foreign Adoption Q & A

To:
Cc:

*Why adopt a foreign-born child?*

International adoption is sometimes easier than domestic adoption because many agencies in this country have restricted or discouraged parents from adopting if they are single or over 40, for example. Depending on the country you choose, there may not be such restrictions.

*(continued on next page)*

email

To:
Cc:

# Foreign Adoption Q & A (cont.)

Some agencies impose their own restrictions on adoptive parents, beyond the restrictions imposed by the foreign country. Their motives may be the number of children and/or age of the children currently being referred to them by their foreign facilitators, or it may be based on their own philosophies about child rearing.

We believe that adoptive parents are individuals as are the waiting children whom they adopt. It is up to the parents and the social workers involved in the home study process to discuss and decide what is in the family and child's best interest. Many agencies welcome single parents, older parents and parents with disabilities.

### Is adopting a girl easier?

Yes. If the country only allows one child per family, for example, China. The birth parents may abandon or place for adoption their female child, hoping the next birth will be a male. Many cultures feel a male child is more capable of caring for his parents than a female. For the family interested in girls only, India at **http://www.ichild.org** and China at **http://www.asiadopt.org** are good choices.

### What countries allow you to view photos?

Some governments prohibit it while others allow it, like Russia at **http://www.kids4us.org/Russia.htm**. For any country, your adoption agency can obtain photographs or videos of waiting children and mail them to you personally.

email

## Foreign Adoption Q & A (cont.)

To:
Cc:

### Is closed adoption easier in another country?

If fear of openness and relating to a birth mother occupy your thoughts, you need to know why and to resolve this issue before you adopt any child. Some adoptive parents are terribly afraid that a birth mother may try to reclaim her baby and feel more secure adopting a child commonly abandoned to an orphanage, mother unknown. Most international adoptions are indeed closed. Unfortunately, for your child, you may not have much to tell about his or her origins; this difficulty is slowly changing but something we accept in adopting foreign born children.

For a time, Russian adoptions were in legal limbo and agencies were using unregulated and sometimes shady characters to assist them in the country. In the spring of 2000, new regulations required that government ministries accredit all adoption agencies working in Russia. Adopting a Russian orphan is always a complicated process. For approved agencies with experience in Russia, point your browser to **http://www.jcics.org**. Each country has its own requirements, which can change quickly. Closely monitor forums and sites dedicated to tracking adoption rules and red tape in various countries, such as **http://www.jcics.org**. If you pick up reports and mutterings that trouble's afoot in the country of your potential adoptive child, proceed with caution. ๑๏

http://www.cradlehope.org

# East European Survey

Cradle of Hope Adoption Center, a non-profit agency founded by adoptive parents in 1998 spearheaded a survey by 19 intercountry agencies of parents who adopted orphans from Romania, Bulgaria, Russia and other former Soviet Republics.

Supervised by researcher Mary Essley, DSW, of the University of New Hampshire, questionnaires were sent to 2,159 families and 1,246 of them were completed and returned.

The results:

- Parents reported their child's overall adjustment was very good (84 percent) or good (11 percent) or very poor (less than 2 percent).

- Has your child shown any symptoms of attachment problems, that is fear or hesitance to trust and love? Children adopted younger than age three: 10 percent. Older than three: 28 percent.

- Parents who said they were very pleased their child had become a member of their family: 93 percent.

- Parents said that two years after adoption, 95 percent of the children showed no delay or only mild delay in motor skills.

- For emotional maturity, 88 percent reported no delay or only mild delay.

- The median age of the children at adoption was two years.

- One-fourth of the children were four years or older. ∞

Internet zone

## Medical Concerns

On the other hand, too many adoptive parents wear rose-colored glasses when they view a photograph of their prospective child from overseas. The big pleading eyes of an orphan can pull at sympathetic hearts and sometimes, only after they bring the child home, do they see that poor diet, neglect and unsanitary living conditions have caused chronic disorders. I can't tell you how many times I've heard, "But they told me she'd be just fine with some good food and love."

The children came to the orphanage because they were abandoned; their parents died or were sick or too poor to provide for them. They likely received little medical care, may be malnourished or have parasites, or, for example, tuberculosis or developmental delays and behavioral problems.

When your agency finds a child for you to consider, they will send you a referral that includes a child's medical file, background information and photographs. Choose an agency that will send you a current videotape of the child and any medical reports needing to be translated. Seek out a physician experienced with intercountry adoption. See Adoption Hotlinks in the back of the book for additional resources.

An Internet search for <physicians international intercountry adoption> will turn up some doctors who do intercountry adoption assessments. For example, at **http://www.familyhelper.net/ad/adclin.html** there is a list of 20 American doctors in a number of different locales, including Seattle, Los Angeles and the state of Maine. At **http://www.come-unity.com/adoption/health/index.html** there is a directory of international adoption medical clinics, articles about health problems such as parasites, scabies, malnutrition and information on the tests and vaccinations that a child from China will need.

Prior to adoption you should have a doctor in the child's country examine your child and run medical tests. Medical records often need to be translated and then you should have a pediatrician in the United States review them. For a list of English-speaking doctors in more than 300 cities worldwide go to **http://www.iamat.org** and click on <Membership Benefits>.

# Special Needs Foreign Adoptions

See **http://www.comeunity.com/adoption/waiting/cleft-story.html**. This is a story on the Internet about a couple who spent four years trying to adopt. It is a story that is uniquely moving and inspiring.

In April of 1993 this particular couple read about children in Vietnam with cleft lips and palates who were available for adoption.

They did their research, talking to people at an Iowa City Otolaryngology Clinic. There, they were informed that modern surgery for these children is so successful that it is considered primarily cosmetic.

After much consideration, they called their agency and said they wanted to adopt one of these special needs children. The baby was only four months old. On Thanksgiving Day in 1993, they went to the airport to meet their new daughter.

The following week, this admirable couple took their new daughter to a clinic in Iowa City for an evaluation. The baby's unilateral cleft ran from the front of her mouth almost to the back of her throat. There would be three separate surgeries: first on the lip, then on the palate, and the third procedure, where doctors would take marrow from the baby's hipbone to graft into her tooth socket, would take three hours.

After some months the surgeons repaired her lip, palate and later did the bone graft. After each surgery, the little girl bounced right back.

It is amazing to see how these children turn out. Except for a small scar, most if not all babies and/or children look quite normal; some don't even have a scar.

So, please, don't overlook special needs children. Each one has a unique personality, each one his or her own special soul. ☯☯

Internet zone

## Your International Home Study

Foreign governments take a huge leap of faith in placing young lives into the hands of strangers from thousands of miles away. They are relying on the immigration service and your home study provider to vouch that you'll make good parents.

You do not need to have a home that passes a white glove test. Your social worker will not expect you to be perfect. They may, for example, check to see if your home is childproofed.

Home studies are an opportunity for you to learn from social workers with adoption expertise, who are familiar with inter-country placements and licensed by the state. They are there to help you in achieving your goal of creating your family. You can express concerns to them and, if needed, find support and guidance. They serve as your advocate.

> ### Great Books on International Adoption!
>
> For a description and reviews, go to **http://www.amazon.com**
>
> - *How to Adopt Internationally* by Jean Nelsen-Erichsen and Heino R. Erichsen.
>
> - *A Passage to the Heart: Writings from Families with Children from China*, edited by Amy Klatzkin.
>
> - *Help for the Hopeless Child* by Dr. Ronald S. Federici.

## The Dossier

As soon as you are *paper ready*, in a process that can take from two to five months, you can have a child designated for you. There are so many waiting children that, for prospective parents willing to adopt a toddler or any child older than two years, there is very little wait time. It may take longer to adopt an infant.

You will need to compile a variety of documents for your home study and for your dossier for the foreign court. You will need your agency to

## What's in Your Dossier?

- Birth certificates.
- Marriage license.
- Divorce decrees for previous marriages.
- Financial statements.
- Letter from your accountant or bank.
- Letter to verify employment and salary.
- Health report from your doctor on your health.
- Letter of intent to adopt.
- Recommendation to adopt.
- Certification of residency.
- Copies of passports.
- Home study report.
- INS approval (I-171H).
- Post placement agreement.

assist you, because you must assume documents are specific to the country, and exact legal or medical forms will be required.

## Traveling to Meet Your Child

Your adoption professional will let you know when you can expect to travel to meet your child. Some countries require one trip and others require two to finalize most adoptions. You will usually appear before a judge in court before you can leave the country with your child.

The time required to stay in your child's country can vary from three to four days in Romania to seven full days in Russia. In some countries, such as the Ukraine, you may have to stay up to one month.

You may encounter problems because you don't speak the language, but here is a tip! Learn to say: *Thank you, please and you're welcome.* You would be amazed to see how far these three simple sentences can get you.

Staying for a few weeks or longer in a foreign land is stressful for some people. In some countries you can hire an adoption escort or more often, your agency will include one for you. Always check with your agency or go online to **http://www.childrenshope.com/russia.htm** for Russia, or **http://www.rainbowkids.com/adoptionchina21.html** for China.

Traveling to the foreign country of your child's birth offers you the chance to become familiar with your child's culture. It provides you the opportunity to take pictures you can later share with your child.

## The Orphan Petition

The courts in the native country will, with few exceptions, make your adoption legal, with the advice and consent of the U.S. Immigration and Naturalization Service. The INS controls adoption of foreign-born children, in part, because it's charged with deciding who can enter our country, who can stay and who can become a citizen.

Moreover, the INS is the *Central Authority* designated by our government to oversee our promise to implement the Hague Convention. Signatories to this international agreement are to make certain that intercountry adoptions are in the child's best interest and that the receiving country has verified that *prospective adoptive parents are eligible and suited to adopt.* Please note that the INS is now a part of Homeland Security.

One can most clearly see how the INS goes about doing its job, by taking a look at the forms online that you will file for your adoption:

---

### Documents to Have When You Travel

*(Check with your adoption professional to determine which documents need to be certified or original):*

- Marriage certificate.

- Birth certificate or proof of age.

- Bank references.

- If needed, the adoption decree of previously adopted children.

- Medical certificates on all people (children included) that are traveling.

- At least three reference letters recommending the adoptive parents.

- Tax returns or documents verifying your income.

- Photographs.

- Your completed home study (If international, it must be done by a government approved agency).

## The Hague Convention

Improvements have taken place in the way we conduct and look at international adoptions both legally and morally. In 1993 The Hague Convention set the standards for international adoptions by instituting the protection of children and cooperation in regards to the way intercountry adoptions are handled. It has been a most important step in international adoption. It came to be as the result of a meeting of world representatives who agreed to a treaty to protect the rights of the children. The treaty standardizes adoption requirements and the requirements of adoptive parents, simplifies the international adoption process and improves the overall procedure to ensure that intercountry adoptions take place in the best interests of the child.

To participate in international adoptions, agencies that handle intercountry adoptions must be accredited. For additional information you may want to visit http://travel.state.gov/hague_childabduction.html.

- I-600 is the principal form used in what is known as the orphan petition process to obtain INS approval to bring a foreign child into this country for adoption. Its title is Petition to Classify Orphan as an Immediate Relative.

- I-600A asks the INS to proceed with qualifying you to adopt, even though a foreign child is not yet identified. It takes about three months to process and when done in advance, the INS need only confirm that the adoptee, when identified, meets certain requirements and can enter the country.

- In cases where a child has already been identified, you will use I-600. With either of these forms you must attach a favorable home study report and documents like your marriage and birth certificates, and your fingerprints for a child abuse clearance.

- I-171H is the notice sent to you advising that the INS has provisionally determined you are able to properly care for an orphan. In some cases the INS may still deny a visa to the child by later rejecting your orphan petition because the child does not qualify as an orphan or for a few other specific reasons.

- I-700 is the notice that the INS has decided you are able to care for the child properly and that the child is, in fact, an orphan defined in immigration law and that all other legal requirements to adopt have been met.

■ N-643 is filed to obtain a certificate of U.S. citizenship, as adoption does not automatically confer citizenship.

Your child's adoption in the foreign country as approved by the INS is usually accepted as a final adoption in the United States. But many adoption attorneys recommend and some states require, that you re-adopt the child under the laws of your state. Always make sure you check with your adoption professional and/or your attorney when you return home.

# 11

# Safe and Secure

The adoption of your child can be one of the happiest moments of your life. In order to make it so, certain precautions must be taken to ensure that you and your family remain safe and secure, and to avoid being the victim of fraud.

## Flirting with Fraud

Adopting online does not mean that you are going to sign up for a baby at a website and give them your credit card number. Rather, it is using your computer to do these things:

- access information
- connect with birth mothers
- locate and check out adoption professionals
- network with people who will help you
- monitor reports of and rumblings about scams to watch out for

You will open yourself up to fraud if you use the Internet without taking the proper care. You should, if at all possible, meet the adoption professional you choose and always get references. If you make online transactions,

like sending money for a promised service and you have not done the
proper research on the adoption professional, social worker or lawyer,
you are at risk. Visit chat rooms and forums on adoption. Learn who is
reputable and who is not. Always protect yourself first.

# Steps to Avoiding Online Fraud

To protect yourself from online fraud, take these proven steps:

## Safety Internet Tips

• Know that because you are vulnerable, you are a potential victim.
Work hard at being practical; proceed with caution and use good sense.

• Always employ adoption professionals to match you with a birth
mother and finalize your adoption in court. Check their references,
meet with them if possible.

• Ask for names and numbers, and then call clients who have adopted
through them.

• Be wary of any organization promising to find you a birth mother
within a short amount of time.

• Never choose a professional who makes unrealistic promises or
promises that seem too good to be true.

• Use the Internet and consult with your attorney until you
understand the laws of your state and those of the birth mother
so you can recognize any illegal activity.

• Always choose an ethical path for your adoption, not necessarily
the shortest, easiest path.

• Travel to meet with your birth parents, look over their situation
and get to know them.

- Use the Internet to learn about the process of adoption and understand what is ethical and what is not.

- Go online to forums, chat rooms and adoption websites to get reports of scams in the works.

- Protect your privacy: in online profiles, don't mention your employer, salary, home or work phone numbers. Use your adoption professional's toll-free telephone number for birth mothers to call. Be very cautious about revealing personal information in chat rooms.

- Never transfer a sizeable amount of money under pressure without assurance either through references, signed contracts and legal advice to make certain you will get what you are paying for.

- If any party to your adoption asks for a quick decision or quick payment, that's a red flag.

- Con artists will typically play on your emotions, convincing you that time is short and you need to take action quickly. Don't fall for it.

- If a professional promises to place a healthy infant with you within three to six months, be skeptical as most such adoptions take between six and eighteen months.

- Avoid anyone who tells you to send money now or they will allow the child to be adopted by another family.

- Don't make a hasty decision, no matter how anxious you are for a child. Don't work with anyone until you have time to check him or her out.

- Why take a chance? There is a child out there, perhaps yet unborn, who is waiting patiently for you. ☺☺

In almost every case of adoption fraud I have known about, the adoptive parents later said something like, "The alarm bells were going off but I didn't hear them."

If you work at putting your emotions aside to think clearly and if you know what to look for, it's pretty easy to spot attempted fraud. By following the basic safety rules in this chapter, you can cut down the chances you will be a victim.

## Know the Law

Two common frauds encountered on the Internet are: 1) The offer by someone to provide you with a baby if you send money and 2) The demand by a purported birth mother for money. Simply knowing what is allowed as an adoption expense in your state laws will help protect you from these scams.

All of the states, in what's known as their baby broker acts, regulate the purposes for which money can change hands. Adoption professionals are allowed to charge reasonable fees. You can pay for:

■ Social workers to do home studies

■ The posting of online profiles

■ Agencies or intermediaries to match you with birth mothers

■ Attorneys who do legal work and prepare documents

Money cannot go directly to the birth mother to buy a baby, but expenses are commonly allowed when, as the law sees it, money flows toward the child, through paying for the birth mother's maternity care, for example, or living and medical expenses during pregnancy. Check with your attorney and look up the laws of your state at one of the sites in

Adoption Hotlinks to see which, if any, expenses are allowed in the state where your birth mother resides.

Never give money directly to your birth mother for any reason. Let your adoption attorney or agency handle all the transactions. He/she will approve only legal expenses and disburse funds directly to the appropriate person: to a landlord, as an example, to a physician, or to the utility company.

Persons who try to charge money for other than approved expenses may face criminal charges. Let's say a teenage girl is pregnant and chooses to place her child for adoption. "Don't worry," her uncle says. "I'll find a wonderful home for the baby and get you some money too." He puts an ad on a personals website: *White newborn baby available to good parents, $10,000.* That's baby selling and it's illegal.

If you end up in a hotel room in a distant city and someone says, "Hand me the check and I'll give you the baby," you will know by your understanding of the law that this is illegal and you won't be scammed. Walk away.

## Screening Your Birth Mother

As a prospective adopting parent, your main worry will be whether the birth parent you connect with, most likely the birth mother, will complete the adoption. Your first task is to confirm her sincerity in the adoption. This can be tough, especially if she is located far from where you live, making a face-to-face meeting unlikely in your early contacts.

In your first phone call, find out where she is calling from, both the location and phone number. With this information, you may be able to enlist the help of an adoption attorney or social worker in her area to meet with her and verify that what she is claiming is true. (See Adoption

Hotlinks for a listing of professionals by state.) Most scammers will be scared away when you tell them you have someone coming to see them.

Ask a birth mother to provide information on her doctor and then take the time or ask your adoption professional to call the doctor's office and find out if she is a current patient. If she tells you where she lives, you can try to verify that the address is real. Go to the Internet and search for that address at **http://www.mapquest.com or http://maps.yahoo.com**.

## "Are You Serious?"

In response to your online profile, you may receive e-mails from people who claim to represent a birth mother. At our center, we say, "Great, have her contact us. We'd like to talk and we'll send you some information you can give her."

If this person says, "You can only go through me to reach her," consider that a red flag and move cautiously.

To birth mothers or their friends we say: these are the steps you must take if you are really serious about adoption. They have to fill out forms, provide proof of pregnancy and if they live nearby, meet with a coordinator or counselor.

If they live out of the area or the state, we arrange to have a professional nearby see them. Adoption professionals agree, approximately two out of ten birth mothers will follow through with an adoption plan. This can keep reclaims down.

If you are trying to match with a birth mother on your own and she is out of your state or area, to be safe and secure, I recommend you travel to meet her.

# Birth Mother Red Flags

Many legitimate prospective birth mothers may be in desperate straits and look to you for money to help with expenses during pregnancy. This is not unusual and it doesn't make her a bad person. She is, after all, carrying this baby to place it for adoption. And it's hard work.

Other women who claim to be birth mothers may not be pregnant at all or are trying to get money from a number of adoptive parents. Here are some red flags. They don't always mean fraud, so use your intuition and judgment, but they may help you to know when a scammer is on the line and you should just say, "No thank you."

- A birth mother who matches too quickly with you.

- Will match with you only if you send money.

- Immediately asks for help with expenses.

- Says you're just perfect but knows little about you.

- Doesn't ask about you, your family or your interests.

- Needs expenses paid immediately.

- Makes you feel guilty or desperate.

- Plays heavily on your sympathies, appears emotionally fragile.

- Threatens to place the child with another family or get an abortion if you don't do something now, like send money.

- Tells incredible and convincing hard-luck stories.

- Calls often, desperately wanting money.

- Seems detached from the pregnancy.

(continued on next page)

- **The focus is not on baby but on herself.**

- **She's evasive about giving her home phone number or other details.**

- **Won't tell you where she's getting prenatal care.**

- **Doesn't want you to speak to her doctor.**

- **She cries uncontrollably. (You can tell it's an act if her sobs stop when you ask how much money she's looking for.)** ∞

## Birth Mother Scams

In the middle of the night you may receive a call from a woman you don't know. She has put off her decision to place the child for adoption until the last possible moment. She is in the hospital and going into labor. This is possible and I have seen it a number of times and these women turn out to be excellent birth mothers.

Usually you can verify her situation by asking the name of the hospital, her doctor and so on. Then you can verify the information with a phone call to the nurse's station in the maternity ward.

Some homeless birth mothers are legitimate and will need help. You will want her safe and, if your state laws allow, you may need to provide her with an apartment during the pregnancy and help set her up with a food bank, social services, state medical plans and other services. Ask your adoption professional to verify the birth mother's story before spending any money.

Attempted fraud on the Internet is not what it's cracked up to be. Yes, fraud does exist and that's why one must be careful. But the numbers of big scams the perpetrators actually pull off are few. Over the years, in the hundreds of Internet adoptions we've completed through our center, when adoptive parents are formally matched with a birth parent, the success rate has been about 95 percent. That makes Internet adoption as safe as any other method.

It's infuriating to me that con artists try to take advantage of those of us who are vulnerable because we are desperately trying to build a family through adoption. I know from personal experience that it's easy to let emotions take over. We follow our hopeful hearts instead of thinking with our heads when offered a situation that seems too good to be true. We desperately want it to work out, so we allow ourselves to believe that the person promising us a newborn baby is trustworthy.

### The Avoider

A birth mother who does not want to give you contact information and insists that all communication be by e-mail could be a scammer or an unwilling participant in a scheme to get money. She may not even be pregnant. Question closely any prospective birth mother who contacts you directly and prefers to talk and work only through you. She may be afraid, because an adoption professional will see right through her. A woman who is sincere about placing her child should be willing to provide you with specific contact information and to talk with your adoption professional.

### The Charmer

Be extremely cautious of the birth mother who flatters you, saying things like, "You are so cute," or "You are the perfect couple." Her charm is her way of luring you into a sense of security before she makes demands for money.

After the birth, she may evade signing over her parental rights. She cancels appointments, promising to sign the papers next time. She'll have your money but she may never consent to the adoption.

### The Puppy Dog Sale

The most obvious form of fraud involves supposed birth parents who accept money from an adoptive family knowing that they will never place their child for adoption. They may promise the child to several families, collecting money from each.

In a common scam known as a puppy dog sale, the birth mother places the child in the care of a prospective adoptive family. A few days later, she calls unexpectedly to demand more money, knowing the family has bonded and is likely to pay. The next day she calls back, saying she's changed her mind and wants the baby back. She then takes the child to her next victim.

### Psychological Fraud

It's rare, but I have seen it: fraud not for money, but for attention or to inflict harm. Most of the perpetrators are not birth mothers at all. In need of psychological help, desperately lonely, they want someone to talk with intimately and know they can find emotionally fragile adoptive parents who will care deeply about them and stay on the phone when they call. Their victims are manipulated into longing for the child. Sometimes they will taunt and harass the adopting couple with stories about a threatened miscarriage or a change of heart about the placement. The game lasts only until they are asked to document the pregnancy or to meet in person.

## How to Check Out an Online Professional

- **Get to know the adoption sites on the Net. Before working with anyone in cyberspace, verify their existence in a "brick and mortar" building.**

## How to Check Out an Online Professional (cont.)

- On visiting the website of a professional, see if they display memberships in organizations like the Better Business Bureau and local Chamber of Commerce. That's a good sign.

- They should list a phone number and a real address, not just a post office box. If they don't, move on.

- Call! Ask questions. On any inkling of doubt, move on.

- If you sense they're trustworthy, ask for five references of clients who have adopted successfully through them. If they won't give this to you, look elsewhere.

- Call the references. Ask questions. If you always get an answering machine and few timely returned calls, question this reference.

- Go online. Enter the precise firm name in a general search engine and check the adoption websites to see if any bad reports come up.

- Visit several adoption forums and post messages asking if anyone has worked with the firm and to relate their experiences.

- Do the e-mail test: dispatch a simple question of substance and see if they respond in a timely, professional way. Look to see if their e-mail signature is consistent. If it all checks out, keep them on your list of candidates. Call the organization again. Ask them to send their contract by mail. If they won't, drop them. If they do, review it: Their contract should be extensive but clear and glowing with professionalism. In our center we don't send out a contract until the applying family has been approved for our program. Be cautious of any organization that takes just anyone. ☺☺

Internet zone

### Don't Be Paranoid

Most adoption professionals are ethical, so be cautious but not paranoid.

- If a business isn't listed when you call information, it could mean they're fairly new and have not yet made it into directory assistance or the yellow page listings.

- If a business is not found, it could be they are not listed in the search engine you are using. Try others.

- Many legitimate attorneys, facilitators and licensed social workers work out of home offices to control costs.

- If the organization uses answering machines and voice mail systems, remember, for the small business owner, the cost of a receptionist can be prohibitive.

- Adoption professionals sometimes combine their talents, as when agencies use facilitators to find birth mothers. Don't be alarmed, but check out each member of the team.

# Friend of a Friend

Some desperate prospective parents will send money when someone e-mails saying, "My friend is pregnant and if you're interested, please send $500 and I'll see that she gets your phone number."

These individuals are not in the adoption field but are trying to coordinate an adoption to make some money.

They know nothing about adoption or the law. This is trouble waiting to happen. To be safe in a situation like this, all you can do is ask for the birth mother's name and phone number and have your adoption professional contact her.

# Intercountry Adoption Fraud

In the Ukraine, between 1992 and 1994, two doctors and two high-ranking government officials used fake death certificates to show eager prospective parents that their designated child had died. They kept the money and later smuggled the children out of the country to sell elsewhere.

In some cases, a defrauder in a specific country connects over the Internet with adoptive parents. He sends photographs of available children. These couples, responding with emotion and bypassing an agency to *save money,* travel to pick up their child. When they hand over an exorbitant amount of money, the scammer goes into another room to *get the little one,* but slips out a door, vanishing into the night.

Work only with a reputable agency that has a history of successful adoptions in the country of your prospective child. Be especially careful about adoptions in Mexico, Romania, Indonesia and Moldavia. Avoid any solicitation directly to you from Nigeria or Sierra Leone.

## A Baby for You Now!

Whether you hear it from an adoption professional or from a birth parent, there is nothing more seductive than the words, *there's a baby for you now!*

You may receive an e-mail from someone in Mexico who informs you of a starving child needing a home. And if you just send $5,000 we can get this child to you right away.

I get e-mails from South Africa: "I have access to children, just send money." One gentleman called me on our 800 number and said he was calling from South Africa.

> ## Blunt Questions the Professionals Ask
>
> If any answer comes with hesitancy, is flat-out wrong or doesn't ring true, forget about it. If you seem to get legitimate answers you may wish to pursue it further with your adoption professional.
>
> If you believe that a party unknown to you may really have a baby to adopt, ask these questions:
>
> - Do you have references?
> - What is your phone number and address?
> - What's the child's name and age?
> - Who and where are his birth parents?
> - Why is this child being placed for adoption now?
> - Do you have and will you send me medical records?
> - Can you send me copies of legal documents related to parental rights?
> - Who is the agency or attorney handling the legal work?

Later on, I checked our phone statement. He was calling from New York and just looking for a vulnerable and naive person to defraud.

If you are offered a child from somebody you don't know or trust, back off. Say, "No, thank you."

I know that it's hard to be objective when the promise of your dream is about to be fulfilled. It's easy to rush into a bad situation. Remember the golden rule of a safe and secure adoption: If it sounds too good to be true, it probably is. Check it out first!

## Troubled but Legitimate

Some adoptive parents you come across in chat rooms and forums may claim a birth mother has taken advantage of them when they lost contact with her. They have assumed they were misled when the reasons for the birth mother's disappearance were due to her situation, a miscarriage, for example, or a decision to parent the child.

## Top Adoption Safety Sites

- Better Business Bureau—Check for complaints on an organization or professional. http://www.bbb.org

- National Council for Adoption—http://www.adoptioncouncil.org

- International Concerns for Children—Find out if the agency you are considering is listed in the Report on Intercountry Adoption. http://www.iccadopt.org/#Report

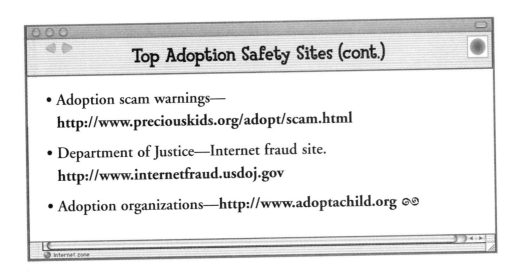

**Top Adoption Safety Sites (cont.)**

- Adoption scam warnings—
  http://www.preciouskids.org/adopt/scam.html

- Department of Justice—Internet fraud site.
  http://www.internetfraud.usdoj.gov

- Adoption organizations—http://www.adoptachild.org

Internet zone

## Meeting Your Professional

Adopting a child is perhaps the most important thing you will do in your life. To be safe and secure, you should travel to meet with your adoption professional and whenever possible with your birth mother or birth parents.

If you were building your dream house, you wouldn't work with an architect clear across the country unless you went to see that he was legitimate and qualified. You'd shake hands, look him in the eye and sit down for a chat. You would want to feel good about him before you signed a contract and wrote out a check.

If you have someone you trust recommending your professional, or if you have talked with several references who say, "Oh, he or she worked so hard for us and he's as honest as the day is long," then perhaps you'd be okay without going to meet him personally.

When I look at cases of Internet adoption, I often see people that have engaged supposed adoption professionals whom they have never met and never checked out. If they had gone to see them and checked references they would have seen that their *professional* was an imposter.

## When Is It OK to Pay Fees Upfront?

At our center and with many adoption professionals, the client pays fees when we begin working together, which is at the start. The professional is saying, "We are going to put our entire effort into this adoption." In response, you are saying, "I am willing to make myself available to look at each of the birth mother situations you present." If you have that commitment on both sides, the adoption will almost always succeed.

### What to Ask Your Attorney

Don't be shy about asking questions of the adoption attorney you're considering.

• How many adoptions do you complete per year?

• Do you have any lawsuits pending?

• Have you ever had any lawsuits filed against you?

• Where do your birth mothers come from?

• What can we expect from your service?

• Have you done interstate adoptions?

• Can you provide me with names of other adoptive families you've worked with?

Some people may say, "Well, if we pay up front, the professional has no incentive." But, remember, if they have a good track record and want to keep it, they need to keep their clients happy! As an adoption professional of Lifetime Adoption, I can say that has always been our incentive.

Another organization may have you pay a small fee up front and another one with a match, and another one when the child comes home. I have seen this fee structure work against the adoptive parents. The organization may be motivated to get a match, any match at all, even if it's not a good one. If the adoption doesn't work out, they keep the fee and the next time there's a match, they'll charge you again.

If you pay $2,000 to start, $4,000 at the match and a balance of $8,000 when the child comes to your home, what if the first match doesn't work out? Next time you get matched will you have to pay another $4,000? Remember that matches don't always work out and that adoptions do fall through because we're dealing with human nature, but that does not constitute a fraud.

I recommend that you find an organization that will charge you one flat fee for the work it does to find you a child. You will want one who will work with you for a period of time, maybe two years, or until a match is found. A clear contract is a must!

## Excessive Fees

An adoption professional may try to take advantage of a hopeful parent by charging excessive fees, either from the outset or by adding on costs over the course of the adoption process. Overcharging can be hard to judge as adoptions can be expensive. Your professional should always be clear on what you will be charged and why. Check with at least three similar adoption professionals and compare fees.

When an adoption agency, attorney or facilitator charges exorbitant fees without any explanation, there is cause for concern. As a general reference, more than $15,000 paid to any one adoption professional should be questioned.

Combined adoption fees covering the home study, legal and agency or facilitator fees could range upwards of $15,000 to $20,000 for some adoptions. In those few states, such as Massachusetts, which do not allow independent adoptions, paying a high fee to an agency may be your only choice.

## Wrongful Adoption

I knew an adoptive couple who went to a public agency that, after only four months, found the child they wanted to adopt, a healthy toddler. A

---

### Teaming Up for Safety

Professional adoption organizations with good reputations and pride in their success stories will be pleased to provide you plenty of information. They will offer to e-mail or fax to you a list of 20 references and their proof of membership in such groups as the Chamber of Commerce and the Better Business Bureau and other professional organizations.

Choose an adoption agency, attorney or facilitator only when you are confident they can get the job done, that they want to work hard and with enthusiasm with you as a member of the team. When you find an organization like this, your adoption will be much more safe and secure.

---

few years later the little girl started showing signs of cerebral palsy and the agency told them, "Oh, we didn't think that would matter to you."

This is known as a wrongful adoption, where the agency neglects to disclose pertinent information about the child's medical or psychological history, or information on the birth parents.

Most agencies are keenly aware of lawsuits filed in such cases and willingly disclose all information, as it's long been the practice of ethical adoption professionals. State to your professional clearly at the outset that you expect a full disclosure of all information in the file, and this includes background on the birth parents including such things as mental and physical disorders.

With older children, acquiring enough medical information can be difficult. Some have been to 20 different doctors in several states. A birth mother can sometimes provide medical information, but some may not be able to remember the number of doctors their child has seen. An older child with problems has often been medically neglected so there isn't much history. If records are missing in such a case, it is not fraud.

You can try to arrange for a medical and psychological evaluation or as some families do, you may choose to adopt a special needs child, knowing the child may have problems and you are willing to accept what they are.

When it comes right down to it, careful planning is the answer. Try not to allow your emotions to rule you. Think before you act, check, then double check everything you are told. When you are comfortable with the adoption professional of your choice and you are comfortable with all the homework you have done, only then can you feel *safe and secure*.

# 12

# Funding Your Adoption

*"I just want a child to love, why does it have to cost so much?"*

Economists have estimated the cost of raising a child from birth to 18 years. For a boy it's $224,000 and for a girl, $234,000. If you add in the cost of an adoption, it can represent approximately 5 percent of the total cost of raising your child. But the value of your investment, a life enriched by sharing your life with a child cannot be measured.

## Agency Fees

If you are completing your adoption through an agency, you'll find fees from $3,500 to $30,000 and up depending on your state of residence and the extent of services offered. Eastern states tend to have higher fees. Some agencies offer a flat fee and others a sliding scale based on your combined income averaged over one to three years. Ask if you'll need to hire an attorney for the birth mother's consent or if that's included.

Your agency fee typically provides: Locating birth mothers and children, and counseling and support for birth mothers and adoptive parents. It also may include parenting classes, birth mother expenses, including prenatal and delivery care if not paid by insurance, post-placement visits and the finalization report for the court.

## Cost Factors in Adoption

- A typical U.S. adoption costs between $10,500 and $18,000.

- On the East Coast it can reach $25,000 to $35,000 and more.

- Tax credits can reduce your costs by as much as $10,000.

- Interstate adoptions are higher.

- Your employer may provide adoption benefits. The benefits usually run $1,000 to $5,000.

- Government subsidies can reduce the cost of special needs adoptions to little or nothing.

- Sliding-scale agency fees based on family income can lower your costs if your income is not high.

- Adopting a foreign-born child can be expensive in certain countries.

- With an independent adoption, you can save money by finding your own birth mother, hiring an attorney for the legal work and if allowed in your state, hiring a private social worker for your home study.

Some families locate a birth mother on their own, or through a qualified facilitator. This is commonly called a *designated adoption*, which saves money as full fees are not charged. However, some agencies charge the same fee whether you find your child or they do. So ask.

In some agency adoptions, where most legal costs are covered by your fee, you may still need to hire an attorney to obtain consent from the birth father.

## Public Agency Fees

To some families, adopting an infant is not a priority. By choosing an older child who is waiting for a loving home, they can save a lot of money. The adoption itself, through a state agency or licensed private agency, can be free or very reasonable. The agency may take payments and you may receive a reimbursement of adoption costs, through programs that provide incentives for parents to provide permanency to children in foster care and adoption subsidies. These older children usually have special needs or are in sibling groups of multi-ethnic heritage.

### Facilitator Fees

Facilitator fees vary from $2,500 to $13,000 and more. The full-service facilitator, normally well staffed with extended hours, offers a variety of services, such as counseling and support groups, acquiring medical records, advertising and screening for birth mothers.

Each facilitator has its own policies, but most outline in their contract a period of 12 to 24 months for adoptive parents to match with a birth mother. They normally ask for fees when services begin.

A second type of facilitator, a locator, specializes in finding birth mothers and children through other professionals such as attorneys, agencies and other facilitators. They may ask for an initial deposit at first, a second payment at the time of your match and a third and final payment at the time of placement. Because more than one professional is involved, you may pay comparatively higher fees.

A third kind of facilitator, an advertiser, will only find a birth mother, leaving the screening, paperwork and negotiating to you. As most adoptions require a team of professionals working together, this is not the best option and usually turns out to be quite expensive.

Most facilitators will continue to work with an adoptive family, without additional fees, in the event an adoption falls through after a match.

---

### How Much Does It Cost to Adopt?

- Fees for public agency adoptions of special needs and older children range from no cost to $3,500.

- Some private agencies offer sliding-scale fees based on income.

- Domestic private agency adoptions are expensive and can run to $30,000 and higher in several Eastern states.

- Independent adoptions, arranged through an attorney, facilitator or other intermediary, are usually less expensive.

- Intercountry adoption, through private agencies, runs $13,000 to $25,000. Add in costs for such items as medical exams and travel or an escort to bring your child home.

## Adoption Fee Guide

• Many agencies, lawyers and facilitators list services offered and explain fees on their websites.

• Compare fees and services of adoption professionals you are considering, as they vary considerably.

• Clarify up front and in writing exactly what services the stated adoption fees will and will not cover.

• Some organizations may quote a fee but later add charges for services like post-placement, travel, postage or court costs.

• Some professionals require the entire fee to be paid when services start. As soon as the contract is signed, they begin searching for your child.

• Since you are paying for services and not for a baby (which is unlawful), use only reputable professionals and sign a contract which clearly specifies what you're paying for.

• The contract should spell out your responsibilities as well.

• Be wary of any adoption professional who will accept you as a client without first reviewing your application or home study.

### Home Study Fees

Home study fees can vary considerably, depending on the state where you live; from as low as $750 in Texas to as high as $20,000 in Massachusetts. A home study for independent adoption is normally less than for an agency adoption and averages about $2,000 or more across the United States. Please keep in mind that these figures are estimates and may be more or less in some areas.

Most domestic public agency adoptions charge a reduced or no home study fee if you adopt a waiting child through their program. Some states allow private social workers, instead of social service department workers, to do home studies for nonagency adoptions.

Many states offer home study services through their social service departments. Some social workers licensed to conduct home studies in your state advertise fees on their websites.

## Interstate Adoption Costs

If you adopt from another state, you'll need to have an adoption professional, an attorney, an agency, or in some states a licensed social worker or paralegal to take birth mother signatures. Your home state adoption attorney will normally coordinate paperwork for the Interstate Compact.

Some agencies will charge a few thousand dollars just to take birth mother signatures and mail them to your agency in your state. Others will charge only a few hundred dollars!

## Birth Mother Expenses

Some birth mothers who have health insurance and good jobs and can afford rent or who live with parents or with boyfriends will ask for no expense money. Others are poor and need help.

In 43 of the 50 states, you can normally pay, during the pregnancy, for food, rent, medical care, counseling, and other expenses such as maternity clothes, gas, oil and minor expenses for her car. But check with at least three adoption attorneys in your state as laws vary greatly.

Over the years, I would estimate that about half of all birth mothers do ask for help with expenses which average about $2,000 total for some and only $100 for others.

You will usually place a budgeted amount into a trust fund and it is the attorney who will disperse the checks for expenses. Such payments are considered gifts and if the adoption is not completed, birth parents are not required to repay them.

---

### How Much Are Legal Fees

- Most attorneys will provide you with a list of fees and services.
- Most require a retainer up front.
- Some have a flat fee for one adoption and a reasonable charge is $4,000-$7,500.
- Others charge by the hour, from $125 to $375 and up per hour. This can be expensive.
- Most attorneys will not refund money for legal work performed if the adoption fails after a match.

# Mardie's 7 Tips on Birth Mother Expenses

1) Deposit money into a trust fund with your adoption attorney for paying birth mother expenses.

2) If your birth mother asks for payments not allowed by state law, let your adoption professional be the bad guy. Keep your distance from big money issues.

3) If allowable by law, many attorneys will allow you to pay minor incidental expenses out of your own pocket, the types of things you might buy for a friend.

4) If working with an agency, your social worker will usually handle all aspects of paying birth mother expenses.

5) Use an adoption professional who will help your birth mother get state aid for medical care, WIC, and other state funded help before asking you to help with pregnancy medical expenses.

6) Some birth mothers are reticent to ask for help, so be caring and concerned: ask if she needs it.

7) When your state laws allow gifts, buy your birth mother a small present or two to show your appreciation and acknowledgment that what she is doing for you is special. ☯

## Medical Expenses

If your birth mother doesn't have health insurance, your adoption professional or you should help her apply. Many birth mothers will qualify for Medicaid (MediCal in California). Your health insurance company may cover the pregnancy related medical expenses of the birth mother as if she were a member of your own family. If her insurance or yours will not pay, most state adoption laws allow you to pay for her prenatal care, counseling, and labor and delivery. Most states require counseling for the birth mother, which you may also need to pay for.

In the early stages of matching, find out who will pay medical expenses. In the excitement of the moment, adoptive couples often make the mistake of overlooking this matter. If you do not have the budget for this expense, you may want to consider matching with another birth mother, one who has medical insurance or state aid. I personally recommend that if you are paying for medical care, that you pay as much as possible of the hospital/medical after signatures are taken and you know you will be adopting the child. Often hospitals will discount up to 50 percent of the bill if you pay in full versus payments. Don't be afraid to ask.

## Care of Your Birth Mother

When adoptive couple Dale and Cindy Fuller first met their birth mother, Laurie, they agreed to cover some of her living expenses during pregnancy, as allowed by California law. Dale, a prudent businessman, decided that he, rather than his adoption attorney, could best manage these costs. He combed through Laurie's receipts. He questioned her $25 phone bill and voiced concern over the $212 she spent on food in one month.

Laurie called me. Feeling belittled by Dale's nitpicking and condescension, she said, "I can't place this baby with a father like him." She chose another adoptive couple, one that cared about her and not just about getting the child.

If you were having a baby in your family, you'd have expenses like those of your birth mother. You would not deny to your pregnant wife or daughter the medical care, food and shelter she needs to give birth to a healthy baby. Treat your birth mother well. She is carrying and giving birth to your child.

# Are These Birth Mother Expenses Allowable?

| Acceptable Expenses | Unacceptable Expenses |
|---|---|
| • Maternity Clothes | • Vet Bill |
| • Food | • New Carpet |
| • Rent | • Dental Work |
| • Phone | • Tummy Tuck |
| • Utilities | • Limo to Prom |
| • Car Insurance | • Hawaiian Vacation |
| • Transportation—Bus, Cab | • Highlights in Hair |
| • Insurance Copayments | • Satellite TV Service |
| • Pregnancy Medical Care | • Pay Off Student Loan |
| • Pregnancy-related Child Care | • Boyfriend's Christmas Present |
| • Foster Care for the Child | • Traffic Tickets or Violations |

*(Believe it or not, I've been asked about each of these!)* ☺☺

## Sensible Saving

You are the best source for funding your adoption and a savings account is your best option. It is better to start your search for your child with the funds in place. This eliminates the stress of money and allows you to concentrate on the adoption process. There will be no interest to pay, no paperwork, no approval needed from a loan officer.

If you don't have a large savings account, remember that most families starting out don't have these funds on hand. But, if you think creatively, you may surprise yourself by the amount of money you can save and raise.

Estimate the cost of caring for a child in one month, the diapers, food, clothing, baby equipment, day care, doctor bills and insurance premiums, then start setting aside that amount each month. Not only will this help you build up substantial savings but it will also help you see how the cost of raising a child will impact your life.

## Creative Fundraising

Get your community and family involved. Clean out your garage and home and then plan a garage sale. Ask friends, family, and neighbors to pitch in with donations. One of our adoptive parents advertised in the newspaper: "Funding Our Adoption Garage Sale". Many well-wishers came to buy things and make donations. On one weekend she raised $750.

If you have unwanted items in your home and garage that are very nice, try selling them on http://www.ebay.com. Items for sale on these sites include clothing, books, accessories, jewelry, CDs and videotapes. Tupperware sells very well as does camping and boating equipment, antiques and collectibles. I know of two women who sell used children's clothing on eBay and make over $1,200 per month each!

One of our adoptive mothers bought items at garage and estate sales and resold them online. She learned to spot rare items including antique books that she bought for a few dollars and sold at the market value of $50. After three months she had made $4,500. For some adoptive mothers who stay at home, selling items on online auctions has allowed them to pay for half of their adoption expenses.

# eBay Fundraising

To: Jessica@skylight.net
From: From: Mardie@lifetimeadoption.com
Date: January 10, 2003

Jessica:

I see you're selling on eBay to pay for your adoption, can you tell me more?

Hi Mardie:

We originally thought that the sale of a rental house we had would fund our adoption so we started the process. The buyer backed out in escrow, after we had identified our adoptive children. Our house is again on the market, but our adoption expenses are on our charge cards (ick).

I have sold on eBay for a couple years, just casually. Now I have a purpose. First I went through all our closets and sold clothing, then books. We now have many of our VHS videos listed and they are up to over $500 as of now. These items are just things I have around the house. I made around $225 for books that are on the shelves. I have friends from my church asking how they can help. I may ask for donations of items to sell, things they don't need and would give away.

My hope is to be able to pay down the debt, but I would really like to be able to fly our whole family to pick up our girls. We are adopting twins from Africa. 👓

## Borrowing Money

Because of the Internet, the borrowing of money has become a competitive market, as lenders compete with other lenders for your business! Knowing that you are just a mouse click away from finding the lowest possible interest rate and the best possible terms, they will offer you their best deal right away.

Online financing puts you in a favorable position that people needing to borrow a decade ago never dreamed possible. No longer do you need to drag yourself around to banks or finance companies, fill out applications and, over the next few days, wait anxiously for approval.

You simply go to a website like **http://www.loanhounds.com** which specializes in advertising your needs and creditworthiness to scores of lenders. Complete the online application and sit back. Within hours, you'll receive offers and conditional terms from a number of lenders, all through e-mail.

With mortgage and related interest rates at record lows, as of this writing, the most sensible way to borrow money for adoption may be a home equity loan. If you do a search at **http://www.google.com** for <home equity loan> and also enter your state, you will find a dozen websites or more where you can borrow on your house and most will e-mail you conditional rates and loan amounts based on your online application.

Many families turn to their local banks for an adoption loan. They walk in the door and negotiate terms the old-fashioned way. Conservative lenders require collateral, strong credit, employment and income history. Call around because some banks have special adoption loan programs with low interest rates.

Some people borrow from credit cards but this is only logical if it's short-term; that is, if you are anticipating enough income in the months ahead to pay off such a high interest loan.

Many prospective grandparents happily contribute to the cost of adoptions by their children. This may have a drawback if your parents consider the acceptance of their funds as an invitation to voice their opinion about your adoption choices or the raising of your children.

## Ask Mardie

*Dear Mardie,*

*After several years of fertility treatment costing lots of money, my wife and I have decided to adopt. We want to get started right away. Should we take out a loan for adoption?*

If you're already having trouble making your car or house payment or paying on credit cards, try to get these expenses under control. Then you might consider a loan. But don't borrow money to adopt if you're adding to a budget already stretched thin.

With a child, you'll have medical expenses, childcare, preschool, the cost of food, clothing and toys. Making the loan payment every month in addition to taking on the expense of the child may be too much to handle.

We've recommended family members take two jobs for a while. With the extra money, they have paid off their debts and saved up for the adoption. But when your child comes, he or she will need you at home. Then you can't be working two jobs, exhausted all the time and trying to enjoy life with your child.

We have childless couples tell us they're going to put off adopting until they pay off an expensive car. They are wasting precious time they could spend with a child. If they really want to build a family, they should sell the car!

### Ask Mardie (cont.)

*Dear Mardie,*

*After paying our adoption agency that has now matched us with a birth mother, my wife is thinking she should go back to work. Is it a good idea for us both to work with a baby in our lives?*

Both adoptive parents sometimes have to work, just as do parents who have a biological child. But you might want to take time off work when your child first comes into your family. This will be an exciting time and important too, for bonding. A few private agencies require that at least one of the adoptive parents stay home with the child for at least six months after the adoption. In some independent adoptions, the birth mother may request that the adoptive mother stay with the child at first or she may want a stay-at-home mom. Consider a job where you work from home. ೦೨

# A Little Grant Goes a Long Way

A few organizations offer grants to families who meet their criteria. These are grants and, usually, you are not required to repay them.

- *AdoptShare:* **http://www.adoptshare.org, a Christian ministry** offers help with the expenses of adoption.

- *Lifetime Foundation:* **http://www.lifetimefoundation.org, offers** grants up to $5,200 for specific adoptions.

*(continued on next page)*

- *African American Adoptions:* http://www.africanamericanadoptions online.com, has an African American Enrichment Adoption Program—Grants help with specific African American, special needs and biracial adoptions. Grant amounts vary.

- *Bright Futures:* http://www.homestead.com/brightfutures/ or e-mail to brightfutures@alltel.net for information on small grants to help with adoption fees.

- *Hebrew Free Loan Association:* http://www.hflasf.org grants interest free loans of up to $10,000 to Jewish couples with financial need and a strong desire to adopt.

- *The Ibsen Adoption Network:* http://www.childadopt.com/funding.htm, grants of $1,000 for special needs adoptions to residents of Washington State.

- *JSW Foundation:* http://www.jsw-adoption.org, provides cash grants of $2,000 or more to defray adoption expenses. Awarded monthly, based on financial hardship.

- *National Adoption Foundation:* http://www.nafadopt.org/nafgrants.htm, awards cash grants four times each year from $500 to $4,000 to selected applicants.

- *Our Chinese Daughters:* http://www.ocdf.org, awards grants and loans to single mothers adopting from China.

- *Project Oz Adoptions:* http://www.projectoz.com/Financing.htm, offers grants up to $8,000 for families adopting foreign-born children through the nonprofit Project Oz agency. ๑๑

# Online Home Equity Loans

Searched the web for <Home equity loan>. Results 1-10 of about 263,000. Search took 0.10 seconds.

- *ING DIRECT:* **http://www.home.ingdirect.com/,** offers Home Equity Line of Credit as low as 4.25% variable APR.

- *Compare Home Equity Loans:* **http://www.100bestlenders.com,** major banks compete at Lending Tree. 4% APR Easy Qualify. Bad Credit OK.

- *Home Equity Loans:* **http://www.ameriquest.com,** refinance with Ameriquest Mortgage. Bad Credit OK.

- *Find The Lowest Rates:* **http://www.LendersCompete.com,** over 15,000 mortgage lenders competing for your loan!

- *Home Equity Loans 10 Days:* **http://www.refinance.com. No upfront fees. No Obligation. Easy application and fast answers.** ☜☞

Internet zone

## Adoption Assistance Programs

Adoption assistance programs vary significantly from state to state. For detailed information about your state's program, visit http://www.nacac.org/subsidy_stateprofiles.html. For a chart comparing

### Medical Coverage

Tim and Chancy adopted a young child who had a history of neglect and had lived in 12 foster homes before being adopted. Tom felt their company medical insurance would be sufficient and decided not to go through more paperwork to see if they could qualify for Medicaid. Their social worker urged them to reconsider. Their adoption finalized without a problem, but Tom and Chancy never completed their paperwork for the adoption subsidy program. Two years later their daughter began to have ongoing problems in school and at home. Their insurance company would only cover a small portion of therapy. The medical expenses were overwhelming. When Tom and Chancy tried to submit their AAP (Adoption Assistance Program) application they were turned down.

http://www.nacac.org/subsidy_stateprofiles.html. For a chart comparing major aspects of the state programs, visit http://www.nacac.org/AAPchart.html.

The Federal Children's Bureau recently prepared a manual for adoptive parents and professionals that clarifies aspects of the Title IV-E Adoption Assistance Program. It's available online with other current and accurate information on subsidies for special needs children and other child welfare topics. Go to http://www.acf.dhhs.gov/programs/cb/ or visit http://www.adoptionquestions.com.

## Military Benefits

The military will reimburse active-duty personnel up to $2,000 per adopted child, whether a healthy infant, special needs or foreign-born child. The maximum benefit is $5,000 in a given year, even if both parents are enlisted. A state agency or non-profit private agency must complete the adoption and the benefit is paid after finalization. When our center assists military families in locating a child, we have to complete it through an agency unless the savings to the family in an independent adoption is greater than $2,000.

Parents who adopt a disabled child may also be eligible for up to $1,000 per month in assistance under the military's Program for Persons with Disabilities. Also, parents of these adoptive children are often assigned to duty stations where the child's special needs can be met.

The military provides free health care for an adopted child as soon as he is placed in your home. You may also take advantage of a leave policy that will provide you with time to be with your new child.

Benefits apply whether the parent is single or married and whether the adoption is completed in the United States or overseas.

## Employee Benefits

When *Working Mother* magazine recently listed the best 100 companies for working women, one of the editor's criteria was financial assistance for adoption, which 85 percent of the companies provided.

When employers offer financial assistance and time off for adoption, it not only makes it possible for more working men and women to adopt, but also improves relations with employees by providing them help at such an important time in their lives. Each year more employers provide this benefit.

At **http://www.adoptionfriendlyworkplace.org**, a group advocating employer adoption benefits, you will find information about the advantages to employee morale that come from providing this benefit and a list of hundreds of employers that do, including big ones like Bank of America, PepsiCo, and State Farm, to name a few. Also, smaller employers are becoming involved, including hospitals and school districts, building contractors and retail outlets.

Those benefits provided by most companies usually include reimbursement for adoption costs of $1,000 to $5,000, which are non-taxable for most families. The companies typically provide resource and referral services and time off for both the adoption effort and time to bond with the child, sometimes paid, sometimes not.

Federal law requires that employers of 50 or more people must grant unpaid leave for family and medical purposes, including adoption and foster care if they have worked 1,250 hours or one year or more. Federal employees are entitled to 12 work weeks of unpaid leave during the year for certain family and medical needs, including adoption.

http://www.adoptionfriendlyworkplace.org

## Portrait of a Champion, SAS Institute, Inc.

A world leader in business-intelligence software and services, focused on its employees, SAS provides benefits to employees that include a $5,000 financial reimbursement for adoption, child care, health care and four weeks of paid leave.

The company also offers to its adoptive families an extensive resource and referral service, a support network and adoption seminars.

Congratulations from the adoption community to our Champion of Adoption Benefits! ☜☞

# 13

# Government Assistance
# in Adoption

As of late, there have been numerous governmental changes to the adoption laws nationwide. Attorney John J. Spina has kindly agreed to note some of the changes that may be applicable to you. Please remember that laws vary from state to state and may or may not relate to your current situation. Please be advised to check with your adoption attorney and/or accountant before filing for adoption credit on your taxes.

## Recent Tax Law Changes Encourage Adoptions
© *2004 by John J. Spina, Esq.*

This information is provided as a general guideline on the new tax benefits available in connection with the adoption of a child. This discussion is not intended as legal advice nor should such information be relied on without consulting your tax advisor or adoption attorney regarding your particular facts and circumstances.

In June 2001, President Bush signed into law a tax relief package that included the permanent extension of the Adoption Tax Credit (ATC) and income exclusion under an employer-sponsored adoption assistance program. Both provisions were set to expire at the end of 2001. Although the new ATC and income exclusion are similar to the provisions enacted in

1996, there are important changes in the law that you should be aware of. The discussion below attempts to explain the new tax benefits, and in the process, answers some frequently asked questions.

### 1. What is the ATC and exclusion?

The ATC is a tax credit for 100 percent of "qualifying adoption expenses" (discussed below) up to a maximum amount of $10,000 (adjusted for inflation after 2002). This means that if you incurred $4,000 in adoption expenses in 2002, you were eligible for a $4,000 credit. However, if you incurred $12,000 in adoption expenses in 2002, you could only claim a $10,000 credit, the maximum amount allowed. (A tax credit reduces your tax liability dollar for dollar and thus is much more valuable than a tax deduction that only reduces the amount of income on which you have to pay tax.)

In addition to the ATC, if your employer has implemented an adoption assistance program, you may be able to exclude from gross income the employer's payments or reimbursements for your expenses in adopting a child. As with the ATC, this amount is limited to a maximum exclusion of $10,000 (adjusted for inflation after 2002). Amounts your employer pays for your adoption expenses are considered income paid to you by the employer (like salary) on which you otherwise would have to pay tax. The exclusion allows you to reduce your income by the amount of the employer payments or reimbursements.

An adoption assistance program is a written plan of the employer that must meet certain federal tax law requirements. For information on these requirements, consult IRS Publication 968 or your tax advisor. You cannot exclude employer payments or reimbursements for adoption expenses that you incurred before the employer's adoption assistance program was in effect.

You may claim both the $10,000 ATC and the $10,000 exclusion for the same adoption, but not for the same expense. Thus, if you incurred

$15,000 in adoption expenses, $8,000 of which you paid and $7,000 of which your employer paid through an adoption assistance program, you would be eligible to claim an $8,000 tax credit for the amounts you paid and exclude from income the $7,000 the employer paid on your behalf.

## II. Who qualifies for the ATC and exclusion?

The ATC and exclusion are available for persons in the process of adopting a child, persons who have adopted a child or who are considering adopting a child. There are income limitations that phase out the ATC and exclusion for higher income earners; however, the dollar amounts have been significantly increased under the new law.

The income limitations are based on modified adjusted gross income (modified AGI), and will be adjusted for inflation after 2002. IRS Form 8839 and the accompanying instructions will tell you how to figure your modified AGI for the purpose of the credit and exclusion and will provide the amount by which you would have to reduce your credit or exclusion if your modified AGI is greater than $150,000.

Note that married couples must file a joint tax return to take the ATC or exclusion. The income limits in the table below apply equally to income reported on the joint return of a married couple as well as income reported on an individual tax return.

| If your modified AGI is: | Then you will be eligible for: |
| --- | --- |
| $150,000 or less | The full credit or exclusion. |
| $150,001 to $189,999 | A reduced credit or exclusion. |
| $190,000 or more | No credit or exclusion. |

For example, assume you had $10,000 of qualifying expenses for 2002 and your modified AGI for 2002 was $165,000. Under the income limitation, your ATC for 2002 would be reduced by an amount provided on IRS Form 8839. If your modified AGI for 2002 was, for example, $195,000, you would be ineligible to claim the ATC or exclusion.

### III. What are "qualifying adoption expenses"?

Qualifying adoption expenses are reasonable and necessary adoption fees, court costs, attorney fees, traveling expenses (including amounts spent for meals and lodging) while away from home, and other expenses directly related to, and whose principal purpose is for, the legal adoption of an "eligible child." An eligible child is under 18 years old or physically or mentally incapable of caring for himself or herself. For a foreign adoptee to be considered an eligible child, he or she must be under 18 years old. It is important to note that as with other credits and exclusions in the tax law, the IRS will be looking to prevent taxpayers from abusing the ATC and exclusion by fraudulently claiming expenses that did not exist or by "padding" actual expenses. Thus, when the tax law provides that qualifying adoption expenses must be "reasonable and necessary," and "directly related to, and whose principal purpose is for" a legal adoption, these are legal standards by which the IRS will review your tax return and determine whether your claim for the ATC or exclusion is valid. For example, the expense for chartering a private jet to take you overseas to meet your adopted child probably is not a reasonable expense for which you could claim the credit or exclusion. In addition, such a claim would likely serve as a "red flag" to the IRS and may prompt an audit of your tax return. Thus, as you incur adoption expenses, you should keep in mind the legal standard when determining what is a qualifying adoption expense.

Non-qualifying expenses include, among other things, expenses that violate state or federal law, expenses for the adoption of your spouse's child, expenses paid using funds received from any federal, state, or local program, expenses allowed as a credit or deduction under any other federal income tax rule, or expenses paid or reimbursed by your employer (except for amounts paid or reimbursed under an adoption assistance program).

### IV. When can you take the ATC and/or exclusion?

There are important differences regarding if and when you could claim the ATC or exclusion depending on whether the eligible child is a U.S. citizen or resident. If the eligible child is a U.S. citizen or resident, you can claim the credit or exclusion even if the adoption is never finalized. However, if you are adopting a foreign child, you cannot take the adoption credit or exclusion unless and until the adoption becomes final. You may claim the credit and/or exclusion as shown in the following tables.

## Adoption of a child who is a U.S. citizen or resident

| If you pay qualifying expenses in: | Then take a credit in: |
|---|---|
| Any year before the year the adoption becomes final. | The year after the year of the payment. |
| The year the adoption becomes final. | The year the adoption becomes final. |
| Any year after the year the adoption becomes final. | The year of the payment. |
| If your employer pays for qualifying expenses under an adoption assistance program in any year. | Then take the exclusion in the year of the payment. |

## Adoption of a child who is <u>not</u> a U.S. citizen or resident

| If you pay qualifying expenses in: | Then take a credit in: |
|---|---|
| Any year before the year the adoption becomes final. | The year the adoption becomes final. |
| The year the adoption becomes final. | The year the adoption becomes final. |
| Any year after the year the adoption becomes final. | The year of the payment. |
| If your employer pays for qualifying expenses under an adoption assistance program in any year before the year the adoption becomes final. | The year the adoption becomes final. |
| The year the adoption becomes final. | The year the adoption becomes final. |
| Any year after the year the adoption becomes final. | The year of the payment. |

If your employer makes adoption assistance payments in a year before the adoption of a foreign child becomes final, you must make an adjustment on your tax return for the earlier year to include the payments in your income. Then, on your return for the year the adoption becomes final, you may make an adjustment to take the exclusion.

Prior dollar limits continue to apply to expenses paid before 2002, and the ATC is not available for expenses incurred before the ATC was enacted. For example, assume you had $7,000 of expenses in 2001 (when the maximum ATC was $5,000) and $3,000 of expenses in 2002. You finalize the adoption of a child in 2002 and now can claim the credit. You would be eligible to take an $8,000 credit—$5,000 for expenses incurred in 2001 (the maximum amount allowed under the old law), and $3,000 for expenses incurred in 2002.

If your tax liability is less than your available credit, you may carry forward the amount of credit left over, until it is used, for a period of five years. For example, assume in 2002 your tax liability was $4,000 but you had $7,000 in adoption expenses. You could claim a $4,000 credit for 2002 and could carry forward the remaining $3,000 of credit to offset tax liability for the next five tax years, if necessary.

You can also apply the credit to offset any taxes owed under the alternative minimum tax.

### V. How to take the ATC or exclusion

You must file IRS Form 8839 with either IRS Form 1040 or Form 1040A to take the credit or exclusion. As noted above, if you are married, you must file a joint return to take the adoption credit or exclusion.

You must provide an identifying number for the child on Form 8839. For this, you must use either a social security number if the child has one or if you will be able to obtain one prior to filing your tax return, or an adoption taxpayer identification number (ATIN) if you are adopting a U.S. citizen or resident and cannot obtain a social security number prior to filing your tax return. You must use an individual taxpayer identification number (ITIN) if the child is a resident or nonresident alien and not eligible for a social security number. An ATIN is not available for a foreign adoptee. The amount of your adoption credit or exclusion is limited to

$10,000 for each effort to adopt an eligible child. If you can take a credit and exclusion, this dollar limit applies separately to each. The $10,000 amount is the total amount of qualifying expenses you may take into account whether, for example, your adoption takes one year or four years. That is, the $10,000 credit must be reduced by the amount of qualifying expenses taken into account in previous years for the same adoption effort.

For example, assume that in your effort to adopt a child, your qualifying adoption expenses for 2002 were $3,000. The maximum amount of expenses you can take into account for future years will be reduced by the expenses you took into account for 2002. Therefore, the maximum amount of expenses you could take into account for future years with respect to this adoption effort is $7,000.

Assume now that you pay $6,000 of qualifying adoption expenses in an effort to adopt an eligible child. However, the adoption is not successful. You then pay an additional $7,000 of qualifying adoption expenses for the successful adoption of a different eligible child. With respect to the dollar limit on the credit, the IRS views the $13,000 of expenses as paid in one adoption effort. Therefore, because the maximum amount of expenses you can take into account is $10,000, you would not be able to take the ATC for $3,000 of qualifying adoption expenses.

## VI. Special rules for adopting a child with special needs

For children with "special needs," the credit or exclusion will be allowed regardless of whether you have qualifying adoption expenses.

A child qualifies as a special needs child if he or she is (1) otherwise an "eligible child" (as defined above), (2) a U.S. citizen or resident, and (3) a state determines that the child cannot or should not be returned to his or her home and probably would not be adopted unless adoption assistance is provided to the adoptive parents.

You should consult your tax advisor, adoption attorney and relevant state agency regarding adoptions of children with special needs.

## VII. What documentation should be kept?

As noted above, the IRS will likely review a tax return claiming the ATC or exclusion with the same careful attention it reviews tax returns claiming other tax credits and exclusions. Therefore, it is important that you retain all of your receipts and records showing payments made in connection with adoption expenses incurred. You should also keep copies of your tax returns that you file each year.

## VIII. For additional information

For additional information on the ATC and income exclusion under an employer sponsored adoption assistance program, you should consult your tax advisor or adoption attorney. You may also consult IRS Publication 968 which provides a fairly clear explanation of the ATC and exclusion as understood by the agency that will be reviewing your tax return and enforcing the requirements of these tax provisions. Additional information may also be found on the IRS web site at **www.irs.gov**, or by calling the IRS at 1-800-829-1040.

## Adoption Law Sites Online

Again, remember that adoption laws can change daily. To date there is no national

---

### Tax Help Online

• To search for tax forms, find help and publications, point your browser to **http://www.irs.gov**.

• To download publications and forms, go to **http://www.irs.gov/form-spubs/index.html**.

• For news about changing taxes and rules, for help finding tax information, forms and booklets, go to **http://www.1040.com**.

• The American Bar Association's page of links to sites with help for taxpayers is at **http://www.abanet.org/tax/sites.html**.

adoption law that would bring all states into compliance as one unit. Therefore, all states have different laws and it will greatly benefit you to contact an adoption attorney in your state of residence. The following sites will give you more access to federal regulation and some state law. We advise you to know the laws of your state thoroughly before adopting.

- **http://www.adoptioncouncil.org**: National Counsel For Adoption.

- **http://www.law.cornell.edu/topics/adoption.html**: Adoption law overview.

- **http://www.lawresearch.com/v2/practice/ctadopt.htm**: Adoption law research.

- **http://www.megalaw.com/top/adoption.php**: More on adoption law.

- **http://family-law.freeadvice.com/adoption_law/**: Adoption law and federal tax credits.

- **http://www.abcadoptions.com/uslaw.htm**: State by state adoption law.

# Your Child's Social Security Number

For your child to qualify as a dependent or to receive adoption benefits or the earned income and other tax credits, you must provide the IRS with the child's social security number. Getting this number for your adopted child is the same as getting it for a biological child. While you can get the number before the adoption is completed, you may want to wait. Then you can apply for the number with your names as the parents and with your child's new name. You will use Form SS-5. For a foreign-born adoptee, you will need to provide evidence of age, identity, citizenship or alien status.

For complete instructions about acquiring a social security number, go to **http://www.ssa.gov/ssnumber**. The forms you need are available for download at **http://www.ssa.gov/online**. If you want to claim your child for tax purposes while the adoption is pending, visit **http://www.irs.gov/formspubs** and download Form W-7A which is an application for a taxpayer identification number for pending adoptions. ෴

# 14

# Your Adoption Budget

## Keeping Track of Your Adoption Expenses

Develop a budget for your expenses. Once you begin to do this, it will make tax time so much easier. You can use a program like Quick Books or one of the financial software programs that comes with your computer or even an old-fashioned ledger book.

So many expenses involved in adopting are deductible, but they are only deductible if you take advantage of them. Believe me, the government isn't going to tell you if you've forgotten a deduction. Check with your accountant as well. Make sure your tax preparer is aware that you are adopting so he can assist you in your tax preparation.

### Things to Remember When Budgeting

- Use an accounting program if at all possible.

- Balance your checkbook each month. Having accurate totals will help ease your adoption stress.

- Watch your ATM usage! Even though they're so easy to use and so convenient!

- Do you really need a big screen TV, new furniture, a new updated microwave?

- Stick to the necessities until your adoption is final.

- Discover the difference between what you need and what you want!

# What's Deductible?

The following items are deductible off your income taxes. This list is for example purposes, and you need to check with your tax preparer to make sure you have left nothing out.

- Legal Fees

- Home Study Fees

- Justice Department Fees for Fingerprinting

- Facilitator Fees

- Agency Fees

- Advertising Costs

- Toll-free Phone Charges

- Calling Cards/Long Distance Charges

- Mileage

- Postage

- Any Medical and/or Psychological Evaluations Required

- Transportation

- Photocopying of Documents

- Lodging and Meals

*Always ask for and do not leave without receipts to add to your growing file of deductible expenses!* ☜☞

## Adoption Planning Budget

Over the years I have compiled a generic list of typical expenses. Not all adoptions will have these expenses. Please add and subtract as needed. Use the adoption budget planning sheet to get you started:

| Adoptive Family Expenses | Budgeted Amounts | Actual Costs |
|---|---|---|
| Home Study | | |
| Medical/Physical | | |
| Filing Fees | | |
| Attorney Fees | | |
| Fingerprinting | | |
| Birth Parent Signatures of Release (Legal) | | |
| Facilitation Fees | | |
| Travel/Lodging/Food | | |
| Resumé Printing | | |
| Postage | | |
| Toll-Free Number | | |
| Advertising | | |
| Faxing | | |
| Copying | | |
| Photography | | |
| Counseling | | |
| Website Design | | |
| Misc. | | |
| **Birth Mother Expenses** | | |
| Pregnancy/Medical Care | | |
| Pregnancy/Child Care | | |
| Maternity Clothes | | |
| Food | | |
| Rent | | |
| Utilities | | |
| Car Insurance | | |
| Insurance Copayments | | |
| Misc. | | |
| | *Total:* | *Total:* |

I've become quite familiar with adoption expenses and formatted this budget form to assist you in your adoption journey. I hope this helps you with your financial planning efforts. Money issues can add to the stress of your adoption if you allow them to. Good planning reduces the stress you are under and will let you enjoy the good times that are just ahead!

# 15

# Adoption Hotlinks
## Your Guide to Over 1,200 Adoption Related Websites

## What Are Adoption Hotlinks?

The Adoption Hotlink section of AdoptingOnline.com includes web addresses to over 1,200 adoption resources both in the United States and Canada. These resources are divided up into 29 categories. Some of these categories include:

1. Attorneys

2. Private and Public Agencies

3. Facilitators

4. Social Workers

5. Special Needs Services and Resources

6. Financial Resources

7. Magazines and Newsletters

8. Support Services

9. Travel Information

Most of the resources you may select by state. Many resources provide services nationwide or to surrounding states. You may also use Adoption Hotlinks to discover the type of adoption process you wish to pursue. Below is a description of each icon found in AdoptingOnline.com that will make the use of Hotlinks a snap.

## How Do I Use Hotlinks?

Once you get the feel of the Internet, you look up the Web addresses that fit your current needs. You can do this in most cases by state or by listing. Enter the address into your Web browser and click. That's all there is to it. Always remember to have a notebook and pen by your side to write down pertinent information gleaned from the site. Or cut and paste the information to your notepad or Word document for future reference.

**Adoption Hotlinks Disclaimer:** AdoptingOnline.com *provides numerous links to websites. It is impossible to know all the content on each site, therefore, AdoptingOnline.com is not liable for any damages resulting from following any of the links provided nor is AdoptingOnline.com responsible for any information provided on these sites. Every attempt has been made to provide accurate information, however, additional information on adoption may be found online. While every effort has been made to ensure that this resource listing is as up-to-date as possible, AdoptingOnline.com cannot be held responsible for the content or services offered on these sites.*

*The Internet is constantly changing. We have made every attempt to verify each address before going to print. We are not responsible for any changes and/or guarantee an organization or individual will continue to maintain a site. We are not able to verify that the content or services of each site will continue or still be offered as at any time changes can be made in regards to policy and fees.*

*The Internet is unregulated and the nature of the Internet is such that no guarantees can be made on the use of a particular site. We do not offer endorsements or recommendations of the services or organizations that are listed within this publication. Modifications can be made which can change the site completely. More important, any person considering adoption should consult with a qualified adoption professional in their state for current laws and guidance before embarking on any adoption. You may also check with the Better Business Bureau at **www.bbbonline.org.***

## ICONS USED IN THIS BOOK

 International Adoptions and/or Services

 Home Study Providers

 Faith-based Organizations

 Magazines, Newsletters or Information by E-mail Available

 Surrogacy Adoptions and Information

 Domestic Adoption Services—Operates Throughout the U.S.

 Ethnic Groups, Transracial Adoptions or Information in Spanish

 Photo Listing of Waiting Children

 Experienced in Single Parent Adoptions

 Interstate Compact Information, Resources and/or Assistance

 Financial Information and Resources

 Military Information and Resources

 Support Services–Adoption and Internet Support Services, Medical and Health

 Profile Services

 Attorney Services

# Adoption Hotlinks

# Adoption Exchanges & Photo Listings

**Alaska Adoption Exchange**                                907.465.3631
*Waiting children photo listing; frequently asked questions; newsletter.*
**http://www.akae.org**
Juneau, AK

**Children Awaiting Parents, Inc.**                         585.232.5110
*Waiting children photo listing; recruitment and referral services; working with the children who have waited the longest; adoption information; non-profit.*
**http://www.capbook.org**
Rochester, NY

**Jewish Children's Adoption Network**                      303.573.8113
*Matches families with specific children in need of a home; primarily special needs children; assists in the application process for subsidy; non-profit.*
**http://www.users.qwest.net/~jcan**
Denver, CO

**MARE, Massachusetts Adoption Resource Exchange, Inc.**    617.542.3678
*Waiting children photo listing; extensive resources related to older and special needs adoption; non-profit; information in Spanish.*
**http://www.mareinc.org**
Boston, MA

**MARN, Minnesota Adoption Resource Network**              612.861.7115
*Waiting children photo listing; advocacy and awareness of the state's special children; listing of agencies; post-adoption support; non-profit.*
**http://www.mnadopt.org**
St. Paul, MN

### My Turn Now, Inc.                                        404.657.3479
*Waiting children photo listing; adoption information, referrals, support and advocacy; non-profit.*
**http://www.myturnnow.com**
Atlanta, GA

### National Adoption Center                                 215.735.9988
*Waiting children photo listing; special needs children; brings children and families together; agency referral; online parenting program; public awareness of waiting children; non-profit.*
**http://www.adopt.org**
Philadelphia, PA

### Northwest Adoption Exchange                              800.927.9411
*Waiting children photo listing; matches state foster children with adoptive families; information for prospective adoptive parents and references to adoption agencies.*
**http://www.nwae.org**
Seattle, WA

### Oklahoma Adoption Exchange                               405.521.2475
*Waiting children photo listing; adoption information; foster care.*
**http://www.okdhs.org/adopt**
Oklahoma City, OK

### Special Needs Adoptive Parent Services, Inc.             208.345.6646
*Adoption promotion organization; find out about available children; waiting children photo listing; special needs children; home study information and agency listing; resource links; non-profit.*
**http://www.idahowednesdayschild.org**
Boise, ID

### TARE Family Network                                      800.233.3405
*Registry for home studied adoptive families from all states; waiting children photo listing; special needs children.*
**http://www.tdprs.state.tx.us/Adoption and Foster Care/TARE Family Network**
TX

**The Adoption Exchange**                                     303.755.4756
*Recruitment of families for waiting children; adoption agency listing; waiting children photo listing; information in Spanish; non-profit.*
**http://www.adoptex.org**
Aurora, CO

---

**The Adoption Exchange**                                     866.872.7212
*Recruitment of families for waiting children; waiting children photo listing; information in Spanish; non-profit.*
**http://www.adoptex.org**
Murray, UT

---

**The Adoption Exchange**                                     505.247.1769
*Recruitment of families for waiting children; waiting children photo listing; information in Spanish; non-profit.*
**http://www.adoptex.org**
Albuquerque, NM

---

**The Adoption Exchange**                                     314.367.3343
*Recruitment of families for waiting children; waiting children photo listing; information in Spanish; non-profit.*
**http://www.adoptex.org**
St. Louis, MO

---

**The Adoption Exchange**                                     702.436.6335
*Recruitment of families for waiting children; waiting children photo listing; information in Spanish; non-profit.*
**http://www.adoptex.org**
Las Vegas, NV

---

**Treasure Book**                                             406.442.3411
*Waiting children photo listing; biracial and special needs children; referral service; non-profit.*
**http://www.treasurebook.org**
Helena, MT

# Adoptive Family Resources

### Adopting Families Profile

*Services to create your personally tailored birth parent letter, photo profile, digital life book and more.*

---

### Adoption Homestudy in Cincinnati, Ohio            513.793.1885

*Home studies; online documents, websites and resources to assist with completing home studies as quickly as possible.*

**http://www.ohiohomestudy.com**
Cincinnati, OH

---

### Adoption Home Study Services for Oklahoma          918.585.2039

*Home study provider; post-placement services; pre- and post-adoption counseling; educational resources; parenting issues; tax credit information; referral to adoption resources.*

**http://adoptionoklahoma.com**

---

### Adoption by Design

*Services to design appealing birth parent profiles; designers are adoptive parents themselves.*

---

### Adoption Designs                                   724.238.9408

*Domain registration and hosting services; professional services to create* Dear Birth Mother *letter, brochures and fliers; website design.*
Champion, PA

---

### Adoption Information Services, Inc.                770.339.7236

*Adoptive parents guidance services; jump-starts the adoption process; education; referrals; advocacy; assessment and support services.*

**http://www.adoptioninfosvcs.com**
Lawrenceville, GA

**Adoption Mailings**  408.927.0100

*Direct mail organization; helps adoptive parents find a baby; taps into obstetricians.*

**http://www.adoptionmailings.com**

San Jose, CA

---

**Adoption Resource Center of Connecticut, Inc.**  860.657.2626

*Domestic and international services; home studies; post-legal adoption services; adoptive parent education agency networking; referrals; non-profit.*

**http://www.arcct.org**

Glastonbury, CT

---

**Ametz Adoption Program of JCCA**  212.558.9949

*Home studies; post-placement services; consultations and education for all parties in an adoption; foster care services; non-profit.*

**http://www.jewishchildcareny.org**

New York, NY

---

**Assistant Stork**  540.659.6845

*Dossier preparation and adoption documents courier; international adoption.*

**http://www.asststork.com**

Stafford, VA

---

**Child and Home Study Associates**  610.565.1544

*Home studies for domestic and international adoptions; educational preparation; network with adoption professionals; post-placement supervision; non-profit.*

**http://www.chsadoptions.org**

Media, PA & Wilmington, DE

---

**Christian Adoption**  316.251.4405

*Profile letters and photos of Christian families who wish to adopt; adoption information.*

**http://www.christianadoption.com**

Coffeyville, KS

### Connections/Reachsource Adoption Services  800.892.4523

*Birth mother referral program; adoption assistance and resources.*

**http://www.pivot.net/~adoptcon**
Windham, ME

---

### Dossier Express

*Assists in obtaining vital records and documents to complete international adoptions.*

---

### Family Adoption Consultants Specialists  617.332.9984

*Consulting service that offers: resources; attorneys and agencies; advertising information; adoption-related reading materials; assistance with writing* Dear Birth Parent *letters.*

**http://www.adoption-consultant.com**
West Newton Hills, MA

---

### Harrah Family (Adoption) Services, Inc.  936.321.5221

*China adoption consultants, including guides and interpreters to travel with adoptive parents in the country; non-profit.*

**http://www.rainbowkids.com/page2/ha11752m.html**
Spring, TX

---

### HopeToAdopt.com  888.481.7252

*Adoptive family support and resources; guidelines on how to write a great profile; forum and chat room.*

**http://www.hopetoadopt.com**
Mesa, AZ

---

### International Concerns for Children, Inc.  303.494.8333

*Comprehensive resource for international adoption; order online "Report on Inter-Country Adoption"; adoption counseling; agency listing; non-profit.*

**http://www.iccadopt.org**
Boulder, CO

---

**Kingdom Kids Adoption Ministries**                509.465.3520

*Christ-centered adoption conferences; assistance for families to raise finances*
*for adoption; local support groups.*

**http://www.kkadoption.com**
Spokane, WA

**Kmetko and Associates, Ltd.**                773.561.6196

*Child welfare agency; interstate compact information; home studies.*

**http://www.kmetko.com**
Chicago, IL

**Link National Adoption Registry, LNAR**                704.792.2229

*Referral service; profiles of waiting Christian families; non-profit.*

**http://www.linkadoption.com**
Concord, NC

**May We Adopt?**                903.923.8077

*Waiting family profiles; links to agencies and other resources; forums;*
*adoption stories.*

**http://www.mayweadopt.com**
Garland, TX

**Nathanson Adoption Services**                704.553.9506

*Adoption services agency; specializing in home studies; does not offer child*
*placement.*

**http://nathansonadopt.com**
Charlotte, NC

**NightLight Foundation**                714.278.1020

*Continuing support for children relocating to U.S.; aid to the orphans and at-risk*
*children of St. Petersburg, Russia, and to families in distress from St. Petersburg's*
*inner city.*

**http://www.toadoptkids.org/nl_found.htm**
Fullerton, CA

### New York Home Study Services                516.333.4999

*Social workers affiliated with authorized agencies to provide home studies for domestic and international adoptions.*

**http://techease.com/nyhomestudy**
NY

### O'Keeffe & McCann, L.L.P.                845.615.8500

*Assist families upon their return home from an international adoption; tips on pediatrician visits; social security applications, tax issues and more.*

**http://www.readoptiononline.com**
Goshen, NY

### Open Adoption Services                425.861.4772

*Open adoption resources; brings birth mothers and qualified adoptive parents together; waiting families profiles.*

http://www.open-adoption-services.com/adopt
Redmond, WA

### ReachSOURCE                207.741.2794

*Advertising services for adoptive parents to reach birth parents through newspapers and the Internet; also connects birth parents with adoptive families.*

**http://www.gwi.net/~reach**

### Real Moms Adoption Newsletter

*Adoptive mothers newsletter; information and links about the adoptive process; photo listing of special needs waiting children.*

**http://www.comeunity.com/adoption/realmoms**
Mooresville, NC

### Southern Social Works, Inc.                256.831.4005

*Social service agency specializing in adoption issues; provides home studies.*

**http://southernsocialworks.com/pages/824178/index.htm**
Anniston, AL

**Spokane Consultants in Family Living**                    509.328.6274
*Specializes in open adoption; family counseling; home studies; foster care; special needs resources.*
**http://host33.com/scfl**
Spokane ,WA

**USAadoptions.com**                    800.923.6784
*Birth and adoptive parent resources; domestic adoption services; counseling, housing and financial assistance; open adoption articles; special needs advocacy.*
**http://www.usaadoptions.com**
Nevada City, CA

# Agencies, Private

## Alabama

**Children of the World**                    251.990.3550
*International: children from Asia, Eastern Europe and Latin America; adoption information; home studies.*
**http://www.childrenoftheworld.com**
Fairhope, AL

**Lifeline Adoption Services**                    205.967.0811
*Domestic and international: children from China and Ukraine; home studies; birth mother services; maternity home; counseling; legal assistance.*
**http://www.lifelineadoption.org**
Birmingham, AL

**Villa Hope International Adoption**                    205.870.7359
*International: children in Asia, Eastern Europe, South and Latin America; home studies; resource links.*
**http://www.villahope.org**
Birmingham, AL

## Alaska

Alaska International Adoption Agency          907.677.2888

*Domestic and international, specializes in children from Russia; adoption services including home studies; non-profit.*

**http://www.akadoptions.com**
Anchorage, AK

Fairbanks Counseling and Adoption          907.456.4729

*Domestic adoption; family counseling; pregnancy services; home studies; post-placement services; non-profit.*

**http://www.ptialaska.net/~fca**
Fairbanks, AK

## Arizona

Arizona Family Adoption Services, Inc.          602.254.2271

*Domestic adoptions; work with families who want to adopt internationally; home studies; referrals to educational, counseling and legal services.*

**http://www.azadoptions.com**
Phoenix, AZ

Commonwealth Adoptions Int'l          520.327.7574

*International: children from Eastern Europe and Latin America; education and social events; home studies; adoptive family stories; travel information; information in Spanish; non-profit.*

**http://www.commonwealthadoption.org**
Tucson, AZ

Dillon Southwest          480.945.2221

*International, children from Korea; home studies; non-profit.*

**http://www.dillonsouthwest.org**
Scottsdale, AZ

Hand in Hand International Adoptions          480.892.5550

*International: children from Asia, Latin America and Eastern Europe; home studies; non-profit.*

**http://www.hihiadopt.org**
Mesa, AZ

## Arkansas

. . . . . . . . . . . . . . . . . . . . . . . . . . . . . . . . . . . . . . . . . . . . . . . . . . . . . . . . . . . . . . . . . . . . .

Adoption Choices, Inc.                                    800.898.6028

*Domestic infants; international, children from Guatemala; home studies;*
*adoption information; travel resources; non-profit.*

**http://www.adoptionchoices.org**
Little Rock, AR

Bethany Christian Services                               501.664.5729

*Christian; domestic infants; international; foster care services; home studies;*
*waiting families profiles; pregnancy counseling; non-profit.*

**http://www.bethany.org/A55798/bethanyWWW.nsf/**
**BCS/littlerockar**
Little Rock, AR

Dillon International                                      501.791.9300

*International: children from Eastern Europe, Latin America and Asia; home*
*studies; pre- and post-placement services; financial information; non-profit.*

**http://www.dillonadopt.com**
Little Rock, AR

## California

. . . . . . . . . . . . . . . . . . . . . . . . . . . . . . . . . . . . . . . . . . . . . . . . . . . . . . . . . . . . . . . . . . . . .

ACCEPT (An Adoption and Counseling Center)              650.321.6916

*International: children from Eastern Europe, Latin America and Asia;*
*homes studies; long-term support and counseling; non-profit.*

**http://www.acceptadoptions.org**
Los Altos, CA

Across the World Adoptions                               925.356.6260

*International: children from Latin America, Russia, Kazakhstan and China;*
*home studies; educational classes; financial information; non-profit.*

**http://www.adopting.com/atwa**
Pleasant Hill, CA

### Adopt International
**650.369.7300**

*Domestic and international: children from Eastern Europe, China, Guatemala and Nepal; home studies; waiting families profiles; post-adoption services.*

**http://www.adopt-intl.org**
Redwood City, CA

---

### Adoptions and Aid International
**925.934.1090**

*International: children from Eastern Europe; single parent adoption; non-profit.*

**http://www.russianadoption.com**
Walnut Creek, CA

---

### America-World Adoption Association West
**714.557.1065**

*Christian; international: children from China, Russia, Ukraine and Vietnam; home studies; financial information; non-profit.*

**http://www.america-china.org**
Santa Ana, CA

---

### Bal Jagat Children's World, Inc.
**818.709.4737**

*International: children from Asia, Eastern Europe and Guatemala; pre- and post-adoption services; home studies; non-profit.*

**http://www.baljagat.org**
Chatsworth, CA

---

### Bay Area Adoption Services, Inc.
**650.964.3800**

*International: children from Asia, Eastern Europe and Latin America; home studies; serving 12 counties in Northern California; non-profit.*

**http://www.baas.org**
Mountain View, CA

---

### Bethany Christian Services
**209.522.5121**

*Christian; domestic infants; international; foster care services; home studies; waiting families profiles; pregnancy counseling; non-profit.*

**http://www.bethany.org/A55798/bethanyWWW.nef/**
**BCS/modestoca**
Modesto, CA

Catholic Charities Adoption Agency                    619.231.2828

*Domestic including transracial adoptions; adoption information; pregnancy coun-*
*seling; information in Spanish.*
**http://www.ccdsd.org/preg.html**
San Diego, CA & San Fancisco, CA

Family Connections Adoptions                          209.524.8844

*Christian; domestic special needs and international; home studies;*
*offices in several locations in the state; non-profit.*
Modesto, CA

Family Network Inc.                                   831.663.5428

*Domestic infants and special needs children; international: children from Asia,*
*Eastern Europe, Latin America and Africa; home studies; interstate compact*
*information; non-profit.*
**http://www.adopt-familynetwork.com**
Monterey, CA

God's Families International Adoption Agency          949.858.7621

*Christian; international: children from Asia, Eastern Europe and Latin America;*
*home studies; financial information; glossary; non-profit.*
**http://www.webworldinc.com/gciaa**
Trabuco Canyon, CA

Heartsent Adoptions, Inc.                             925.254.8883

*International: children from Eastern Europe, Guatemala and Asia; home studies;*
*education; articles; cultural events for adoptive families; non-profit.*
**http://www.heartsent.org**
Orinda, CA

Holy Family Services, Adoption & Foster Care          626.578.1156

*Domestic infants and special needs children; interim infant foster care; home*
*studies; non-profit.*
**http://www.holyfamilyservices.org**
Pasadena, CA

Independent Adoption Center                                925.827.2229

*Domestic infants; international services; home studies; counseling and support
groups; interstate compact information; nationwide services; non-profit.*

**http://www.IndependentAdoptionCenter.org**
Pleasant Hill, CA

---

Infant of Prague                                          559.447.3333

*Domestic infants and special needs children; home studies; counseling and
post-adoption services; non-profit.*

**http://www.infantofprague.org**
Fresno, CA

---

International Christian Adoptions                          909.695.3336

*Christian; domestic infants, special needs and foster care services; international:
children from Eastern Europe, Asia and Latin America; home studies; non-profit.*

**http://www.4achild.com**
Temecula, CA

---

Kinship Center                                           800.454.6744

*Domestic infants and special needs children; foster care; home studies;
relative care and support; counseling; non-profit.*

**http://www.kinshipcenter.org**
Salinas, CA

---

Lifetime Adoption                                        530.271.1740

*Domestic adoption infants and older children; newsletter; profile services.*

**http://www.lifetimeadoption.com**
Grass Valley, CA

---

Lilliput Children's Services                              916.923.5444

*Domestic; foster children; home studies; education, resources and links;
reading list; local support groups; offices in other cities; non-profit.*

**http://www.lilliput.org**
Sacramento, CA

---

North Bay Adoptions                                      707.570.2940

*International: children from Asia, Latin America, Russia and Eastern Europe;
home studies; pre-adoption classes; non-profit.*

**http://www.northbayadoptions.com**
Santa Rosa, CA

**PACT, an Adoption Alliance**                          510.243.9460

*Domestic infants of color and transracial newborns; pre- and post-adopt education programs; support groups; newsletter; non-profit.*

**http://www.pactadopt.org**
Richmond, CA

---

**Sierra Adoption Services**                           530.272.9600

*International adoptions; domestic, special needs children; home studies; information and resources; foster care services; non-profit.*

**http://www.sierraadoption.org**
Grass Valley, CA

---

**Vista Del Mar Child and Family Services**            310.836.1223

*Domestic infants and special needs children; international services; foster care; pregnancy counseling; monthly support groups.*

**http://www.vistadelmar.org**
Los Angeles, CA

---

## Colorado

**AAC Adoption & Family Network, Inc.**                970.532.3576

*International: children from China and Korea; home studies; waiting children photo listing; counseling; education; cultural activities; non-profit.*

**http://www.aacadoption.com**
Berthoud, CO

---

**Adoption Choices, Inc.**                             303.670.4401

*Domestic infants; international: children from Vietnam and Guatemala; home studies; adoption information; travel resources; non-profit.*

**http://www.adoptionchoices.org**
Evergreen, CO

---

**Bethany Christian Services of Colorado**            303.221.0734

*Christian; domestic infants; international; foster care services; home studies; waiting families profiles; pregnancy counseling; non-profit.*

**http://www.bethany.org/colorado**
Denver, CO

### Chinese Children Adoption International          303.850.9998

*International: Chinese children and special needs Chinese adoptions; home studies; waiting children info packets; resources; non-profit.*

**http://www.chinesechildren.org**
Englewood, CO

### Hand in Hand International Adoptions          970.586.6866

*International: children from Asia, Latin America and Eastern Europe; home studies; non-profit.*

**http://www.hihiadopt.org**
Estes Park, CO

### Hope's Promise          303.660.0277

*Domestic infants; international: children from Ukraine, Nepal, Sierra Leone, India and Cambodia; waiting children photo listing; home studies; non-profit.*

**http://www.hopespromise.com**
Castle Rock, CO

### Littlest Angels International          970.856.6177

*Domestic infants and special needs children; international: children from Asia, Latin America and Eastern Europe; home studies; non-profit.*

**http://www.co-biz.com/angelsinternational**
Cedaredge, CO

### Lutheran Family Services of Colorado          303.922.3433

*Domestic infants and special needs children; international: children from Asia, Eastern Europe and South America; home studies; foster care services; non-profit.*

**http://www.lfsco.org**

### MAPS Colorado          970.262.2998

*International and domestic; home studies; foster care services; parenting and adoption support services; counseling services; non-profit.*

**http://www.mapsadopt.org**
Silverthorne, CO

Small Miracles                                          303.220.7611

*International, primarily children from Guatemala; home studies; nationwide*
*services; resources; non-profit.*

**http://www.smallmiracles.org**
Englewood, CO

## Connecticut

Adoption Services of Lutheran Social Services of        860.257.9899
New England

*Domestic infants and special needs children; international: children from Asia*
*and Eastern Europe; home studies; non-profit.*

**http://www.adoptlss.org/conn.html**
Rocky Hill, CT

Adoptions From The Heart                                203.256.0046

*Domestic infants and biracial children; international, children from ten countries;*
*home studies; waiting family profiles; links; newsletter; non-profit.*

**http://www.adoptionsfromtheheart.com**
Green Farms, CT

Catholic Charities of Fairfield County                 203.372.4301

*Domestic infants; international, children from China; home studies; birth parent*
*counseling; foster care; non-profit.*

**http://www.ccfc-ct.org**
Bridgeport, CT

Family and Children's Agency Inc.                      203.855.8765

*Domestic special needs children; international: children from Russia, Ukraine,*
*Taiwan, Vietnam, Korea and China; home studies; newsletter.*

**http://www.familyanDChildrensagency.org**
Norwalk ,CT

Thursday's Child Adoption Agency                       860.242.5941

*Domestic and international infants and older children from Bulgaria, China,*
*Guatemala, Russia, Vietnam and India; home studies; non-profit.*

**http://www.tcadoption.org**
Bloomfield, CT

## Delaware

Adoptions From The Heart                                                302.658.8883

*Domestic infants and biracial children; international, children from ten countries; home studies; waiting families profiles; links; newsletter; non-profit.*

**http://www.adoptionsfromtheheart.com**
Wilmington, DE

Bethany Christian Services                                             302.369.3470

*Christian; Domestic infants; international; foster care services; home studies; waiting families profiles; pregnancy counseling; non-profit.*

**http://www.bethany.org/ftwash**
Newark, DE

## District of Columbia

Adoption Service Information Agency, Inc. (ASIA)            202.726.7193

*Domestic infants; international: children from Asia; home studies; counseling; newsletter; non-profit.*

**http://www.asia-adopt.org**
Washington, D.C.

CASI Foundation for Children                                          202.974.0970

*Domestic and international: children from Latin America, Asia and Eastern Europe; Chinese special needs children; home studies; non-profit.*

**http://www.adoptcasi.org**
Washington, D.C.

Lutheran Social Services, National Capital Area              202.723.3000

*Domestic infants and special needs children; international services; foster care; home studies; pregnancy and birth parent counseling; non-profit.*

**http://www.lssnca.org**
Washington, D.C.

## Florida

................................................................

### A Bond of Love Adoption Agency, Inc.  941.957.0064

*Domestic infants; home studies; counseling and
support services; non-profit.*
Sarasota, FL

### Adoption Placement, Inc.  954.474.8494

*Domestic and international: children from Russia, Guatemala and China;
home studies; nationwide services; non-profit.*
**http://www.adoptionplacement.com**
Plantation, FL

### Adoption Resources of Florida  941.779.1632

*Domestic infants and special needs children; international: children from Asia,
Eastern Europe and Guatemala; home studies; parenting and adoption support
services; newsletter; non-profit.*
**http://www.mapsadopt.org**
Holmes Beach, FL

### Advocates for Children and Families  305.653.2474

*Domestic; special needs; home studies; counseling; housing; legal services;
interstate compact; Spanish-speaking staff; non-profit.*
**http://www.adoptionflorida.org**
North Miami Beach, FL

### Bethany Christian Services  407.667.9393

*Christian; domestic infants; international; foster care services; home studies;
waiting families profiles; pregnancy counseling; non-profit.*
**http://www.bethany.org/maitland**
Maitland, FL

### Children of the Nations International Adoptions  727.859.0365

*International: children from Asia, Eastern Europe and Latin America;
home studies; adoption information; non-profit.*
**http://www.cotni.org**
New Port Richey, FL

### Children's Home Society of Florida                    407.895.5800
*Pregnancy counseling; foster care; special needs children; home studies; waiting children photo listing; more than 200 offices in the state; non-profit.*
**http://www.chsfl.org**
Orlando, FL

### Gift of Life Adoption Services                        727.549.1416
*Domestic infants and special needs children; home studies; counseling center including attachment issues; pre- and post-adoption services.*
**http://www.giftoflifeinc.org**
Pinellas Park, FL

### Intercountry Adoption Center                          941.761.1345
*International: children from Asia, Guatemala and Russia; waiting children photo listing; non-profit.*
**http://www.intercountryadopt.com**
Bradenton, FL

### International Adoption Resource                        954.825.0470
*International: children from Colombia, Vietnam, Romania and Peru; home studies; waiting children photo listing.*
Coral Springs, FL

### Lifelink Child and Family Services Corporation        941.957.1614
*Christian; international: children from Asia, Eastern Europe and Guatemala; foster adoptions; home studies; information in Spanish; non-profit.*
**http://www.lifelink.org**
Sarasota, FL

### New Beginnings Family & Children's Services           727.584.5262
*International: children from Asia, Peru and Russia; financial resources; home studies; non-profit.*
**http://www.new-beginnings.org**
Largo, FL

**Universal Aid for Children**                        954.785.0033

*International: children from Eastern Europe, Asia and Latin America; home studies; non-profit.*

**http://www.uacadoption.org**
Pompano Beach, FL

## Georgia

**AAA Partners in Adoption**                        770.740.0045

*Domestic African American infants; international: orphans from Africa; home studies; counseling; education; non-profit.*

**http://www.aaapia.org**
Alpharetta, GA

**Bethany Christian Services**                        770.455.7111

*Christian; domestic infants; international; foster care services; home studies; waiting families profiles; pregnancy counseling; non-profit.*

**http://www.bethany.org/atlanta**
Atlanta, GA

**Covenant Care Services, Inc.**                        478.475.4990

*Christian; domestic adoption; international adoption services; home studies; non-profit.*

**http://www.covenantcareadoptions.com**
Macon, GA

**Elina International Adoption Services, Inc.**                        770.650.0730

*International: children from Ukraine, Russia and Kazakhstan; home studies; travel arrangement; nonprofit.*

**http://www.elinaadoption.org**
Atlanta, GA

**Families First**                        404.853.2800

*Adoption services; home studies; foster care; links to family related services.*

**http://www.familiesfirst.org**
Atlanta, GA

### Genesis Adoptions                                                          678.393.7300
*International; children from Eastern Europe; home studies; travel arrangements and assistance with cultural issues; non-profit.*
**http://www.GenesisAdoptions.org**
Alpharetta, GA

### Georgia AGAPE                                                              770.452.9995
*Christian; domestic infants; unplanned pregnancy assistance and counseling; foster care and special needs children; non-profit.*
**http://www.georgiaagape.org**
Atlanta, GA

### Hope for Children, Inc.                                                    800.522.2913
*Christian; domestic and international: children from India, Russia and China; home studies; counseling; non-profit.*
**http://www.hopeforchildren.org**
Atlanta, GA

### Illien Adoptions International Inc.                                         404.815.1599
*International: children from 10 countries; home studies; single-parent adoption; nationwide; non-profit.*
**http://www.illienadoptions.org**
Atlanta, GA

### Independent Adoption Center                                                404.321.6900
*Domestic infants; international services; home studies; counseling and support groups; interstate compact information; nationwide services; non-profit.*
**http://www.adoptionhelp.org**
Tucker, GA

### Lutheran Ministries of Georgia                                             404.875.0201
*Domestic, infants and special needs children; international services; foster care services; home studies; non-profit.*
**http://www.lsga.org/Programs/adoption.htm**
Atlanta, GA

**Open Door Adoption Agency**                                    229.228.6339

*Christian; domestic infants; international: children from Eastern Europe, Asia and Latin America; African American program; home studies; non-profit.*

**http://www.opendooradoption.com**
Thomasville, GA

---

**World Partners Adoption, Inc.**                                770.962.7860

*International: children from Asia, Eastern Europe and Latin America; resource links; non-profit.*

**http://www.worldpartnersadoption.org**
Lawrenceville, GA

---

## Hawaii

**Adopt International**                                          650.369.7300

*Domestic infants; international: children from China, Guatemala and Nepal; home studies; waiting family profiles; post-adoption services; non-profit.*

**http://www.adopt-intl.org**
Honolulu, HI

---

**Adoption Choices, Inc.**                                      800.898.6028

*Domestic infants; international, children from Guatemala; home studies; adoption information; travel resources; non-profit.*

**http://www.adoptionchoices.org**
Honolulu, HI

---

**Hawaii International Child Placement and Family Services, Inc.**   808.589.2367

*Domestic and international: children from China, Ukraine, Azerbaijan, Kazakhstan and Vietnam; home studies; non-profit.*

**http://www.h-i-c.org**
Honolulu, HI

## Idaho

### CASI Foundation for Children
208.376.0558

*Domestic and international: children from Latin America, Asia and Eastern Europe; special needs children; home studies; seminars; non-profit.*

**http://www.adoptcasi.org**
Boise, ID

### Idaho Youth Ranch Adoption Services
208.377.2613

*Domestic infants and special needs children; international adoptions services; home studies; non-profit.*

**http://www.youthranch.org**
Boise, ID

## Illinois

### Bethany Christian Services
773.233.7600

*Christian; domestic infants; international; foster care services; home studies; waiting families profiles; pregnancy counseling; non-profit.*

**http://www.bethany.org**
Chicago, IL

### Center for Family Building, Inc.
847.869.1518

*International and domestic infant, toddler and transracial adoptions; birth mother counseling; adoption information; home studies.*

**http://www.centerforfamily.com**
Evanston, IL

### Cradle Society
847.475.5800

*Domestic infants; international: children from any country that allows adoption; home studies; education and support; resources; non-profit.*

**http://www.cradle.org**
Evanston, IL

**Family Resource Center**                                    773.334.2300

*Domestic infants; African American program; international: children from China and Ukraine; home studies; foster care; educational programs; non-profit.*

**http://www.adoptillinois.org**
Chicago, IL

---

**Finally Family**                                           312.939.9399

*International: children from Bulgaria, Russia, Ukraine and Guatemala; home studies; financial information; non-profit.*

**http://www.finallyfamily.com**
Chicago, IL

---

**Journeys of the Heart**                                    630.469.4367

*Domestic infants; international: children from Eastern Europe, Asia and Guatemala; home studies; non-profit.*

**http://www.journeysoftheheart.net**
Glen Ellyn, IL

---

**Lifelink International Adoption**                           630.521.8281

*Christian; international: children from Asia, Eastern Europe and Guatemala; foster adoptions; home studies; information in Spanish: non-profit.*

**http://www.lifelink.org**
Bensenville, IL

---

**Lutheran Child and Family Services of Illinois**           708.763.0700

*Domestic infant and special needs children; international: children from Asia, Eastern Europe, Latin America and Africa; foster care services; home studies; non-profit.*

**http://www.lcfs.org**
River Forest, IL

---

**Lutheran Social Services of Illinois**                     847.635.4600

*Domestic infants and special needs children; international adoption; foster care services; pregnancy counseling; home studies; non-profit.*

**http://www.lssi.org**
Des Plaines, IL

---

### Sunny Ridge Family Center, Inc                    630.668.5117
*Domestic infants, biracial and special needs children; international adoptions; children from many different countries; home studies; newsletter; non-profit.*
**http://www.sunnyridge.org**
Wheaton, IL

### Uniting Families Foundation                    847.356.1452
*International: children from Guatemala, El Salvador and Romania; home studies; education on international adoption; non-profit.*
**http://www.members.aol.com/UnitingFam**
Lake Villa, IL

## Indiana

### Americans for African Adoptions, Inc. (AFAA)    317.271.4567
*International: children from Ethiopia, East Africa and Liberia and Mali, West Africa; home studies; publications; single parents; non-profit.*
**http://www.africanadoptions.org**
Indianapolis, IN

### Bethany Christian Services                    317.568.1000
*Christian; domestic infants; international; foster care services; home studies; waiting families profiles; pregnancy counseling; non-profit.*
**http://www.bethany.org/indiana**
Indianapolis, IN

### Center for Family Building, Inc.                    219.836.0163
*International and domestic infant, toddler and transracial adoptions; birth mother counseling; adoption information; home studies.*
**http://www.centerforfamily.com**
Munster, IN

### Childplace, Inc.                    812.282.8248
*Domestic infants; African American biracial children; home studies; international adoption services; foster care services; maternity home; non-profit.*
**http://www.childplace.org**
Jeffersonville, IN

**Children's Bureau of Indianapolis**                   317.264.2700

*Specializes in special needs adoption; also domestic infants; foster care; home studies; outreach to recruit African-American adoptive parents; teen pregnancy services.*

**http://www.childrensbureau.org**
Indianapolis, IN

---

**Coleman Adoption Agency**                   317.638.0965

*Domestic; biracial, special needs and minority infants; home studies; counseling and support; non-profit.*

**http://www.colemanadopt.org**
Indianapolis, IN

---

**Compassionate Care**                   812.749.4152

*Domestic infants; international: children from Eastern Europe, Asia and Latin America; crisis pregnancy counseling; home studies; nonprofit.*

**http://www.compassionatecareadopt.org**
Oakland City, IN

---

**Families Thru International Adoption**                   812.479.9900

*International and special needs; children from seven countries; home studies; forum; travel information; financial resources; non-profit.*

**http://www.ftia.org**
Evansville, IN

---

**Hand in Hand International Adoptions**                   260.636.3566

*International: children from Asia, Latin America and Eastern Europe; home studies; non-profit.*

**http://www.hihiadopt.org**
Albion, IN

---

**Independent Adoption Center**                   800.877.6736

*Domestic infants; international services; home studies; counseling and support groups; interstate compact information; nationwide services; non-profit.*

**http://www.adoptionhelp.org**
Indianapolis, IN

### Lutheran Child and Family Services                317.359.5467
*Domestic infants and special needs children; international; foster care services; home studies; post-adoption services; non-profit.*
**http://www.lutheranfamily.org**
Indianapolis, IN

### St. Elizabeth's Pregnancy & Adoption Services        317.787.3412
*Pregnancy testing; support and counseling; international and domestic adoptions; home studies; non-profit.*
**http://www.stelizabeths.org**
Indianapolis, IN

### Sunny Ridge Family Center, Inc.                  219.836.2117
*Domestic infants, biracial and special needs children; international: children from many different countries; home studies; newsletter; non-profit.*
**http://www.sunnyridge.org**
Munster, IN

## Iowa

### Adoption International, Inc.                      515.727.5840
*International: children from Russia and Ukraine; single parents; non-profit.*
**http://www.adoptchild.com**
Clive, IA

### Bethany Christian Services                       515.270.0824
*Christian; domestic infants; international; foster care services; home studies; waiting families profiles; pregnancy counseling; non-profit.*
**http://www.bethany.org/desmoines**
Des Moines, IA

### Crittenton Center                                712.255.4321
*Domestic infants and special needs; home studies; counseling; pre- and post-adoption services; foster care; maternity care; non-profit.*
**http://www.crittentoncenter.org**
Sioux City, IA

### Family Resources Adoption Network

*International: children from Eastern Europe, Central America and China;*
*home studies; resources; non-profit.*

**http://www.familyres.net**
New Hampton, IA

---

### Gift of Love International Adoptions, Inc. 515.255.3388

*International: children from Eastern Europe, Asia and Guatemala; chat room;*
*nationwide services; home studies; non-profit.*

**http://www.giftoflove.org**
De Moines, IA

---

### Lifelink International Adoption 563.441.0165

*Christian; international: children from Asia, Eastern Europe and Guatemala;*
*foster adoptions; home studies; information in Spanish: non-profit.*

**http://www.lifelinkadoption.org**
Davenport, IA

## Kansas

### Adoption and Beyond, Inc. 913.381.6919

*Domestic, embryo, special needs and international adoption; home studies;*
*pre- and post-adoption counseling and services; infertility information; non-profit.*

**http://www.adoption-beyond.org**
Overland Park, KS

---

### Adoption Centre of Kansas 316.265.5289

*Domestic infants; birth mother counseling services; home studies.*

**http://www.adoptioncentre.com**
Wichita, KS

---

### Adoption Choices, Inc. 800.898.6028

*Domestic infants; international: children from Guatemala; home studies;*
*adoption information; travel resources; non-profit.*

**http://www.adoptionchoices.org**
Wichita, KS

### Adoption of Babies and Children, Inc.
913.894.2223

*Domestic infants; international: children from Russia; home studies; counseling; non-profit.*

**http://www.abcadoption.org**
Lenexa, KS

### Kansas Children's Service League Manhattan
877.530.5275

*Domestic infants and special needs adoption; foster care; home studies; child advocacy; statewide services in many locations; non-profit.*

**http://www.kcsl.org**
Topeka, KS

### Special Additions
913.681.9604

*Domestic special needs infants; international: children from Asia, Eastern Europe and Guatemala; home studies; non-profit.*

**http://www.specialad.org**
Stilwell, KS

## Kentucky

### A Helping Hand Adoption Agency
800.525.0871

*Christian; international: children from China, Guatemala, Kazakhstan and Ukraine; home studies; forum; financial information; single parents; non-profit.*

**http://www.ahh.to**
Lexington, KY

### Adopt! Inc.
859.276.6249

*Domestic infants; international and domestic home studies; support, counseling and post-placement services; non-profit.*

**http://www.adoptinc.org**
Lexington, KY

**Adoption and Home Study Specialists**      502.423.7713

*Christian; domestic with focus on minority children; international services; home studies; post-placement services; support groups; non-profit.*

**http://www.iglou.com/kac/adoption_home-study_specialists.html**

Louisville, KY

---

**Adoption Assistance**      859.236.2761

*Domestic and international; home studies; counseling and post-placement services; financial information; non-profit.*

**http://www.adoptionassistance.com**

Danville, KY

---

**Bluegrass Christian Adoption Services**      859.276.2222

*Domestic infants; home studies; international services, home studies and post-placement; non-profit.*

**http://www.iglou.com/kac/bluegrass.html**

Lexington, KY

---

**Catholic Charities Adoption Services**      502.637.9786

*Domestic infants; home studies; pregnancy and adoption counseling; international adoption services; non-profit.*

**http://www.iglou.com/kac/cathcharities.html**

Louisville, KY

---

**Catholic Social Service Bureau**      859.253.1993

*Domestic infants; foster care program; associate of Kentucky Adoption Coalition.*

**http://cssb.cdlex.org**

Lexington, KY

---

**Catholic Social Services of Northern Kentucky**      859.581.8974

*Domestic infants and special needs children; home studies; crisis pregnancy resources; post-adoption services; monthly support groups; non-profit.*

**http://www.cssnky.org**

Covington, KY

### Children's Home of Northern Kentucky                    859.261.8768
*Domestic, infants and special needs children; international: children from Korea,
China and Guatemala; home studies; post-placement services; non-profit.*
**http://www.chnk.org**
Covington, KY

### Kentucky Adoption Coalition
*Coalition of private adoption agencies; membership agencies provide domestic
and international adoptions, open and closed adoptions, home studies,
pregnancy counseling and maternity services.*
**http://www.iglou.com/kac**
Louisville, KY

### Kentucky Baptist Homes for Children                     800.928.5242
*Christian; domestic infants and special needs children; foster care services;
home studies; pregnancy services; counseling; adoption classes
and training; non-profit.*
**http://www.kbhc.org**
Louisville, KY

### Mary Kendall Family Services                            270.683.3723
*Domestic special needs children; international: children from Asia,
Eastern Europe and Guatemala; home studies; post-placement
services; non-profit.*
**http://www.marykendall.org**
Owensboro, KY

## Louisiana

### Acorn Adoption, Inc.                                    985.626.3800
*Domestic infants; home studies; counseling; post-placement services;
legal information; non-profit.*
**http://www.acornadoption.org**
Mandeville, LA

## Maine

MAPS, Maine Adoption Placement Service International    207.775.4101
*International: children from Asia, Eastern Europe, Guatemala and Sierra Leone;*
*home studies; parenting, adoption support and counseling services; non-profit.*
**http://www.mapsadopt.org**
Portland, ME

## Maryland

Adoption Resource Center, Inc.    410.744.6393
*International: children from Asia, Eastern Europe and Guatemala; home studies;*
*post-placement services; non-profit.*
**http://www.adoptionresource.com**
Baltimore, MD

Adoption Service Information Agency, Inc. (ASIA)    301.587.7068
*Domestic infants; international: children from Asia; home studies; counseling;*
*newsletter; non-profit.*
**http://www.asia-adopt.org**
Silver Spring, MD

Adoptions Forever    301.468.1818
*Domestic infants; international: children from Eastern Europe, China and*
*El Salvador; home studies; counseling; travel information; non-profit.*
**http://www.adoptionsforever.com**
Rockville, MD

Adoptions Together, Inc.    301.439.2900
*Domestic and international; home studies; counseling and educational services;*
*foster care; financial information including military; newsletter.*
**http://www.adoptionstogether.org**
Silver Spring, MD

### Barker Foundation

301.229.8300

*Domestic infants; international: children from Asia and Latin America; home studies; support groups and counseling; non-profit.*

**http://www.barkerfoundation.org**
Cabin John, MD

### Bethany Christian Services

410.721.2835

*Christian; domestic infants; international; foster care services; home studies; waiting families profiles; pregnancy counseling; non-profit.*

**http://www.bethany.org/maryland**
Crofton, MD

### CASI Foundation for Children

301.570.9600

*Domestic and international: children from Latin America, Asia and Eastern Europe; special needs children; home studies; seminars; non-profit.*

**http://www.adoptcasi.org**
Olney, MD

### Creative Adoptions, Inc.

301.596.1521

*International: children from China, Jamaica, Ukraine, and Russia; home studies; pre- and post-placement services; non-profit.*

**http://www.creativeadoptions.org**
Columbia, MD

### Frank Adoption Center, Inc.

301.682.5025

*International: children from Russia and Kazakhstan; home studies; newsletter; non-profit.*

**http://www.fortheloveofachild.org**
Frederick, MD

### International Children's Alliance

301.495.9710

*International: children from China and Eastern Europe; home studies; non-profit.*

**http://www.adoptica.org**
Silver Spring, MD

Jewish Family Services—Adoption Alliances            410.581.1031

  *Domestic infants; international: children from Eastern Europe and Guatemala;*
  *home studies; non-profit.*
  **http://www.jfs.org/index.htm**
  Owings Mills, MD

World Child International                              301.588.3000

  *International: children from Eastern Europe, Asia and Latin America;*
  *home studies; links; non-profit.*
  **http://www.worldchild.org**
  Silver Spring, MD

## Massachusetts

Adoption Choices/Jewish Family Service of Metrowest     508.875.3100

  *Domestic infants and special needs children; international: children from Russia*
  *and China; home studies; counseling and education; pre- and post-placement*
  *services; non-profit.*
  **http://www.jfsmw.org**
  Framingham, MA

Adoption Resource Center at Brightside                413.827.4315

  *Domestic infants; international: children from Russia, Ukraine, Kazakhstan,*
  *Poland and China; home studies; nationwide services; non-profit.*
  **http://www.brightsideadoption.org**
  West Springfield, MA

Adoption Services of Lutheran Social Services of       508.791.4488
New England

  *Domestic infants and special needs children; international: children from Asia*
  *and Eastern Europe; home studies; non-profit.*
  **http://www.adoptlss.org/mass.html**
  Worcester, MA

### Adoptions with Love, Inc.    800.722.7731

*Domestic infant adoption; home studies; birth mother resources; non-profit.*

**http://www.adoptionswithlove.org**
Newton, MA

### American-International Children's Alliance (AICA)    781.631.7900

*International: children from Romania, Russia, Ukraine, Azerbaijan and Guatemala; home studies; pre- and post-adoption counseling services; non-profit.*

**http://www.adopting.com/aica**
Marblehead, MA

### Bethany Christian Services    978.794.9800

*Christian; domestic infants; international; foster care services; home studies; waiting families profiles; pregnancy counseling; non-profit.*

**http://www.bethany.org/nandover_ma**
North Andover, MA

### Bright Futures Adoption Center, Inc.    978.263.5400

*Domestic infants; home studies; successful adoption stories; newsletter; counseling and support; non-profit.*

**http://www.bright-futures.org**
Acton, MA

### Cambridge Family and Children's Services    617.876.4210

*Domestic infants, special needs and biracial children; international: children from Asia, Eastern Europe and Guatemala; home studies; training; pre- and post-placement services; newsletter; non-profit.*

**http://www.helpfamilies.org**
Cambridge, MA

### China Adoption with Love, Inc.    800.888.9812

*International: children from China; home studies; post-adoption services; local support groups; travel information; newsletter; non-profit.*

**http://www.chinaadoption.org**
Brookline, MA

**Florence Crittenton League**                                    978.452.9671

*International: children from China, Guatemala and Eastern Europe;*
*home studies; counseling; non-profit.*

**http://www.fcleague.org**
Lowell, MA

---

**Full Circle Adoptions**                                         413.587.0007

*Domestic adoption; international and domestic home studies; newsletter;*
*nationwide; non-profit.*

**http://www.fullcircleadoptions.org**
Northampton, MA

---

**Home for Little Wanderers**                                     617.428.0440

*Domestic infants and special needs children; international: children from Asia,*
*Central America and Eastern Europe; home studies; non-profit.*

**http://www.thehome.org**
Boston, MA

---

**MAPS International**                                             617.267.2222

*Domestic, infants and special needs children; international: children from Asia,*
*Eastern Europe, Guatemala and Sierra Leone; home studies; non-profit.*

**http://www.mapsadopt.org**
Boston, MA

---

**Wide Horizons for Children**                                    800.729.5330

*Domestic infants; international: children from Asia, Eastern Europe and*
*Latin America; home studies; nationwide services; non-profit.*

**http://www.whfc.org**
Waltham, MA

---

## Michigan
· · · · · · · · · · · · · · · · · · · · · · · · · · · · · · · · · · · · · · · · · · · · · ·

**Adoption Associates, Inc.**                                     616.667.0677

*Domestic infants; international: children from Eastern Europe, Latin America and*
*China; home studies; education; non-profit.*

**http://www.adoptassoc.com**
Jenison, MI

---

### Adoption Consultants Inc.                                284.737.0336
*International: children from Eastern Europe; domestic adoption services;*
*home studies; counseling; non-profit.*
**http://www.aciadoption.com**
Farmington Hills, MI

---

### Americans for International Aid & Adoption              248.362.1207
*International: children from Asia, Eastern Europe and Latin America;*
*special needs; parenting education; newsletter; non-profit.*
**http://www.aiaaadopt.org**
Troy, MI

---

### Bethany Christian Services, National Office            616.224.7617
*Christian; domestic infants; international; foster care services; home studies;*
*waiting families profiles; pregnancy counseling; non-profit.*
**http://www.bethany.org**
Grand Rapids, MI

---

### Family Adoption Consultants                            269.343.3316
*Domestic infants and special needs children; international: children from Korea,*
*China, Guatemala and Philippines; home studies; education, counseling and*
*support groups; non-profit.*
**http://www.facadopt.org**
Kalamazoo, MI

---

### Hands Across the Water                                 734.477.0135
*Domestic infants and special needs children; international: children from*
*Guatemala, Eastern Europe and Brazil; home studies; education and resources;*
*non-profit.*
**http://www.hatw.org**
Ann Arbor, MI

---

### International Adoption Association                      888.546.4046
*Domestic infants; international: children from Russia and Eastern Europe;*
*home studies; financial and travel information; non-profit.*
**http://www.adoptionpros.com**
Jenison, MI

International Family Services, Inc.                    248.349.3811
*International: children from Asia, Eastern Europe and Latin America;*
*home studies; non-profit.*
**http://www.ifservices.org**
Northville, MI

Lutheran Adoption Services                            248.423.2770
*Domestic infants and special needs children; international adoptions;*
*home studies; post-placement services; non-profit.*
**http://www.lasadoption.org**
Southfield, MI

M.C. International Adoptions                          248.593.6636
*International: children from Romania and Eastern Europe; home studies;*
*cultural information; non-profit.*
Bloomfield Hills, MI

## Minnesota

Adoption Miracle International, Inc.                  952.470.6141
*International: children from Eastern Europe, Asia, and Central America;*
*home studies; waiting children photo listing; links; book store; non-profit.*
**http://www.adoptionmiracle.org**
Minnetonka, MN

Bethany Christian Services                           763.553.0344
*Christian; domestic infants; international; foster care services; home studies;*
*waiting families profiles; pregnancy counseling; non-profit.*
**http://www.bethany.org**
Plymouth, MN

Child Link International                              612.861.9048
*Christian; international: children from Russia; home studies; store with Russian*
*handmade items; newsletter; non-profit.*
**http://www.child-link.com**
Richfield, MN

Children's Home Society of Minnesota     651.646.6393
*Domestic and international; adoption services; waiting families profiles;*
*directory of professional service providers; non-profit.*
**http://www.chsm.com**
St. Paul, MN

Crossroads Adoption Services     952.831.5707
*International: children from Eastern Europe, Asia and Latin America;*
*home studies; informational meetings; non-profit.*
**http://www.crossroadsadoption.com**
Minneapolis, MN

Family Resources     763.422.8590
*International: children from Eastern Europe, Central America and China;*
*home studies; resources; non-profit.*
**http://www.familyres.net**
Anoka, MN

Hand in Hand International Adoption     651.917.0384
*International: children from Asia, Latin America and Eastern Europe;*
*home studies; non-profit.*
**http://www.hihiadopt.org**
St. Paul, MN

International Adoption Services     952.893.1343
*International: children from Guatemala, Russia, Vietnam, and China; counseling;*
*home studies; non-profit.*
**http://www.ias-ww.com**
Edina, MN

Lutheran Social Services     651.642.5990
*Domestic, infants and special needs children; international; home studies;*
*pregnancy counseling; post-adoption services; non-profit.*
**http://www.lssmn.org**
Minneapolis, MN

Permanent Family Resource Center 218.998.3400

*Domestic infants and special needs children; foster care services; home studies; information and resources; non-profit.*

**http://www.permanentfamily.org**
Fergus Falls, MN

Reaching Arms International, Inc. 763.591.0791

*Domestic and international: children from Eastern Europe and Guatemala; home studies; non-profit.*

**http://www.raiadopt.org**
New Hope, MN

Summit Adoption Home Studies, Inc. 651.645.6657

*Domestic and international adoptions; home studies; non-profit.*

**http://www.summitadoption.com**
St. Paul, MN

## Mississippi

Acorn Adoption, Inc. 888.221.1370

*Domestic infants; home studies; counseling; post-placement services; legal information; non-profit.*

**http://www.acornadoption.org**
Bay St. Louis, MS

Bethany Christian Services 601.366.4282

*Christian; domestic infants; international; foster care services; home studies; waiting families profiles; pregnancy counseling; non-profit.*

**http://www.bethany.org/mississippi**
Jackson, MS

Mississippi Children's Home Society 601.352.7784

*Domestic infants, special needs and biracial children; home studies; international adoption services; non-profit.*

**http://www.mchsfsa.org/adoption.html**
Jackson, MS

## Missouri

. . . . . . . . . . . . . . . . . . . . . . . . . . . . . . . . . . . . . . . . . . . . . . . . . . . . . . . . . . . . . . . . . . . . . .

**Adoption and Beyond, Inc.**                                816.822.2800

*Domestic infants, embryo, special needs adoption; international;
home studies; pre- and post-adoption counseling and services;
infertility info; non-profit.*

**http://www.adoption-beyond.org**
Kansas City, MO

**Americans Adopting Orphans**                              314.963.7100

*International: children from China, Ukraine, Cambodia and Vietnam;
home studies; waiting children photo listing; newsletter; non-profit.*

**http://www.orphans.com**
St. Louis, MO

**Bethany Christian Services**                              636.536.6363

*Christian; domestic infants; international; foster care services; home studies;
waiting families profiles; pregnancy counseling; non-profit.*

**http://www.bethany.org/missouri**
Chesterfield, MO

**Children's Hope International**                            314.890.0086

*International: children from Asia, Eastern Europe and Latin America; home
studies; free adoption guide; financial information; non-profit.*

**http://www.ChildrensHope.com**
St. Louis, MO

**Dillon International**                                     314.576.4100

*International: children from Eastern Europe, Latin America and Asia; home
studies; pre- and post-placement services; financial information; non-profit.*

**http://www.dillonadopt.com**
St. Louis, MO

**Future, Inc.**                                            636.391.8868

*International, children from Russia; home studies; non-profit.*

**http://www.futureadopt.com**
Ballwin, MO

**Love Basket, Inc.** 636.797.4100

*Domestic infants; international: children from India, Romania, Ukraine and Guatemala; home studies; financial assistance fund; non-profit.*

**http://www.lovebasket.org**
Hillsboro, MO

---

**Lutheran Family and Children's Services** 314.787.5100

*Christian; domestic infants and special needs children; international adoption; home studies; pregnancy counseling; publication; non-profit.*

**http://www.lfcsmo.org**
St. Louis, MO

---

**Small World Adoption Foundation, Inc.** 636.207.9229

*International: children from Belarus, Russia and Ukraine; home studies; non-profit*

**http://www.swaf.com**
Ballwin, MO

---

## Montana
· · · · · · · · · · · · · · · · · · · · · · · · · · · · · · · · · · · · · · · · · · · · · · · · · · · · · · · · · · · · · · · · · · · · · · ·

**A New Arrival** 406.287.2114

*Domestic infants; international: children from Eastern Europe, Asia, Latin America and South Africa; home studies; military information; non-profit.*

**http://www.anewarrival.com**
Silver Star, MT

---

**Global Adoption Services, Inc.** 406.889.3106

*Christian; international: children from Russia and Ukraine; home studies; single parents; non-profit.*

**http://www.adoptglobal.org**
Eureka, MT

---

**Lutheran Social Services** 406.761.4341

*Christian; domestic infants; international and domestic home studies; pregnancy counseling; post-adoption studies; non-profit.*

**http://www.lssmt.org**
Great Falls, MT

---

## Nebraska

Lutheran Family Services                                402.342.7038

*Christian; domestic, infants and special needs children; International: children from Eastern Europe and Asia; waiting children photo listing; home studies; non-profit.*

**http://www.lfsneb.org**
Omaha, NE

Nebraska Children's Home Society                         402.451.0787

*Domestic infants and special needs children; pregnancy education and support; behavioral intervention program; foster care; home studies; non-profit.*

**http://www.nchs.org**
Omaha, NE

## Nevada

Catholic Charities of Southern Nevada                    702.385.3351

*Domestic infants; home studies; non-profit.*

**http://www.catholiccharities.com**
Las Vegas, NV

Catholic Community Services of Northern Nevada           775.322.7073

*Domestic infant adoptions; birth mother services; home studies; non-profit.*

**http://www.catholicreno.com**
Reno, NV

The Adoption Alliance                                    702.968.1986

*Domestic infants; legal services by attorney; referrals for home studies; non-profit.*

**http://www.adoption-alliance.com**
Las Vegas, NV

## New Hampshire

Adoption Services of Lutheran Social Services of                603.224.8111
New England

*Domestic, infants and special needs children; international: children from Asia and Eastern Europe; birth parent services; home studies; non-profit.*

**http://www.adoptlss.org/new_hampshire.html**
Concord, NH

Bethany Christian Services of New England              603.483.2886

*Christian; domestic infants; international; foster care services; home studies; waiting families profiles; pregnancy counseling; non-profit.*

**http://www.bethany.org/nandover_ma**
Candia, NH

## New Jersey

Adoptions from the Heart              856.665.5655

*Domestic infants and biracial children; international: children from ten countries; home studies; waiting families profiles; links; newsletter; non-profit.*

**http://www.adoptionsfromtheheart.com**
Cherry Hill, NJ

Bethany Christian Services              201.444.7775

*Christian; domestic infants; international; foster care services; home studies; waiting families profiles; pregnancy counseling; non-profit.*

**http://www.bethany.org/newjersey**
Midland Park, NJ

Children's Home Society of New Jersey              908.735.9458

*Domestic, infants and special needs children; international: children from Eastern Europe, China and Guatemala; home studies; non-profit.*

**http://www.chsofnj.org**
Clinton, NJ

### Golden Cradle                                          856.667.2229
*Domestic infants; international: children from Eastern Europe, China and Guatemala; home studies; legal services; post-adoption services; non-profit.*
**http://www.goldencradle.org**
Cherry Hill, NJ

### Homestudies and Adoption Placement Services            201.836.5554
*Domestic infants; international: children from China, Guatemala, Romania and Russia; home studies; post-placement services; non-profit.*
**http://www.haps.org**
Teaneck, NJ

### Lutheran Social Ministries of New Jersey               609.386.7171
*Christian; domestic infants and special needs children; international adoption; birth parent counseling; post-placement services; home studies; non-profit.*
**http://www.lsmnj.org**
Burlington, NJ

### Small World Adoption Programs                          856.829.2769
*Domestic infants; international: children from Asia and Eastern Europe; home studies; non-profit.*
**http://www.swa.net**
Palmyra, NJ

## New Mexico
............................................................

### A.M.O.R. Adoptions, Inc.                               505.831.0888
*Domestic infants; international children; operates an orphanage in Guatemala; home studies; waiting children photo listing; non-profit.*
**http://www.amoradoptions.com**
Albuquerque, NM

### La Familia                                             505.766.9361
*Domestic infants; African American, grandparent and stepparent adoptions; treatment foster care; home studies; ICPC studies; non-profit.*
**http://www.la-familia-inc.org**
Albuquerque, NM

Rainbow House International                                   505.861.1234

*International: children from Eastern Europe, Asia, Central and South America; home studies; non-profit.*

**http://www.rhi.org**
Belen, NM

## New York

Adoption S.T.A.R.                                            716.691.3300

*Domestic: infants, at-risk and special needs children; African American program; home studies; counseling; adoptive parents educational training; non-profit.*

**http://www.adoptionstar.com**
Amherst, NY

Bethany Christian Services                                   845.987.1453

*Christian; domestic infants; international; foster care services; home studies; waiting families profiles; pregnancy counseling; non-profit.*

**http://www.bethany.org/warwick_ny**
Warwick, NY

Catholic Home Bureau for Dependent Children                  212.371.1000

*Domestic infants and special needs children; home studies; crisis pregnancy services incl. medical care, infant and maternity clothing; international services; foster care program; non-profit.*

**http://www.catholichomebureau.org**
New York, NY

Children at Heart Adoption Services, Inc.                    518.664.5988

*International: children from Kazakhstan and Russia; home studies; single-parent adoptions; support and post-adoption services; non-profit.*

**http://www.childrenatheart.com**
Mechanicville, NY

Children of the World Adoption Agency, Inc.                  516.935.1235

*International: children from Russia; home studies; pre- and post-adoption services; knowledge of foreign adoption law; non-profit.*

**http://www.cwaany.org**
Syosset, NY

Creative Adoptions, Inc.     718.369.7337

*International: children from China, Jamaica, Ukraine, and Russia; home studies; pre- and post-placement services; non-profit.*

**http://www.creativeadoptions.org**
Brooklyn, NY

---

Family Services of Westchester     914.948.8004

*Domestic; infants, biracial and special needs children; international adoption services; home studies; counseling; non-profit.*

**http://www.fsw.org**
White Plains, NY

---

Gladney Center for Adoption     212.222.1222

*Domestic infants, biracial and special needs children; international: children from Russia, China, Guatemala, Mexico and Bulgaria; home studies; non-profit.*

**http://www.adoptionsbygladney.com**
New York, NY

---

Happy Families International Center, Inc.     845.265.9272

*International: children from Eastern Europe, China and Guatemala; home studies; non-profit.*

**http://www.happyfamilies.org**
Cold Spring, NY

---

New Beginnings Family and Children's Services     516.747.2204

*International: children from Asia, Peru and Russia; financial resources; home studies; non-profit.*

**http://www.new-beginnings.org**
Mineola, NY

---

New Life Adoption Agency     315.422.7300

*Domestic infants; international: specializes in children from China; post-adoption support; cultural activities; home studies; non-profit.*

**http://www.newlifeadoption.org**
Syracuse, NY

Open Arms Adoption and Family Center                    315.622.3640
   *Domestic infants; biracial children; birth parent counseling and support;*
   *waiting families profiles; home studies; non-profit.*
   **http://www.openarmsadoption.org**
   Liverpool, NY

Spence-Chapin Services to Families and Children          212.369.0300
   *Domestic infants, special needs and biracial children; international: children from*
   *Eastern Europe, Asia and Latin America; home studies; non-profit.*
   **http://www.spence-chapin.org**
   New York, NY

Vida Special Needs Adoption                              518.828.4527
   *Domestic special needs children; international: children from Latin America,*
   *Asia and Eastern Europe; home studies; travel information; non-profit.*
   **http://members.aol.com/vidaadopt/vida.html**
   Hudson, NY

## North Carolina

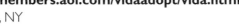

Bethany Christian Services, Inc.                         828.274.7146
   *Christian; domestic infants; international; foster care services; home studies;*
   *waiting families profiles; pregnancy counseling; non-profit.*
   **http://www.bethany.org/ncarolina**
   Asheville, NC

Carolina Adoption Services, Inc.                         336.275.9660
   *International: children from Asia, Eastern Europe and Latin America;*
   *home studies; pre- and post-adoption services; non-profit.*
   **http://www.carolinaadoption.org**
   Greensboro, NC

Children at Heart Adoption Services, Inc.                910.799.6140
   *International: children from Kazakhstan and Russia; home studies; single-parent*
   *adoptions; support and post-adoption services; non-profit.*
   **http://www.childrenatheart.com**
   Wilmington, NC

Children's Home Society of North Carolina, Inc.          800.632.1400
*Domestic infants and special needs children; pregnancy counseling;*
*home studies; post-adoption and international services; non-profit.*
**http://www.chsnc.org**
Greensboro, NC

---

Christian Adoption Services                              704.847.0038
*Christian; domestic infants; international: children from Asia and Russia; home studies;*
*pre- and post-adoption services; newsletter; non-profit.*
**http://www.christianadopt.org**
Matthews, NC

---

Datz Foundation of North Carolina                       800.829.5683
*Domestic infants; international: children from Asia, Eastern Europe and Latin*
*America; home studies; seminars; non-profit.*
**http://www.datzfound.com**
Concord, NC

---

Gladney Center for Adoption                             252.355.6267
*Domestic infants, biracial and special needs children; international: children from*
*Russia, China, Guatemala, Mexico and Bulgaria; home studies; non-profit.*
**http://www.gladney.org**
Greenville, NC

---

Independent Adoption Center                             919.789.0707
*Domestic infants; international services; home studies; counseling and support*
*groups; interstate compact information; nationwide services; non-profit.*
**http://www.adoptionhelp.org**
Raleigh, NC

---

## North Dakota
................................................................

Lutheran Social Services of North Dakota                701.235.7341
*Christian; domestic, special needs children; foster care services; international;*
*home studies; pregnancy counseling; non-profit.*
Fargo, ND

## Ohio

· · · · · · · · · · · · · · · · · · · · · · · · · · · · · · · · · · · · · · · · · · · · · · · · · · · · · · · ·

### Adoption at Adoption Circle                                    614.237.7222

*Domestic, specializes in newborns and children up to six months of age;
biracial and special needs children; home studies; non-profit.*

**http://www.adoptioncircle.org**

Columbus, OH

---

### Adoption Specialists, Inc.                                    216.932.2880

*Domestic and international; experienced in Ohio adoption law; a pilot adoption
agency that participates in AdoptOHIO.*

**http://www.adoption-specialists.com**

Cleveland Heights, OH

---

### Catholic Social Services of the Miami Valley            937.223.7217

*Domestic infants and special needs children; international adoptions; pregnancy
counseling; local support groups; education and training; home studies; non-profit.*

**http://www.cssmv.org**

Dayton, OH

---

### Lutheran Children's Aid and Family Services            216.281.2500

*Domestic infant and special needs adoption; international: children from Russia,
China, Guatemala, Colombia, Mongolia and Bulgaria; infant foster care; home
studies; non-profit.*

**http://www.bright.net/~lcafs**

Cleveland, OH

---

### Private Adoptions Services, Inc.                            513.871.5777

*Domestic, infants and special needs children; international: children from China,
Guatemala and Russia; home studies; legal services; directed by Attorney
Carolyn Franke.*

**http://www.privateadoptionservice.com**

Cincinnati, OH

---

## Oklahoma

**Adoption Choices, Inc.** 800.898.6028

*Domestic infants; international: children from Vietnam and Guatemala;
home studies; adoption information; travel resources; non-profit.*

**http://www.adoptionchoices.org**
Edmond, OK

**Bless This Child, Inc.** 918.473.7045

*International: primarily children from Russia; home studies; single parent
adoption; non-profit.*

**http://www.blessthischild.com**
Checotah, OK

**Dillon International** 918.749.4600

*International: children from Eastern Europe, Latin America and Asia; home
studies; pre- and post-placement services; financial information; non-profit.*

**http://www.dillonadopt.com**
Tulsa, OK

**Small Miracles International** 405.732.7295

*International: children from Guatemala; home studies; non-profit.*

**http://www.smiint.org**
Midwest City, OK

## Oregon

**All God's Children International** 503.282.7652

*Christian; international: children from China, Guatemala and Eastern Europe;
home studies; financial information; non-profit.*

**http://www.allgodschildren.org**
Portland, OR

**Associated Services for International Adoption** 503.697.6863

*International: specializes in children from China; nationwide services; cultural
awareness and support for adoptive parents; home studies; non-profit.*

**http://www.asiadopt.org**
Lake Oswego, OR

**Bethany Christian Services**                    503.533.2002

*Christian; domestic infants; international; foster care services; home studies;*
*waiting families profiles; pregnancy counseling; non-profit.*

**http://www.bethany.org/oregon**
Hillsboro, OR

---

**Christian Family Adoptions**                    503.232.1211

*Domestic infants and special needs children; home studies; international*
*services; birth parent counseling; non-profit.*

**http://www.christianfamilyadoptions.org**
Portland, OR

---

**Dove Adoptions International, Inc.**             503.774.7210

*International: children from Russia, Sierra Leone and Mexico; home studies;*
*travel and visa information; link to the Russian Consulate; non-profit.*

**http://www.adoptions.net**
Portland, OR

---

**Heritage Adoption Services**                    503.233.1099

*Domestic infants and transracial children; international, children from China,*
*Guatemala and Haiti; special needs program; home studies; newsletter;*
*non-profit.*

**http://www.heritageadoption.org**
Portland, OR

---

**Holt International Children's Services**         541.687.2202

*Domestic, infants; international: children from Asia, Eastern Europe and*
*South America; special needs children; home studies; non-profit.*

**http://www.holtintl.org**
Eugene, OR

---

**International Family Services, Inc.**            503.538.3665

*International: children from Asia, Eastern Europe and Latin America;*
*home studies; non-profit.*

**http://www.ifservices.org**
Newberg, OR

**Journeys of the Heart Adoption Services**     503.681.3075

*Domestic infants; international: children from Eastern Europe, Asia and Guatemala; home studies; non-profit.*

**http://www.journeysoftheheart.net**
Hillsboro, OR

**New Hope Child & Family Agency**     503.282.6726

*Domestic infants; international: children from China, Taiwan, Azerbaijan and El Salvador; home studies; foster care services; non-profit.*

**http://www.newhopekids.org**
Portland, OR

**Open Adoption & Family Services, Inc.**     503.226.4870

*Domestic infants; home studies; fears and facts about open adoption; newsletter; non-profit.*

**http://www.openadopt.com**
Portland, OR

**PLAN Loving Adoptions Now, Inc.**     503.472.8452

*Christian; domestic infants and special needs children; African American program; international: children from Asia, Guatemala, Africa and Ukraine; home studies; non-profit.*

**http://www.planlovingadoptions.org**
McMinnville, OR

**Tree of Life Adoption Center**     503.244.7374

*Domestic infants and special needs children; international: children from Eastern Europe; waiting children photo listing; home studies; non-profit.*

**http://www.toladopt.org**
Portland, OR

## Pennsylvania

**1st Steps International Adoptions, Inc.**     570.226.4448

*International: children from Russia, Georgia and Guatemala; waiting children photo listing; home studies; travel resources.*

**http://www.kids4us.org**
Hawley, PA

### Adopt-A-Child
**412.421.1911**

*International: children from Russia; home studies; newsletter; non-profit.*

**http://www.adopt-a-child.org**
Pittsburgh, PA

---

### Adoption Services, Inc.
**717.737.3960**

*Domestic infants; international: children from China, Guatemala and Eastern Europe; home studies; non-profit.*

**http://www.adoptionservices.org**
Harrisburg, PA

---

### Adoptions from the Heart
**610.642.7200**

*Domestic infants and biracial children; international: children from 10 countries; home studies; waiting families profiles; links; newsletter; non-profit.*

**http://www.adoptionsfromtheheart.org**
Wynnewood, PA

---

### Adoptions International, Inc.
**215.238.9057**

*International: children from Guatemala, El Salvador and China; home studies; non-profit.*

Philadelphia, PA

---

### Bethany Christian Services
**412.734.2662**

*Christian; domestic infants; international; foster care services; home studies; waiting families profiles; pregnancy counseling; non-profit.*

**http://www.bethany.org**
Pittsburgh, PA

---

### Children's Aid Society
**814.765.2686**

*Domestic, international and special needs children; home studies; birth parent counseling; non-profit.*

**http://www.childaid.org**
Clearfield, PA

### Common Sense Adoption Services                717.766.6449

*Domestic infants and special needs children; international: children from Russia, China and Guatemala; home studies; training and workshops; local support groups; adoption glossary; non-profit.*

**http://www.csas-swan.org**
Mechanicsburg, PA

### Commonwealth Adoptions Int'l.                724.772.8190

*International: children from Eastern Europe and Latin America; education and social events; home studies; adoptive family stories; travel information; information in Spanish; non-profit.*

**http://www.commonwealthadoption.org**
Cranberry Township, PA

### Diakon Lutheran Services                717.845.9113

*Domestic infants and special needs children; international adoptions; foster care services; pregnancy program; home studies; non-profit.*

**http://www.diakon.org**
York, PA

### Family Health Council's Family Adoption Center                412.288.2138

*Domestic infants; international: children from Russia and Ukraine; home studies; non-profit.*

**http://www.fhcinc.org**
Pittsburgh, PA

### International Adoption Center                215.782.1191

*International: children from Brazil, Colombia and Eastern Europe; legal services; pre- and post-adoption services; non-profit.*

**http://www.adoptlaw.org**
Elkins Park, PA

### International Assistance Group, Inc.                412.828.5800

*International: children from Russia and Belarus; home studies; pre- and post-adoption support and education; mentoring program; non-profit.*

**http://www.iagadoptions.org**
Oakmont, PA

**Jewish Family and Children's Service**          215.673.0100

*International: children from Eastern Europe, Asia and Guatemala; home studies; non-profit.*

**http://www.jfcsphil.org/adopt.htm**
Philadelphia, PA

---

**La Vida Adoption Agency**          610.688.8008

*International: children from China and Vietnam; home studies; listing of waiting children; links to in-depth resources; non-profit.*

**http://www.lavida.org**
King of Prussia, PA

---

**Love the Children**          215.536.4181

*International: specializes in Korean children; home studies; recommended reading list; non-profit.*

**http://www.lovethechildren.com**
Quakertown, PA

---

**New Beginnings Family and Children's Services**          570.491.2366

*International: children from Asia, Peru and Russia; financial resources; home studies; non-profit.*

**http://www.new-beginnings.org**
Matamoras, PA

---

**Pearl S. Buck Foundation Inc.**          215.249.0100

*Domestic infants and special needs children; international, programs primarily in Asia; home studies; child-advocacy; newsletter; non-profit.*

**http://www.pearl-s-buck.org**
Perkasie, PA

---

## Rhode Island

**Adoption Services of Lutheran Social Services of New**          401.785.0015
**England**

*Domestic infants and special needs children; international: children from Asia and Eastern Europe; home studies; non-profit.*

**http://www.adoptlss.org/ri.html**
Cranston, RI

Alliance for Children Foundation                                      781.431.7148

*International: children from China, South America and Europe; home studies;*
*nationwide services; information about each country; non-profit.*
**http://www.allforchildren.org**
Wellesley, RI

Bethany Christian Services                                           401.467.1395

*Christian; domestic infants; international; foster care services; home studies;*
*waiting families profiles; pregnancy counseling; non-profit.*
**http://www.bethany.org**
Warwick, RI

## South Carolina

Bethany Christian Services                                          803.779.0541

*Christian; domestic infants; international; foster care services; home studies;*
*waiting families profiles; pregnancy counseling; non-profit.*
**http://www.bethany.org/columbia_sc**
Columbia, SC

Carolina Adoption Services, Inc.                                    843.946.3577

*International: children from Asia, Eastern Europe and Latin America;*
*home studies; pre- and post-adoption services; non-profit.*
**http://www.carolinaadoption.org**
Myrtle Beach, SC

Carolina Hope Christian Adoption Agency                             864.268.0570

*International: children from Eastern Europe, Asia and Latin America;*
*home studies; resources; waiting children photo listing.*
**http://www.carolinahopeadoption.org**
Greenville, SC

Child of the Heart                                                  843.881.2973

*International: specializes in children from Russia; home studies; non-profit.*
**http://www.childoftheheart.org**
Mount Pleasant, SC

**Small World Adoption Programs** 864.338.4673

*Domestic infants; international: children from Asia and Eastern Europe; home studies; non-profit.*

**http://www.swa.net**
Belton, SC

## South Dakota

**Bethany Christian Services** 605.343.7196

*Christian; domestic infants; international; foster care services; home studies; waiting families profiles; pregnancy counseling; non-profit.*

**http://www.bethany.org/rapidcity**
Rapid City, SD

## Tennessee

**Bethany Christian Services** 901.818.9996

*Christian; domestic infants; international; foster care services; home studies; waiting families profiles; pregnancy counseling; non-profit.*

**http://www.bethany.org/memphis**
Memphis, TN

**Small World Adoption Programs, Inc.** 615.883.4372

*Domestic infants; international: children from Asia and Eastern Europe; home studies; non-profit.*

**http://www.swa.net**
Hermitage, TN

## Texas

**Abrazo Adoption Associates** 210.342.5683

*Christian; domestic infants; special needs children; home studies; nationwide services; forum; non-profit.*

**http://www.abrazo.org**
San Antonio, TX

### Adoption Access                                      214.750.4847

*Infants and older children of all ethnicities; focus on counseling for birth mothers; birth father support; general information; non-profit.*

**http://www.adoptionaccess.com**
Dallas, TX

---

### Adoption Advisory, Inc.                              214.520.0004

*Domestic infant adoption; egg donor program; pre- and post-adoption services; home studies.*

**http://www.texasadoption.com**
Dallas, TX

---

### Adoption Alliance                                    210.349.3761

*Domestic infants; legal services by attorney; offer referrals for home studies; non-profit.*

**http://www.adoption-alliance.com**
San Antonio, TX

---

### Adoption Services Associates (ASA)                   210.699.6094

*Domestic, infants and biracial children; international: children from Russia, Ukraine and Kazakhstan; home studies; counseling; non-profit.*

**http://www.adoptionservicesassociates.org**
San Antonio, TX

---

### Adoption Services Worldwide, Inc.                    210.342.0444

*Domestic infants and international: children from Eastern Europe and Colombia; home studies; tax and finance information.*

**http://www.babyasw.com**
San Antonio, TX

---

### Adoptions and Aid International                      210.651.6623

*International: children from Eastern Europe; home studies; single parent adoption; non-profit.*

**http://www.russianadoption.com**
San Antonio, TX

### Adoptions International, Inc.    214.342.8388

*International: children from Russia, China, Ukraine and Guatemala; home studies; counseling; travel information; cultural awareness seminars; non-profit.*

**http://www.adoptmeinternational.org**
Dallas, TX

### Bethany Christian Services of North Texas    214.373.8797

*Christian; domestic infants; international; foster care services; home studies; waiting families profiles; pregnancy counseling; non-profit.*

**http://www.bethany.org/dallas_tx**
Dallas, TX

### Bless This Child, Inc.    512.329.9280

*International: primarily children from Russia; home studies; single parent adoption; non-profit.*

**http://www.blessthischild.com**
Austin, TX

### DePelchin Children's Center    713.730.2335

*Domestic infant and special needs adoption; home studies; foster care; teen pregnancy counseling; pre- and post-adoption services; non-profit.*

**http://www.depelchin.org**
Houston, TX

### Gladney Center for Adoption    817.922.6088

*Domestic infants, biracial and special needs children; international: children from Russia, China, Guatemala, Mexico and Bulgaria; home studies; non-profit.*

**http://www.adoptionsbygladney.com**
Forth Worth, TX

### Great Wall China Adoption    512.323.9595

*International: children from China; nationwide; home studies; travel and cultural orientation; non-profit.*

**http://www.gwcadopt.org**
Austin, TX

### Hope Cottage Pregnancy & Adoption Center                214.526.8721
*Domestic infants; international; home studies; counseling and resources;*
*newsletter; pregnancy services; non-profit.*
**http://www.hopecottage.org**
Dallas, TX

### Hope International                214.672.9399
*International: children from Russia, Kazakhstan, Ukraine, China and the Marshall*
*Islands; home studies; travel assistance; non-profit.*
**http://www.hopeadoption.com**
Dallas, TX

### Little Miracles International Adoption                806.351.1100
*International: children from Asia and Eastern Europe; home studies; forum;*
*e-mail lists and support; bookstore; non-profit.*
**http://www.littlemiracles.org**
Amarillo, TX

### Los Ninos International Adoption Center                281.363.2892
*International: children from Asia, Caribbean, Eastern Europe and Latin America;*
*home studies; links to in-depth adoption information; non-profit.*
**http://www.losninos.org**
The Woodlands, TX

### Marywood Children and Family Services                512.472.9251
*Domestic infants and special needs children; international services; pregnancy*
*counseling; foster care services; home studies; non-profit.*
**http://www.marywood.org**
Austin, TX

### Methodist Mission Home                210.696.2410
*Christian; international and domestic; infants and special needs children;*
*home studies; post-adoption services.*
**http://www.mfrs.org**
San Antonio, TX

## Utah

**Adopt an Angel**                                     801.537.1622

*Domestic infants; home studies; pregnancy and adoption counseling; maternity home; international adoption services; non-profit.*

**http://www.geocities.com/iadoptanangel**
Salt Lake City, UT

**Adoption Center of Choice, Inc.**                    801.224.2440

*Domestic infants; home studies; birth mother counseling and other services; nationwide.*

**http://www.theadoptioncenter.com**
Orem, UT

**Wasatch International Adoptions**                     801.334.8683

*International: children from Eastern Europe, Latin America and Asia; special needs children; home studies; waiting children photo listing; non-profit.*

**http://www.wiaa.org**
Ogden, UT

## Vermont

**Friends in Adoption**                                800.844.3630

*Domestic healthy infants; home studies; articles and books; waiting families profiles; support groups; non-profit.*

**http://www.friendsinadoption.org**
Middletown Springs, VT

**Lund Family Center**                                 802.864.7467

*Domestic infants and special needs children; international; pre- and post-adoption services; residential programs; home studies; non-profit.*

**http://www.lundfamilycenter.org**
Burlington, VT

Vermont Children's Aid Society                                  800.479.0015

*Domestic infants and special needs children; international: children from China,*
*Korea, Russia and Guatemala; home studies; non-profit.*

**http://www.vtcas.org**
Winooski, VT

## Virginia

A Loving Family                                                703.370.7140

*International: children from Russia and Ukraine; home studies; non-profit.*

**http://www.alovingfamily.org**
Alexandria, VA

Adoption Service Information Agency, Inc. (ASIA)              703.312.0263

*Domestic infants; international: children from Asia; home studies; counseling;*
*newsletter; non-profit.*

**http://www.asia-adopt.org**
Arlington, VA

Adoptions from the Heart                                       757.546.3874

*Domestic infants and biracial children; international: children from 10 countries;*
*home studies; waiting families profiles; links; newsletter; non-profit.*

**http://www.adoptionsfromtheheart.com**
Chesapeake, VA

America-World Adoption Association, East                       800.429.3369

*Christian; international: children from China, Russia, Vietnam and Ukraine; home*
*studies; special needs children; financial information; non-profit.*

**http://www.america-china.org**
McLean, VA

Bethany Christian Services, Inc.                              703.385.5440

*Christian; domestic infants; international; foster care services; home studies;*
*waiting families profiles; pregnancy counseling; non-profit.*
**http://www.bethany.org/virginia**
Fairfax, VA

### Coordinators/2, Inc.                                 800.690.4206
*Domestic infants; international: children from Eastern Europe, Latin America and Asia; special needs adoptions; home studies; education and training; non-profit.*

**http://www.c2adopt.org**
Richmond, VA

### Cradle of Hope Adoption Center                       703.352.4806
*International: children from Russia, China and Guatemala; home studies; e-mail list of adoptive families and stories; financial information; non-profit.*

**http://www.cradlehope.org**
Fairfax, VA

### Datz Foundation                                      703.242.8800
*Domestic infants; international: children from Asia, Eastern Europe and Latin America; home studies; seminars; non-profit.*

**http://www.datzfound.com**
Vienna, VA

### Frost International Adoptions                         703.750.9470
*Domestic infants and special needs children; international adoptions; home studies; financial and travel information; resource links; non-profit.*

**http://www.frostadopt.org**
Falls Church, VA

### Lutheran Family Services, Inc.                        804.288.0122
*Christian; domestic infants and special needs children; international: children from Asia, Eastern Europe and Guatemala; home studies; non-profit.*

**http://www.lfsva.org**
Roanoke, VA

### United Methodist Family Services of Virginia         804.353.4461
*Domestic infants and special needs children; international; foster care services; home studies; crisis pregnancy counseling; non-profit.*

**http://www.umfs.org**
Richmond, VA

## Washington

Adoption Advocates International                     360.452.4777

*Domestic and special needs children; international: children from Haiti, Asia and Africa; home studies; news and articles; also licensed in Alaska; non-profit.*

**http://www.adoptionadvocates.org**
Port Angeles, WA

Americans Adopting Orphans                     206.524.5437

*International: children from China, Ukraine, Cambodia and Vietnam; home studies; waiting children photo listing; newsletter; non-profit.*

**http://www.orphans.com**
Seattle, WA

Bethany Christian Services                     206.367.4604

*Christian; domestic infants; international; foster care services; home studies; waiting families profiles; pregnancy counseling; non-profit.*

**http://www.bethany.org/Washington**
Seattle, WA

Children's Home Society Corporate Headquarters    206.695.3200

*Home studies, post-placement and international services; foster care program; newsletter; many offices in the state.*

**http://www.chs-wa.org**
Seattle, WA

Faith International Adoptions                     253.383.1928

*International: children from China, Vietnam, Panama, Costa Rica, China and Russia; home studies; special needs children; non-profit.*

**http://www.faithadopt.org**
Tacoma, WA

Journeys of the Heart                     360.426.6455

*Domestic infants; international: children from Eastern Europe, Asia and Guatemala; home studies; non-profit.*

**http://www.journeysoftheheart.net**
Shelton, WA

### Medina Children's Services
206.260.1700

*Domestic infant and special needs adoptions; abused, neglected, abandoned children; home studies; pregnancy counseling; non-profit.*

**http://www.medinachild.org**
Seattle, WA

### Open Adoption & Family Services, Inc.
206.782.0442

*Domestic infants; home studies; fears and facts about open adoption; newsletter; services for Canadian birth mothers; non-profit.*

**http://www.openadopt.com**
Seattle, WA

### Polish Business Consultants Group, Ltd.
206.579.7092

*International: children from Poland; information and resources.*

**http://www.polbiznet.com**
Seattle, WA

### World Association for Children and Parents (WACAP)
206.575.4550

*International: children from India, Thailand, Korea, China and Russia; domestic special needs children; home studies; non-profit.*

**http://www.wacap.org**
Seattle, WA

## Wisconsin

### Bethany Christian Services
262.547.6557

*Christian; domestic infants; international; foster care services; home studies; waiting families profiles; pregnancy counseling; non-profit.*

**http://www.bethany.org**
Waukesha, WI

### Catholic Charities—Diocese of La Crosse
608.782.0710

*Domestic, infant and special needs adoption; international; home studies; pregnancy counseling; non-profit.*

**http://www.catholiccharitieslax.org**
La Crosse, WI

Lifelink International Adoption     608.278.4011

*Christian; international: children from Asia, Eastern Europe and Guatemala; foster adoptions; home studies; information in Spanish; non-profit.*

**http://www.lifelinkadoption.org/office_locations.shtml**
Fitchburg, WI

---

Lutheran Counseling and Family Services     414.536.8333

*Christian; domestic infants to Lutheran families; international; home studies; non-profit.*

**http://www.lcfswi.org**
Milwaukee, WI

---

Van Dyke, Inc.     920.452.5358

*International: children from Romania, Ukraine and Lithuania; home studies; legal information.*

**http://www.execpc.com/romanian_adoption_assistance**
Sheboygan, WI

---

## West Virginia

Adoptions from the Heart     304.291.5211

*Domestic infants and biracial children; international: children from 10 countries; home studies; waiting families profiles; links; newsletter; non-profit.*

**http://www.adoptionsfromtheheart.com**
Morgantown, WV

---

## Wyoming

A.D.O.P.P.T., Inc.     307.682.4157

*International: children from Vietnam; travel and cultural information; non-profit.*

**http://www.adopptinc.com**
Gillette, WY

---

Global Adoption Services, Inc.     307.674.6606

*Christian; international: children from Russia and Ukraine; home studies; single parents; non-profit.*

**http://www.adoptglobal.org**
Sheridan, WY

Wyoming Children's Society     307.632.7619
*Domestic, infants and special needs children; international: children from Russia; waiting children photo listing; home studies; non-profit.*
**http://www.wyomingcs.org**
Cheyenne, WY

# Agencies, Public

## Alabama

Alabama Department of Human Resources     334.242.9500
*Adoption services and foster care; special needs children; newsletter.*
**http://www.dhr.state.al.us/**
Montgomery, AL

## Alaska

Alaska Department of Health and Social Services     907.269.3900
*Adoption; guardianship and foster care; interstate compact; resources links; child protective services.*
**http://www.hss.state.ak.us/ocs**
Anchorage, AK

## Arizona

Arizona Department of Economic Security     877.543.7633
*Adoption and foster care services; special needs children; waiting children photo listing; links to more resources.*
**http://www.de.state.az.us/dcyf/adoption**
Phoenix, AZ

## Arkansas

Arkansas Department of Human Services      501.682.8770
*Waiting children photo listing; foster care; child protective services.*
**http://www.state.ar.us/dhs/chilnfam**
Little Rock, AR

## California

California Department of Social Services      916.323.1000
*Waiting children photo listing; adoption and foster care information;*
*agency listing; interstate compact information.*
**http://www.childsworld.ca.gov**
Sacramento, CA

## Colorado

Colorado Department of Human Services      303.866.5932
*Foster care and adoption services; special needs children; waiting children photo*
*listing; interstate compact.*
**http://www.cdhs.state.co.us/cyf/cwelfare/cwweb.html**
Denver, CO

## Connecticut

Connecticut Department of Children and Families      860.550.6578
*Waiting children photo listing; foster care; adoption information; interstate*
*compact; articles.*
**http://www.state.ct.us/dcf/new_fasu/fasu_index.htm**
Hartford, CT

## Delaware

Delaware Department of Services for Children          302.633.2655
*Waiting children photo listing; adoption information; resources links; agency listing.*
**http://www.state.de.us/kids/adoption.htm**
Wilmington, DE

## District of Columbia

Department of Health and Human Services          202.619.0257
*Waiting children photo listing; adoption information; special needs and*
*foster care; financial aid.*
**http://www.os.dhhs.gov**
Washington, D.C.

## Florida

Florida Department of Children and Families          850.487.1111
*Waiting children photo listing; special needs; adoption information.*
**http://www5.myflorida.com/cf_web/myflorida2/health-**
**human/adoption**
Tallahassee, FL

## Georgia

Georgia Department of Human Resources          404.657.3550
*Special needs; waiting children photo listing; adoption information; financial*
*resources; support groups; agency listing.*
**http://www.adoptions.dhr.state.ga.us**
Atlanta, GA

## Hawaii

Hawaii Department of Human Services                    808.586.5698
  *Human services.*
  **http://www.state.hi.us/dhs**
  Honolulu, HI

## Idaho

Idaho Department of Health and Welfare                208.334.2411
  *Adoption and foster care; special needs children; waiting children photo listing;*
  *infant toddler program; foster parent success stories.*
  **http://www2.state.id.us/dhw**
  Boise, ID

## Illinois

Illinois Department of Children and Family Service    217.785.2509
  *Waiting children photo listing; foster care; adoption information; resources links;*
  *child protective services.*
  **http://www.state.il.us/dcfs/adoption/index.shtml**
  Springfield, IL

## Indiana

Indiana Family & Social Services                      888.252.3678
  *Adoption and foster care; special needs children; waiting children photo listing;*
  *legal information; in-depth information on the adoption process.*
  **http://www.in.gov/fssa/adoption**
  Indianapolis, IN

Indiana's Adoption Initiative                         317.264.7793
  *Special needs; waiting children photo listing; adoption information; newsletter.*
  **http://www.state.in.us/fssa/adoption**
  Indianapolis, IN

## Iowa

Iowa Department of Human Services                    515.281.5730
   *Family services including adoption and foster care information.*
   **http://www.dhs.state.ia.us/ACFS/ACFS.asp**
   Des Moines, IA

## Kansas

Kansas Department of Social and Rehabilitation       785.296.2500
   *Adoption and foster care services; special needs children; statewide adoptive*
   *and foster home recruitment; adoptive and foster parent training.*
   **http://www.srskansas.org/services/adoption.htm**
   Topeka, KS

## Kentucky

Kentucky Department for Social Services              502.564.7130
   *Special needs children and foster care; general information; assistance and*
   *support; waiting children photo listing; newsletter.*
   **http://cfc.state.ky.us/help/foster_care.asp**
   Frankfort, KY

## Louisiana

Louisiana Department of Social Services             225.342.4006
   *Adoption services; waiting children photo listing; foster care; child protective services.*
   **http://www.dss.state.la.us**
   Baton Rouge, LA

## Maine

Maine Department of Human Services                    207.287.5060

*Adoption services and foster care; special needs; waiting children photo listing; interstate compact information.*

**http://www.state.me.us/dhs/bcfs**
Augusta, ME

## Maryland

Maryland Department of Human Resources               410.767.7506

*Adoption information; foster care; waiting children photo listing.*

**http://www.dhr.state.md.us/ssa**
Baltimore, MD

## Massachusetts

Massachusetts Department of Social Services          617.748.2248

*Waiting children photo listing; foster care; resource links; child protective services.*

**http://www.state.ma.us/dss/Adoption/AD_Overview.htm**
Boston, MA

Massachusetts Office of Child Care Services          617.626.2000

*Adoption and foster care information links; search engine for agencies and foster care providers.*

**http://www.qualitychildcare.org/adoption.shtml**
Boston, MA

## Michigan

Michigan Family Independence Agency                  517.335.6158

*Information; foster care; child protective services.*

**http://www.michigan.gov/fia**
Lansing, MI

## Minnesota

Minnesota Department of Human Services                651.297.3933

> *Adoption information; interstate compact; adoption agencies listing;*
> *special needs and foster care.*
> **http://www.dhs.state.mn.us/infocenter/children.htm**
> St. Paul, MN

## Mississippi

Mississippi Department of Human Services                601.359.4500

> *Waiting children photo listing; foster care and special needs;*
> *child protective services.*
> **http://www.mdhs.state.ms.us/fcs.html**
> Jackson, MS

## Missouri

Jackson County Division of Family Services              816.889.2326

> *Waiting children photo listing; special needs; foster care; interstate compact;*
> *subsidy programs; educational resources.*
> **http://www.kclinc.org/mdfs**
> Kansas City, MO

Missouri Department of Social Services                573.751.6529

> *Adoption information; waiting children photo listing; interstate compact;*
> *subsidy program; home studies; foster care.*
> **http://www.dss.state.mo.us/dfs/csp.htm**
> Jefferson City, MO

## Montana

Montana Department of Public Health and Services　　406.444.2700

*Adoption information; foster care; waiting children photo listing; enter "adoption" in search engine and follow the links.*

**http://www.dphhs.state.mt.us**
Helena, MT

## Nebraska

Nebraska Department of Health and Human Services　　402.471.2306

*Waiting children photo listing; adoption information; interstate compact information; special needs and foster care.*

**http://www.hhs.state.ne.us/chs/chsindex.htm**
Lincoln, NE

## Nevada

Nevada Division of Child & Family Services　　702.486.7650

*Adoption exchange program; agency listing; information and resources; special needs and foster care; interstate compact; subsidy information.*

**http://www.dcfs.state.nv.us**
Carson City, NV

## New Hampshire

New Hampshire Department of Health and Human Services　603.271.4711

*In-depth foster care information and resources; foster care stories; information for kids.*

**http://www.nhfostercare.org**
Concord, NH

## New Jersey

New Jersey Division of Youth and Family Services          609.984.6800
  *Waiting children photo listing; foster care; adoption information; resources links.*
  **http://www.state.nj.us/humanservices/adoption/adopt.html**
  Trenton, NJ

## New Mexico

New Mexico Children, Youth and Families Department          505.827.4690
  *Waiting children photo listing; foster care; adoption information.*
  **http://www.state.nm.us/cyfd**
  Santa Fe, NM

## New York

New York Department of Family Assistance          518.474.9447
  *Waiting children photo listing; adoption agency listing; information and resources*
  *including subsidy information.*
  **http://www.ocfs.state.ny.us/adopt**
  Albany, NY

## North Carolina

Foster Child Adoption in North Carolina          919.733.3801
  *Information including steps to adoption; special needs and foster care;*
  *waiting children photo listing.*
  **http://www.dhhs.state.nc.us/dss/adopt**
  Raleigh, NC

## North Dakota

North Dakota Department of Human Services          701.328.4805
*Adoption and foster care services; interstate compact information; child protective services.*
**http://www.state.nd.us/humanservices**
Bismarck, ND

## Ohio

Ohio Department of Job and Family Services          614.466.4258
*Waiting children photo listing; foster care; in-depth adoption information; agency listing; reading list.*
**http://jfs.ohio.gov/index.stm**
Columbus, OH

## Oklahoma

Department of Human Services DCFS Adoption Section          877.657.9438
*Waiting children photo listing; special needs; adoption information; foster care.*
**http://www.okdhs.org/adopt/adoptinfo.htm**
Oklahoma City, OK

## Oregon

ACT for Children Today          503.945.5944
*Waiting children photo listing.*
**http://www.naccrra.org/act/contact.htm**
Salem, OR

Oregon Department of Human Services          503.945.5651
*Adoption and foster care; special needs; resources; agency listing; interstate compact information; waiting children photo listing.*
**http://www.dhs.state.or.us/children**
Salem, OR

## Pennsylvania

Pennsylvania Department of Public Welfare                    717.783.6292

*Adoption resources; foster care and special needs; waiting children photo listing;*
*state adoption agency listing.*

**http://www.dpw.state.pa.us/ocyf/ocyfas.asp**

Harrisburg, PA

## Rhode Island

Rhode Island Dept. for Children, Youth and Family          401.254.7020

*Adoption and foster care information; special needs resources;*
*child protective services.*

**http://www.dcyf.state.ri.us**

Bristol, RI

## South Carolina

South Carolina Department of Social Services               888.227.3487

*Waiting children photo listing; foster care; list of agencies; child protective services.*

**http://www.state.sc.us/dss/adoption**

Columbia, SC

## South Dakota

South Dakota Department of Social Services                 605.773.3227

*Waiting children photo listing; foster care; list of agencies; child protective services.*

**http://www.state.sd.us/social/cps/adoption**

Pierre, SD

## Tennessee

Tennessee Department of Children's Services                615.532.5637

*Adoption and foster care; special needs children; waiting children photo listing; adoption agencies; information on the adoption process.*

**http://www.state.tn.us/youth/adoption**

Nashville, TN

## Texas

Texas Department of Protective and Regulatory Services    800.233.3405

*Waiting children photo listing; foster care and special needs children; legal information.*

**http://www.tdprs.state.tx.us**

Austin, TX

## Utah

Utah Department of Human Services                         801.538.4242

*Adoption information; waiting children photo listing; foster care; child protective services.*

**http://www.hsdcfs.utah.gov**

Salt Lake City, UT

## Vermont

Vermont Department of Social Services                     802.241.2139

*Waiting children photo listing; foster care; adoption information; interstate compact; child protective services.*

**http://www.state.vt.us/srs/adoption**

Waterbury, VT

## Virginia

Virginia Department of Social Services                     804.692.1900
   *Adoption information and procedure; foster care and special needs;*
   *waiting children photo listing; home studies; grant program.*
   **http://www.dss.state.va.us/family/children.html**
   Richmond, VA

## Washington State

Washington State Department of Social & Health Services    888.794.1794
   *Adoption and foster care; special needs children; foster parent training.*
   **http://www1.dshs.wa.gov/ca/adoption**
   Olympia, WA

## West Virginia

West Virginia Department of Health and Human Resources    304.558.7980
   *Waiting children photo listing; special needs children.*
   **http://www.wvdhhr.org/oss/adoption**
   Charleston, WV

## Wisconsin

Wisconsin Department of Health and Family Services         608.266.1865
   *Foster care and special needs children; many types of adoptions; post-adoption*
   *services; agency listing; state statutes and codes.*
   **http://www.dhfs.state.wi.us/children/adoption**
   Madison, WI

### Wyoming

Wyoming Children Available for Adoption      307.777.7921

   *Adoption and foster care; waiting children photo listing; agency listing;*
   *foster parent handbook.*

   **http://dfsweb.state.wy.us**
   Cheyenne, WY    

# Attorneys

Adoptive Families/Adoption Attorneys      202.832.2222

   *Attorney locator; experts in adoption law and in the variety of interstate*
   *and international regulations surrounding adoption.*

   **http://www.adoptivefamilies.com/attorney_search_2002.php**  

American Adoption Law

   *Attorney locator; law and state-by-state resources including Canada;*
   *downloadable legal books for sale.*

   **http://www.americanadoptionlaw.com**  

Attorney Search Network, ASN

   *Attorney locator service; referrals to law professionals in most areas*
   *of the law.*

   **http://www.getareferral.com**  

ATTORNEYFIND

   *Attorney locator in all 50 states and worldwide.*

   **http://www.attorneyfind.com**  

Lawyers.com

   *Search engine for finding attorneys; nationwide.*

   **http://www.lawyers.com**

## Alabama

Beth Marietta Lyons                                     251.690.9111
*Adoption law.*
**http://www.adoptionattorneys.org/states/alabama.htm**
Mobile, AL

Bryant (Drew) A. Whitmire, Jr.                          205.324.6631
*Adoption law including interstate adoptions.*
**http://www.adoptionattorneys.org/states/alabama.htm**
Birmingham, AL

David P. Broome                                         251.432.9933
*Civil litigation and family law, including private adoptions.*
**http://www.lawyers.com/broomelaw**
Mobile, AL

Douglas C. Freeman                                      334.264.2000
*Adoption and family law.*
**http://www.lawyers.com/freeman**
Montgomery, AL

Glenn A. Shedd                                          256.845.6300
*Adoption and family law.*
**http://www.lawyers.com/glennashedd**
Fort Payne, AL

Martha Durant Hennessy, P.C.                            251.431.6000
*Adoption and family law; litigation.*
**http://www.lawyers.com/mdhpclaw**
Mobile, AL

## Alaska

Robert B. Flint                                         907.276.1592
*Adoption law.*
**http://www.hartig.com/attorneys/r flint.hml**
Anchorage, AK

Andrew C. Mitton                                         907.276.1592
   *Adoption law.*
   Anchorage, AK

## Arizona

Kerry B. Moore                                           602.271.9899
   *Adoption law; represents only the birth mother.*
   **http://www.arizadoption.com**
   Phoenix, AZ

Phillip (Jay) McCarthy, Attorney at Law                 928.774.1453
   *Adoption law.*
   **http://www.h2m2law.com/practices.html**
   Flagstaff, AZ

## Arkansas

H. Keith Morrison                                        479.575.0808
   *Adoption law.*
   **http://www.adoptionattorneys.org/states/arkansas.htm**
   Fayetteville, AR

Kaye H. McLeod                                           501.663.6224
   *Adoption law.*
   **http://www.adoptionattorneys.org/states/arkansas.htm**
   Little Rock, AR

Law Offices of Gary Green P.A.                           888.442.7947
   *Adoption and family law.*
   **http://www.ggreen.com**
   Little Rock, AR

Patricia Sievers Harris                     501.212.1323
   *Adoption law.*
   **http://www.adoptionattorneys.org/states/arkansas.htm**
   Little Rock, AR

## California

Academy of California Adoption Lawyers        818.501.8355
   *Attorney member listing; adoption law, information and resources.*
   **http://www.acal.org**
   Encino, CA

Adoption Center of Northern California        530.888.1311
   *Adoption services; waiting families profiles; owned by an attorney and*
   *adoptive mother.*
   **http://www.adoption-center.com**
   Auburn, CA

Alison A. Sconyers                            209.579.1978
   *Surrogacy, adoption and family law; links to in-depth articles about infertility.*
   **http://www.surrogacy.com/lawyer/sconyers.html**
   Modesto, CA

David J. Radis                               310.552.0536
   *Adoption law.*
   **http://www.radis-adopt.com**
   Los Angeles, CA

Douglas R. Donnelly                          805.962.0988
   *Adoption law.*
   **http://www.lawyers.com/adoptionlawfirm**
   Santa Barbara, CA

Felice A. Webster                            323.664.5600
   *Adoption law.*
   **http://www.adoptionattorneys.org/states/california.htm**
   Los Angeles, CA

**Jane A. Gorman**                                    650.347.7041
  *Adoption law; litigator.*
  **http://www.adoptionattorneys.org/states/california.htm**
  Burlingame, CA

---

**Law Office of Diane Michelsen**                    925.945.1880
  *Adoption and surrogacy law; ovum donor information.*
  **http://www.lodm.com**
  Lafayette, CA

---

**Law Offices of Jim E. Handy**                      916.941.8128
  *Domestic, Native American and interstate adoptions;*
  *free initial consultation.*
  **http://www.littleangeladoptions.com**
  El Dorado Hills, CA

---

**Law Offices of Schmiesing Blied Stoddart & Mackey**    949.863.0200
  *International and domestic adoption law.*
  **http://www.sbsmlaw.com**
  Irvine, CA

---

**Law Offices of Theresa M. Erickson**               858.577.0358
  *Reproductive (surrogacy), adoption and family law; egg donor and*
  *embryo donation.*
  **http://www.surrogacylawyer.net**
  Los Angeles, CA

---

**Marc Gradstein**                                   800.922.0777
  *Private and agency adoptions; waiting families profiles.*
  **http://www.placebaby4adoption.com**
  Burlingame, CA

---

**O'Neil and Widelock**                              800.677.8675
  *Adoption law and private adoptions; matches birth mothers and adoptive parents.*
  **http://www.thestork.com**
  Bakersfield, CA

---

**Steven W. Lazarus**                                    323.692.7848

*Adoption and surrogacy law; stepparent, relative, special needs and foster adoptions.*

**http://www.lifefocuscenter.com/slazarus.htm**

Los Angeles, CA

---

**Susan Romig**                                          530.273.7800

*Adoption law.*

**http://www.attorneyweb.net/us/ca_grassvalley.html**

Grass Valley, CA

---

**Law Offices of D. Durand Cook**                        323.655.2601

*Adoption law and placement; birth mother and adoptive parents education and counseling; home studies; newsletter; annual social event.*

**http://www.adoption-option.com**

Beverly Hills, CA

---

**Law Offices of David H. Baum**                         818.501.8355

*Adoption and family law; support groups.*

**http://www.adoptlaw.com**

Encino, CA

---

**Law Offices of Theresa M. Erickson**                   858.577.0358

*Reproductive (surrogacy), adoption and family law; egg donor and embryo donation; office also in San Francisco.*

**http://www.surrogacylawyer.net**

Los Angeles, CA

---

**Vorzimer, Masserman & Chapman**                        323.782.1400

*Family and reproductive law including surrogacy and egg donation.*

**http://www.vgme.com**

Beverly Hills, CA

## Colorado

Kevin F. Hughes ............................................................. 303.758.4181
*Adoption and family law.*
**http://www.lawyers.com/kevinhughes**
Denver, CO

Law Offices of Eric P. Ruderman ................................... 303.861.1444
*Adoption and family law.*
**http://www.lawyers.com/rudermanlaw**
Denver, CO

Seth A. Grob ..................................................................... 303.679.8266
*Adoption law.*
**http://www.adoptionattorneys.org/enhanced_directory/grob.htm**
Evergreen, CO

Susan Beth Price ............................................................. 303.893.3111
*Adoption law.*
**http://www.adoptionattorneys.org/states/colorado.htm**
Denver, CO

Patricia Germer-Coolidge ............................................... 719.578.9912
*Adoption and family law.*
**http://www.lawyers.com/pgc**
Colorado Springs, CO

## Connecticut

Donald B. Sherer ............................................................. 203.327.2084
*Adoption law and assisted reproductive technology (ART) law.*
**http://www.donaldsherer.com**
Stamford, CT

Pamela Nolan Dale ........................................................... 203.329.8220
*Adoption law.*
**http://www.adoptionattorneys.org/states/connecticut.htm**
Stamford, CT

## District of Columbia
................................................................................

**American Academy of Adoption Attorneys**                    202.832.2222
*National associations of lawyers in the field of adoption law; member directory;*
*newsletter; annual meetings and educational seminars.*
**http://www.adoptionattorneys.org**
Washington, D.C.

---

**Jody Marten**                                              202.537.0496
*Adoption law.*
**http://www.adoptionattorneys.org/states/districtofcolumbia.htm**
Washington, D.C.

---

**Mark T. McDermott**                                        202.331.1955
*Legal information; also in the states of Virginia and Maryland.*
**http://www.theadoptionadvisor.com/independent.html**
Washington, D.C.

---

**Michael Bentzen, Hughes & Bentzen, PLLC**                 202.293.8975
*Adoption law.*
**http://handb.whatsup.net:82/customers/handb.nsf/home**
Washington, D.C.

---

**Peter J. Wiernicki**                                       202.331.1955
*Adoption law.*
**http://www.adoptionattorneys.org/states/districtofcolumbia.htm**
Washington, D.C.

---

## Delaware
................................................................................

**Ellen Shaffer Meyer**                                      302.429.0344
*Adoption law.*
**http://www.lawyers.com/rsmlaw**
Wilmington, DE

---

Harlan S. Tenenbaum    302.477.0914
*Adoption law.*
**http://www.adoptionattorneys.org/states/delaware.htm**
Wilmington, DE

Joel D. Tenenbaum    302.477.3200
*Family and adoption law.*
**http://www.wtnlaw.com**
Wilmington, DE

## Florida

Irina M. O'Rear, P.A.
*Russian adoption law; member of International Bar Association, St. Petersburg, Russia; author of* Adoption in Russia; *information in Russian.*
**http://www.russialegal.com**
Tampa, FL

L. Jack Gibney, Attorney at Law    904.396.6546
*Adoption law.*
**http://www.adoptionswithcare.com**
Jacksonville, FL

Law Office of Joyce Sibson Dove    850.224.1111
*Private, domestic and international adoption law.*
**http://www.adoptioninternational.com**
Tallahassee, FL

Law Office of Susan L. Stockham    941.378.9000
*Adoption and surrogacy law; international, stepparent and grandparent adoptions.*
**http://www.fladoptlaw.com**
Sarasota, FL

Mary Ann Scherer, P.A.    954.564.6900
*Has practiced adoption law for 20 years; family law.*
**http://www.adoptionflorida.com**
Fort Lauderdale, FL

**Shorstein & Kelly, P.A.**                              888.412.3678

*Adoption law including interstate adoptions.*

**http://www.adoptionattorneyfla.com**

Jacksonville, FL

---

**The Law Office of Madonna Finney Hawken**             850.577.3077

*Comprehensive adoption services; private and intermediary adoption;*
*minority children; stepparent adoption.*

**http://www.madonnaelliott.com**

Tallahassee, FL

---

## Georgia

**Irene Steffas, P.C.**                                  770.642.6075

*Adoption law, international and domestic.*

**http://www.steffaslaw.com**

Roswell, GA

---

**Law Office of Juliette W. Scales**                     770.270.0191

*Domestic and foreign adoption law.*

**http://www.firms.findlaw.com/Adoptlaw**

Atlanta, GA

---

## Hawaii

**Adoption Law Office of Linda E.F. Lach**               808.245.8000

*Adoption and surrogacy law; in-depth information.*

**http://www.youcanadopt.com**

Lihue, HI

---

**Laurie A. Loomis**                                     808.524.5066

*Adoption and surrogacy law: services for birth and adoptive parents; national*
*and international consultation.*

**http://www.adoptionsolutions.com/attorneys/**
**attorney.htm**

Honolulu, HI

## Idaho

Alfred E. Barrus                                         208.678.1155
  *Adoption law.*
  **http://www.adoptionattorneys.org/states/idaho.htm**
  Burley, ID

John T. Hawley Jr.                                       208.336.6686
  *Adoption law; stepparent adoptions.*
  **http://www.adoptionattorneys.org/states/idaho.htm**
  Boise, ID

## Illinois

Ballard, Desai, Bush-Joseph & Horwich                   312.673.5312
  *Adoption law and reproductive technology consulting.*
  **http://www.infertility-law.com**
  Chicago, IL

Law Firm of Braselton and Millard                       630.645.2225
  *Adoption and family law; adoption education.*
  **http://www.illinois-adoption-law.com**
  Oakbrook, IL

Law Office of Denise J. Patton                          847.995.7003
  *Adoption law; educational seminars.*
  **http://www.iladoptionattorney.com**
  Schaumburg, IL

## Indiana

Kirsh & Kirsh                                            800.333.5736
  *Adoption law.*
  **http://www.indianaadoption.com**
  Indianapolis, IN

Steven and Rebecca Bruce, Attorneys at Law        765.286.1776
  *Adoption law.*
  **http://www.adoptindiana.org**
  Muncie, IN

## Iowa

Bray & Klockau, P.L.C.        319.338.7968
  *Adoption and family law.*
  **http://www.lawyers.com/bray&klockau**
  Iowa City, IA

Larry E. Ivers        515.448.3919
  *Adoption law.*
  **http://www.adoptionattorneys.org/states/iowa.htm**
  Eagle Grove, IA

Maxine M. Buckmeier        712.277.1261
  *Adoption law; also practices in South Dakota.*
  **http://www.adoptionattorneys.org/states/southdakota.htm**
  Sioux City, IA

Pasley and Singer Law Firm, L.L.P.        515.232.4732
  *Adoption and family law.*
  **http://singerlaw.lawoffice.com**
  Ames, IA

Ross S. Randall        319.291.6161
  *Adoption law.*
  **http://www.randall-nelson.com**
  Waterloo, IA

## Kansas

Jill Bremyer-Archer                                        620.241.0554
  *Adoption law.*
  **http://www.adoptionattorneys.org/states/kansas.htm**
  McPherson, KS

Martin W. Bauer                                            913.491.5500
  *Adoption law; represents adoptive parents nationally and internationally;*
  *birth parent services.*
  **http://www.martinpringle.com**
  Overland Park, KS

## Kentucky

Elisabeth Goldman                                          859.252.2325
  *Adoption law.*
  **http://www.adoptionattorneys.org/states/kentucky.htm**
  Lexington, KY

Mitchell A. Charney                                        502.589.4440
  *Adoption law.*
  **http://www.adoptionattorneys.org/states/kentucky.htm**
  Louisville, KY

## Louisiana

Adoptions Worldwide, Inc.                                  337.626.9009
  *Adoption law; facilitate adoptions; home studies; legal and financial information;*
  *adoptive parents themselves.*
  **www.adoptionsworldwide.com**
  Sulphur, LA

Fred H. Belcher, Jr.                                       225.291.7000
  *Adoption and family law.*
  **http://www.bplawfirm.com**
  Baton Rouge, LA

Terri Hoover Debnam                                    318.387.8811
  *Adoption law.*
  **http://www.adoptionattorneys.org/states/louisiana.htm**
  West Monroe, LA

## Maine

Judith M. Berry                                        207.839.7004
  *Adoption law.*
  **http://www.adoptionattorneys.org/states/maine.htm**
  Gorham, ME

## Maryland

Ellen Ann Callahan                                     301.258.2664
  *Adoption law; information and resources; adoption agency listing.*
  **http://www.adoptinmaryland.com**
  Gaithersburg, MD

Rena E. Friedman                                       301.776.0300
  *Adoption and family law.*
  **http://www.members.aol.com/RENAATTY**
  Laurel, MD

Schweitzer Scherr & Leichman                           301.961.6464
  *Adoption and family law; provide representation in cases of wrongful adoptions.*
  **http://www.schweitzerlaw.net**
  Bethesda, MD

## Massachusetts

Herbert D. Friedman                                    617.951.9980
  *Over 20 years experience in the field of adoption; adoptive parent.*
  **http://www.massadoption.com**
  Boston, MA

Law Office of Paula B. Mackin    617.332.0781
*Adoption and surrogacy law.*
**http://www.adoptinmassachusetts.com**
Newton, MA

## Michigan

Joanne R. Lax, J.D.    248.203.0816
*Adoption law.*
**http://www.michiganadoption.net**
Bloomfield Hills, MI

Sommers, Schwartz, Silver & Schwartz    800.967.1234
*Adoption and surrogacy law.*
**http://www.s4online.com**
Southfield, MI

Swartz Adoption Attorneys    989.793.0000
*Adoption law; also a full-service agency.*
**http://www.swartzadoptions.com**
Saginaw, MI

## Minnesota

Judith D. Vincent    612.332.7772
*Adoption and surrogacy law; Indian Child Welfare Act (ICWA);*
*interstate compact; agency representation.*
**http://www.adoptionlaw-mn.com**
Minneapolis, MN

Walling & Berg, P.A. Attorneys and Counselors at Law    612.340.1150
*Adoption law.*
**http://www.walling-berg.com**
Minneapolis, MN

## Mississippi

Dan J. Davis                                                    662.841.1090
   *Adoption law.*
   **http://www.adoptionattorneys.org/states/mississippi.htm**
   Tupelo, MS

Lisa Milner                                                    601.948.6100
   *Adoption law*
   **http://www.adoptionattorneys.org/states/mississippi.htm**
   Jackson, MS

## Missouri

Allen S. Russell, Jr. Attorney at Law                          816.753.1500
   *Adoption and family law.*
   **www.kcdivorcelaw.com**
   Kansas City, MO

Law Offices of Gary Green P.A.                                 888.242.7947
   *Adoption and family law.*
   **http://www.ggreen.com**
   Springfield, MO

Mary Beck                                                      573.446.7554
   *Small private practice limited to the adoption of children.*
   **http://www.law.missouri.edu/beck**
   Columbia, MO

## Montana

Dennis E. Lind                                                 406.728.0810
   *Adoption law.*
   **http://www.adoptionattorneys.org/states/montana.htm**
   Missoula, MT

## Nebraska

Michael C. Washburn                                402.397.2200
*Adoption law.*
**http://www.adoptionattorneys.org/states/nebraska.htm**
Omaha, NE

Susan Kubert Sapp                                 402.474.6900
*Adoption law.*
**http://www.adoptionattorneys.org/states/nebraska.htm**
Lincoln, NE

## Nevada

Eric A. Stovall, LTD.                             775.329.4111
*Adoption law.*
**http://www.personalinjurynevada.com**
Reno, NV

Israel "Ishi" L. Kunin                            702.438.8060
*Adoption law.*
**http://www.adoptionattorneys.org/states/nevada.htm**
Las Vegas, NV

Rhonda Mushkin                                    702.474.2400
*Adoption law; litigation.*
**http://www.adoptionattorneys.org/states/nevada.htm**
Las Vegas, NV

## New Hampshire

Philbrook Law Office                              603.673.3933
*Adoption law.*
**http://www.philbrooklaw.com**
Brookline, NH

Quigley Law Offices                                   603.644.8300
*Adoption related services to adoptive parents and birth parents;*
*independent and agency adoptions.*
   **http://www.adoptionnh.com**
   Manchester, NH

## New Jersey
.........................................................................

Carol S. Allenza                                      908.782.5500
*International adoption.*
   **http://www.quickbyte.com/adoptionlaw**
   Flemington, NJ

Deborah Steincolor                                    973.743.7500
*Adoption law; practices also in New York.*
   **http://www.adoptionattorneys.org/states/newjersey.htm**
   Bloomfield, NJ

Law Offices of Laurie B. Goldheim                     732.602.1616
*Private domestic adoption; international adoption; re-adoption;*
*stepparent adoption.*
   **http://www.adoptionrights.com/adoption_4.htm**
   Woodbridge, NJ

Law Office Richard W. Stewart                         609.641.2810
*Adoption and family law.*
   **http://home.pro-usa.net/rstewart**
   Absecon, NJ

Steven B. Sacharow                                    856.661.2272
*Adoption and family law; litigation.*
   **http://www.flastergreenberg.com/bios/sacharow_s.htm**
   Cherry Hill, NJ

## New Mexico

Harold O. Atencio                                      505.839.9111
*Adoption law.*
**http://www.adoptionattorneys.org/states/newmexico.htm**
Albuquerque, NM

## New York

Amy Klein Szymoniak                                    716.632.2546
*Adoption law; information and waiting family profiles.*
**http://www.adopt.net**
Williamsville, NY

Benjamin J. Rosin                                      212.972.5430
*Adoption and family law.*
**http://www.adoptionattorneys.org/states/newyork.htm**
New York, NY

Brendan C. O'Shea                                      518.432.7511
*Adoption law.*
**http://www.adoptionattorneys.org/states/newyork.htm**
Albany, NY

Deborah Steincolor                                     212.421.7807
*Adoption law; practices also in New Jersey.*
**http://www.adoptionattorneys.org/states/newyork.htm**
New York, NY

Denise Seidelman                                       914.962.3001
*Adoption law.*
**http://www.adoptionattorneys.org/states/newyork.htm**
Yorktown Heights, NY

Flory Herman                                           716.691.1706
*Adoption law.*
**http://www.adoptionattorneys.org/states/newyork.htm**
Amherst, NY

Frederick J. Magovern                               212.962.1450
   *Adoption law.*
      **http://www.adoptionattorneys.org/states/newyork.htm**
      New York, NY

Golda Zimmerman                                     315.475.3322
   *Adoption law.*
      **http://www.adoptionattorneys.org/states/newyork.htm**
      Syracuse, NY

Law Office of Laurie B. Goldheim                    845.624.2727
   *Private domestic adoption; international adoption; re-adoption;*
   *stepparent adoption.*
      **http://www.adoptionrights.com/adoption_4.htm**
      Nanuet, NY

Law Office of Sanford M. Bernardo                   212.560.5200
   *Adoption and assisted reproduction law.*
      **http://www.benardo.com**
      New York, NY

Robin A. Fleischner                                 212.362.6945
   *Adoption law.*
      **http://www.adoptionattorneys.org/states/newyork.htm**
      New York, NY

## North Carolina
. . . . . . . . . . . . . . . . . . . . . . . . . . . . . . . . . . . . . . . . . . . . . . . . . . .

Herring McBennett Mills & Finkelstein, PLLC         919.821.1860
   *Adoption law and surrogacy issues.*
      **http://www.hermcb.com**
      Raleigh, NC

W. David Thurman                                      704.377.4164
*Adoption law; independent, agency, interstate and international adoptions;*
*surrogacy situations; represents adoptive parents, birth parents and adoptees.*
**http://www.surrogacy.com/lawyer/thurman.html**
Charlotte, NC

## North Dakota

William P. Harrie                                      701.237.5544
*Adoption and family law.*
**http://www.nilleslaw.com**
Fargo, ND

## Ohio

Mary Catherine Barrett                                440.356.4604
*Adoption and surrogacy law.*
**http://www.mcbadoptions.com**
Rocky River, OH

Michael R. Voorhees                                   513.985.2500
*Adoption law.*
**http://www.phillipslawfirm.com**
Cincinnati, OH

## Oklahoma

Boren & Boren Law                                     405.235.1200
*Adoption and surrogacy law.*
**http://www.borenlaw.com**
Oklahoma City, OK

Julie Demastus                                              405.752.0080
> *Adoption law.*
> **http://www.web-law.com/attorneys/demastus/adopt.html**
> Oklahoma City, OK

## Oregon

Bouneff & Chally Attorneys at Law                          503.238.9720
> *Adoption, litigation and surrogacy law; legal procedures around assisted*
> *reproductive techniques.*
> **http://www.adoptionnorthwest.com**
> Portland, OR

John R. Hassen                                             541.779.8900
> *Adoption law.*
> **http://www.roguelaw.com/partners/hassen.htm**
> Medford, OR

Sandra L. Hodgson                                          503.238.9720
> *Adoption litigation; surrogacy and assisted reproductive technologies;*
> *general adoption.*
> **www.worldstar.com/~bounchal**
> Portland, OR

## Pennsylvania

Craig B. Bluestein                                         215.576.1030
> *Adoption law.*
> **http://www.adoptionattorneys.org/states/pennsylvania.htm**
> Jenkintown, PA

Martin Leventon                                            610.642.7182
> *Adoption law.*
> **http://www.adoptionattorneys.org/states/pennsylvania.htm**
> Wynnewood, PA

Mary Ann Petrillo                                              724.861.8333
   *Adoption and family law.*
   **http://www.petrillo-law.com**
   Irwin, PA

Samuel Totaro, Jr.                                            215.638.9330
   *Adoption law.*
   **http://www.adoptionattorneys.org/states/pennsylvania.htm**
   Bensalem, PA

Tara E. Gutterman                                            215.748.1441
   *Adoption law.*
   **http://www.adoptionattorneys.org/states/pennsylvania.htm**
   Philadelphia, PA

William P. Rosen III                                         610.688.8600
   *Adoption law.*
   **http://www.adoptionattorneys.org/states/pennsylvania.htm**
   King Russia, PA

## Rhode Island

Doris J. Licht                                               401.274.2000
   *Adoption law; intrastate, interstate and international.*
   **http://www.haslaw.com**
   Providence, RI

Nancy J. Oliver                                              401.294.9595
   *Adoption and family law.*
   **http://www.shopcpn.com/webpage/display.cfm?ID=1570**
   Wickford, RI

## South Carolina

Broome & Bromme, Attorneys at Law                            803.788.4478
   *Adoption and family law.*
   **http://firms.findlaw.com/jcbroome**
   Columbia, SC

James Fletcher Thompson                                    864.573.7575
  *Adoption law.*
  **http://www.sc-adopt.org/Sum2000/page8.html**
  Spartanburg, SC

## South Dakota

Hughes Law Offices                                        605.339.3939
  *Adoption law; waiting family profiles.*
  **http://www.adoptionhelp.net**
  Sioux Falls, SD

## Tennessee

Dawn Coppock                                              423.933.8173
  *Adoption law; independent, agency, interstate, state agency, international,*
  *relative adoptions; reproductive technology.*
  **http://www.tba.org/Members_Web/Coppock_Dawn**
  Strawberry Plains, TN

Edward J. Bailey                                          615.263.1980
  *Adoption and family law.*
  **http://www.baileylaw.com**
  Brentwood, TN

Law Offices of Gary Green P.A.                            888.742.7947
  *Adoption and family law.*
  **http://www.ggreen.com**
  Memphis, TN

Law Offices of Rochelle, McCulloch & Aulds, PLLC          615.444.1433
  *Adoption and family law.*
  **http://www.rma-law.com**
  North Lebanon, TN

## Texas

......................................................................................................................

**Calabrese Associates, P.C.**       214.939.3000
    *Adoption law; domestic and international.*
    **http://www.calabreselaw.com**
    Dallas, TX

---

**Charles E. Myers**       915.692.2708
    *Adoption law.*
    **http://www.adoptionattorneys.org/states/texas.htm**
    Abilene, TX

---

**David Charles Cole**       214.363.5117
    *Adoption and surrogacy law; legal information.*
    **http://www.adoptlegal.com**
    Dallas, TX

---

**Irv W. Queal**       214.696.3200
    *Adoption law.*
    **http://www.adoptionattorneys.org/states/texas.htm**
    Dallas, TX

---

**Law Offices of Gary Green P.A.**       888.942.7947
    *Adoption and family law.*
    **http://www.ggreen.com**
    Austin, TX

---

**Michael R. Lackmeyer**       254.690.2223
    *Adoption law.*
    **http://www.adoptionattorneys.org/states/texas.htm**
    Killeen, TX

---

**The Royalls**       713.462.6500
    *Legal services in all types of adoptive services; father/daughter law firm devoted to adoption and family law.*
    **http://www.adoptiontexas.com**
    Houston, TX

Vika Andrel                                          512.448.4605
>   *Adoption law.*
>   **http://www.adoptionattorneys.org/states/texas.htm**
>   Austin, TX

## Utah
· · · · · · · · · · · · · · · · · · · · · · · · · · · · · · · · · · · · · · · · · · · · · · · · · · ·

Dale M. Dorius                                       435.723.5219
>   *Adoption law.*
>   **http://www.adoptionattorneys.org/states/utah.htm**
>   Brigham City, UT

Law Office of Stephen J. Buhler                      801.964.6901
>   *Adoption law.*
>   **http://www.utahadoptionattorney.com**
>   West Valley City, UT

Les F. England                                       435.649.0569
>   *Adoption law.*
>   **http://www.adoptionattorneys.org/states/utah.htm**
>   Park City, UT

## Vermont
· · · · · · · · · · · · · · · · · · · · · · · · · · · · · · · · · · · · · · · · · · · · · · · · · · ·

Hon. Susan L. Fowler (Judicial)                      802.651.1518
>   *Adoption law.*
>   **http://www.adoptionattorneys.org/states/vermont.htm**
>   Burlington, VT

Murdoch & Hughes                                     802.864.9811
>   *Legal services for adoptive families and pregnant women; international*
>   *and interstate placements; private and agency adoptions.*
>   **http://www.adoptvt.com**
>   Burlington, VT

## Virginia

**A Baby for All**
*Law office; adoption services including international adoption.*
**http://www.adopting.com/abf**
Rural Retreat, VA

**Colleen Marea Quinn**        804.343.4375
*Adoption law and legal information.*
**http://www.cantorarkema.com/attorneys/quinn.cfm**
Richmond, VA

**Robert H. Klima**        703.361.5052
*Adoption and family law.*
**http://www.rhklima.com**
Manassas, VA

## Washington

**Gayle Harthcock**        800.903.6141
*Adoption law.*
**http://www.firms.findlaw.com/gmh**
Yakima, WA

**Ron Anderson**        253.581.1234
*Adoption law; adoption information.*
**http://www.attorneyronanderson.com**
Lakewood, WA

**Timothy C. Farris**        360.733.0212
*Children's rights; foster care; litigator in the field of wrongful adoption.*
**http://www.brettlaw.com/tf.html**
Bellingham, WA

## West Virginia

David Allen Barnette                                          304.340.1327
    *Adoption law.*
    **http://www.jacksonkelly.com/html/barnette.html**
    Charleston, WV

## Wisconsin

Carol M. Gapen                                               608.821.8211
    *Adoption law.*
    **http://www.law4kids.com**
    Madison, WI

Lynn J. Bodi                                                 608.821.8212
    *Adoption law.*
    **http://www.adoptionattorneys.org/states/wisconsin.htm**
    Madison, WI

Richard B. Schoenbohm                                        920.735.5858
    *Adoption law.*
    **http://www.adoptionattorneys.org/states/wisconsin.htm**
    Appleton, WI

## Wyoming

Douglas H. Reiniger                                          307.859.8811
    *Adoption law.*
    **http://www.adoptionattorneys.org/states/wyoming.htm**
    Bondurant, WY

Peter J. Feeney                                              307.266.4422
    *Adoption law.*
    **http://www.adoptionattorneys.org/states/wyoming.htm**
    Casper, WY

# Birth Parents Resources

### ABC Adoptions.com

*Waiting family profiles by state; birth mother and open adoption information; resources; forums.*

**http://www.abcadoptions.com**

---

### Adoption Ministry

**888.423.6781**

*Christian adoption resources; encouragement for birth parents; 24-hour services; waiting Christian family profiles; articles; links; prayer request; books and newsletter.*

**http://www.adoptionministry.net/**

---

### AdoptionTree.com

*Birth parent resources; counseling for birth parents; housing or financial assistance; pregnancy and legal referrals; adoption services; waiting family profiles.*

**http://www.adoptiontree.com**

---

### Angel Adoption Talk

*Birth mother forum and chat room; a place for comfort, friendship and support.*

**http://pub10.ezboard.com/bangeladoptiontalk**

---

### Baby Blues Connection

**503.797.2843**

*Information, resources and support to postpartum mothers and families; local support groups; chat room; links.*

**http://www.babybluesconnection.org**

---

### Center for Postpartum Health

**818.887.1312**

*Postpartum Mood Disorder information, and resources and support groups; self-assessment test; chat room and forum.*

**http://www.postpartum.net**
Woodland Hills, CA

**Christian Adoption**                                            316.251.4405

*Profile letters and photos of Christian families who wish to adopt; adoption information.*

**http://www.christianadoption.com**

Coffeyville, KS

---

**Connections/Reachsource Adoption Services**        800.892.4523

*Birth mother referral program; adoption assistance and resources.*

**http://www.pivot.net/~adoptcon**

Windham, ME

---

**CrisisPregnancyOnline.com**

*Birth mother resources; assistance to make an informed decision about pregnancy; pregnancy info; baby development with photos; newsletter.*

**http://www.crisispregnancyonline.com**

---

**Emergency Pregnancy Service, Inc.**                     813.262.6381

*Pregnancy tests and information; medical care referrals; counseling; 24 hour hotline; adoption referral network; baby resources; non-profit.*

**http://www.naples.net/social/eps.htm**

Naples, FL

---

**Lifetime Adoption Foundation**                            530.271.1756

*Educational scholarships for birth mothers; adoption assistance; referrals and counseling; non-profit.*

**http://www.lifetimefoundation.org**

---

**Link National Adoption Registry, LNAR**              704.792.2229

*Referral service; profiles of waiting Christian families; non-profit.*

**http://www.linkadoption.com**

Concord, NC

---

**March of Dimes**                                               888.663.4637

*Advocacy of healthy born infants; provides information and education to prevent premature births that lead to birth defects and infant mortality.*

**http://www.marchofdimes.com**

### May We Adopt?                                              903.923.8077
*Waiting family profiles; links to agencies and other resources; forums;*
*adoption stories.*
**http://www.mayweadopt.com**
Garland, TX

### Oxygen Media
*Online pregnancy calendar; pregnancy and infant*
*developmental information.*
**http://www.oxygen.com/pregnancy_calendar**

### Pregnancy Center of Greater Toledo              419.842.9900
*Christian pregnancy and social services agency; support groups;*
*adoption counseling; 24-hour crisis line.*
**http://www.pregnancycenter.org**
Toledo, OH

### Project Cuddle                                            714.432.9681
*Birth mother advocacy; 24-hour crisis line; non-profit.*
**http://www.projectcuddle.org**
Costa Mesa, CA

### ReachSOURCE                                               207.741.2794
*Advertising services for adoptive parents to reach birth parents through*
*newspapers and the Internet.*
**http://www.gwi.net/~reach**

### Refuge Pregnancy Center, Inc.                    770.922.5939
*Prenatal classes; pregnancy testing; adoption assistance and other services*
*for birth mothers.*
Conyers, GA

### Resource4Women.com
*Pregnancy information and adoption assistance; pregnancy calculator;*
*newsletter, articles and books.*
**http://www.resource4women.com**

**Sunflower Birthmom Support Page**
*Birth mother mailing list; online support group.*
**http://www.bmom.net**

**USAadoptions.com**                                    800.923.6784
*Birth and adoptive parent resources; domestic adoption services; counseling,*
*housing and financial assistance; open adoption articles; special needs advocacy.*
**http://www.usaadoptions.com**
Nevada City, CA

**Women's Resource Guide**                              619.516.3266
*Birth mother and pregnancy resources; crisis hotlines and other women's*
*support services.*
**http://www.wrg.org**
San Diego, CA

# Books & Publications

**Adoptingonline.com**
*Adopting on the Internet; practical, easy-to-follow guidelines; stories from*
*real life; over 1,100 online adoption resources; order online.*
**http://www.adoptingonline.com**

**Adoption Nation Education Initiative**
*Book:* Adoption Nation-How the Adoption Revolution Is Transforming
America; *also seminars, lectures, research, strategy and media.*
**http://www.adoptionnation.com**
Newton, MA

**Carriage House Publishing**                           530.470.0720
*Educational and inspirational adoption books; reports; order online.*
**http://www.carriagehousepublishing.com**
Cedar Ridge, CA

Perspectives Press, Inc.                           317.872.3055
*Fertility, adoption & surrogacy resources through books and publications; publisher.*
**http://www.perspectivespress.com**
Indianapolis, IN

---

Reaching Out
*Writing guide; how to write a terrific Dear Birth Mother letter; order online.*
**http://www.DearBirthmotherLetter.com**

---

Tapestry Books                                     800.765.2367
*Book publisher on the topics of adoption and infertility.*
**http://www.tapestrybooks.com**
Hillsborough, NJ

---

The Adoption Dilemma
The Adoption Dilemma: A Handbook for Adoptive Parents; *clear and concise presentation of emotional problems encountered in adoption; more books on related topics; order online.*
**http://www.arvinpublications.com/adoption.html**

---

The Future of Children                             650.917.7110
*Translates research into better policy and practice for children; each issue examines a single topic of importance from a multidisciplinary perspective.*
**http://www.futureofchildren.org**
Los Altos, CA

---

# Canadian Resources

Access to Justice Network
*Legal information: federal, provincial, and territorial statutes; legal search engine; information in French.*
**http://www.acjnet.org**
Edmonton, AB

**Adoption by Choice** 780.448.1159

*Adoption agency: domestic infants and special needs children; international adoptions; home studies; education for adoptive parents; non-profit.*

**http://www.adoptionbychoice.ab.ca**
Edmonton, AB

**Adoption by Choice** 403.245.8854

*Adoption agency: domestic infants and special needs children; international adoptions; home studies; education for adoptive parents; non-profit.*

**http://www.adoptionbychoice.ab.ca**
Calgary, AB

**Adoption Council of Canada** 613.235.0344

*Umbrella organization for adoption in Canada: raises public awareness of adoption; promotes placement of waiting children; advocacy of post-adoption services; resource library; newsletter.*

**http://www.adoption.ca**
Ottawa, ON

**Adoption Horizon, Inc.** 416.512.7591

*Intercountry child placement agency; international adoptions: children from Russia, Belarus, Ukraine and Georgia; non-profit.*

**http://www.adoptionhorizons.com**
North York, ON

**Adoption Options** 780.433.5656

*Adoption agency: domestic infants and special needs children; home studies; international services; educational seminars; post- placement services; non-profit.*

**http://www.adoptionoptions.com**
Edmonton, AB

**Adoption Options** 403.270.8228

*Adoption agency: international and domestic adoption; information and resources; seminars, support groups and books; post-placement services.*

**http://www.adoptionoptions.com**
Calgary, AB

**Adoptive Families Association of BC**                 604.320.7330
*Support and promotion of adoption: special needs children; information and*
*articles; local support groups; book orders; newsletter.*
**http://www.bcadoption.com**
Burnaby, BC

**Alberta Children's Services**                         780.415.4890
*Public agency; domestic, international and special needs adoption:*
*foster care and resources for disabled children; listing of private agencies.*
**http://www.child.gov.ab.ca**
Edmonton, AB

**British Columbia Vital Statistics Agency**            250.952.2681
*Guide that explains how to file a disclosure veto or no-contact declaration*
*under the new Adoption Act.*
**http://www.vs.gov.bc.ca**
Victoria, BC

**Burgar, Rowe LLP**                                    705.721.3377
*Family and adoption law.*
**http://www.burgarrowe.com/areas.htm#Family**
Barrie, ON

**Burke Robertson Barristers & Solicitors LLP**        613.236.9665
*Family and adoption law.*
**http://www.burkerobertson.com**
Ottawa, ON

**Canada Adopts**
*Adoption information and resources: agency and adoption practitioners listing;*
*myths and facts; forum.*
**http://www.canadaadopts.com/canada/resources_links.shtml**
Toronto, ON

**Canada's Waiting Kids**                               888.542.3678
*Information and referral services: special needs children; support groups;*
*waiting children photo listing.*
**http://www.canadaswaitingkids.ca**

**Canadian Bar Association**                                    613.237.2925

*Legal information.*

**http://www.cba.org/CBA/Info/Main/Contact.asp**

Ottawa, ON

---

**Canadian Legal Resources**

*Legal resources: listing of law firms including firms that practice family and adoption law.*

**http://www.gahtan.com/cdnlaw**

---

**Canadian Parents Online, Inc.**                              519.637.7342

*Parenting resources; pregnancy, baby, toddler and child raising information and more; articles and newsletter; chat room and forum.*

**http://www.canadianparents.com**

St. Thomas, ON

---

**Cheadle Johnson Shanks MacIvor LLP**                         807.622.6821

*Family and adoption law.*

**http://www.cheadle.com/areas.htm#family**

Thunder Bay, ON

---

**Duncan & Craig LLP**                                         780.428.6036

*Family and adoption law.*

**http://www.duncanandcraig.com**

Edmonton, AB

---

**Family Helper.com**

*How-to-adopt guide for Canadians; national adoption publication for domestic and international adoptions; infertility resources; adoption agency directory; support groups; research; statistics.*

**http://www.familyhelper.net**

Southampton, ON

---

**Fillmore Riley**                                             204.956.2970

*Family and adoption law.*

**http://www.fillmoreriley.com/pg/familylaw.html**

Winnipeg, MB

**Human Resources Development Canada**

*Intercountry adoption services; links to federal information.*

**http://www.hrdc-drhc.gc.ca/hrib/sdd-dds/cfc/content/
interAdopt.shtml**

North York, ON

---

**Indigenous Bar Association**                                604.951.8807

*Indigenous legal information.*

**http://www.indigenousbar.ca**

Surrey, BC

---

**International Adoptions for Canadians**

*International adoption resources and links: special needs children;
Canadian agency listing by province; waiting children photo listing.*

**http://www.interlog.com/~ladybug**

---

**Judith M. Blair**                                          204.957.4648

*Family and adoption law.*

**http://www.aikins.com/people/jmb.htm**

Winnipeg, MB

---

**Kitchen Kitchen Simeson Mcfarlane**                        905.579.5302

*Family and adoption law.*

**http://www.kksm.com**

Oshawa, ON

---

**Klein Law Office**                                         905.272.2540

*Licensed to place children for private adoptions within Ontario;
also a family law lawyer.*

**http://www.kleinlawoffice.com/adoption.html**

Mississauga, ON

---

**Lim & Company Lawyers**                                    604.266.1988

*Family and adoption law.*

**http://lim-and-company-law.com**

Vancouver, BC

**LIMIAR**

*Adoption facilitator; international: children from Brazil; profile of Brazil with sights, sounds and travel notes; newsletter; information in Portuguese; non-profit.*

**http://www.limiar.org**

Barrie, ON

---

MacIsaac & Company                                          250.381.5353

*Family and adoption law; litigation.*

**http://bc.macisaacgroup.com/practice.htm**

Victoria, BC

---

Mary Ann Gerhart                                          403.329.6900

*Family and adoption law.*

**http://www.lawpollock.com/Maryann.html**

Lethbridge, AB

---

McConnan Bion O'Connor & Peterson Law Corporation          250.385.1383

*Family and adoption law.*

**http://www.mcbop.com**

Victoria, BC

---

Ontario Bar Association                                          416.869.1047

*Legal information; information in French.*

**http://199.243.163.178/en/main/home_en**

Toronto, ON

---

Open Adoption & Family Services, Inc.                    206.782.0442

*Adoption agency, located in USA, with services for Canadian birth mothers; domestic infants; home studies; fears and facts about open adoption; newsletter; non-profit.*

**http://www.openadopt.com**

Seattle, WA, USA

---

Parentbooks                                          416.537.8334

*Books on all kinds of parenting topics.*

**http://www.parentbookstore.com**

Toronto, ON

**Peterson Stark Scott**                                604.736.9811
    *Family and adoption law; office also in Surrey, BC.*
    **http://www.petersonstark.bc.ca**
    Vancouver, BC

---

**Pushor Mitchell Lawyers**                            250.762.2108
    *Family and adoption law.*
    **http://www.pushormitchell.com/adoption.asp**
    Kelowna, BC

---

**Ricketts, Harris LLP**                               416.364.6211
    *Family and adoption law.*
    **http://www.rickettsharris.com**
    Toronto, ON

---

**Single Parent Adoption (SPA)**                       416.740.7640
    *Single parents support group; meeting bi-monthly in the Toronto area.*
    **http://www.familyhelper.net/join/spa.html**

---

**Sliman, Stander & Company**                          604.533.2300
    *Family law and adoption; office also in Chilliwack.*
    **http://www.slimanstander.com**
    Langley, BC

---

**Terre Des Hommes Canada, Inc.**
    *International adoption: children from Vietnam, Honduras, Nepal, Romania and*
    *Latvia; information and resources; information in French.*
    **http://www.tdh.ca   IN**
    Montreal, QUE

---

**Victoria Bar Association**
    *Legal information.*
    **http://www.vicbar.com**
    Victoria, BC

---

**Wallance Meschisnick Clackson Zawada**               306.933.0004
    *Family and adoption law.*
    **http://www.wmcz.com/aboutus/family.html**
    Saskatoon, SK

**White, Ottenheimer & Baker**                709.722.7584
  *Family and adoption law.*
  **http://www.wob.nf.ca/Practice/practice.htm**
  St. John's, NF

**Yahoo Canada**
  *Search engine and web guide.*
  **http://www.ca.yahoo.com**

# Chat Rooms & Forums

**Adopt Korea**
  *Korean adoption issues.*
  **http://groups.yahoo.com/group/adopt_korea**

**Adopting While Living Abroad**
  *Americans who want to adopt or have adopted internationally while living
  abroad; also for internationally married couples and military;
  Yahoo group.*
  **http://groups.yahoo.com/group/adoptingwhilelivingabroad**

**Adoption Chat-o-Rama**
  *Boards and chat room for the adoption triad.*

**Adoption Solutions**
  *Birth and adoptive parents resources; registry; legal information and laws; attorney
  and agency locator by state; waiting children photo listing; forum.*
  **http://www.adoptionsolutions.com/general/info_home.htm**

**Adoption Support Group for Military Families**
  *Support group for military families, offering encouragement and assistance with
  the process and issues of adoption; Yahoo group.*
  **http://groups.yahoo.com/group/AdoptionSupportGroup
  ForMilitaryFamilies**

### Adoption Triad Outreach Chat Rooms                           414.483.3533

*Support and resources for the adoption triad; legal information; newsletter.*

**http://www.adoptiontriad.org**

### Adoption.About.com

*Articles, newsletter, information and resources on many aspects of adoption and foster care; chat room and forum.*

**http://www.adoption.about.com**

### AdoptionPlan.com

*Adoptive families resources.*

**http://www.adoptionplan.com**

### Adoptions Forums

*Links to many forums.*

**http://www.abcadoptions.com/boards.htm**

### All Experts

*Ask adoption questions of experts.*

**http://www.allexperts.com/getExpert.asp?Category=1467**

### American Infertility Association                             718.621.5083

*Infertility and adoption resources; articles and fact sheets; legal information; newsletter; forum and chat room.*

**http://www.americaninfertility.org/**

### BabyCenter

*Preconception, pregnancy, parenting and topics A-Z.*

**http://www.babycenter.com**

### BabyNet Adoption Forum

*Discuss adoption issues with parents and parents-to-be.*

**http://www.babynet.com/boards/list.htm?num=19&**

### Babyzone

*Resources and links; adoption, foster care, pregnancy, parenting information; newsletter and much more.*

**http://www.babyzone.com**

### Bella Online

*Adoption information including book reviews, articles and news.*
**http://www.bellaonline.com/site/adoption**

### Birthmothers.org

*Waiting family profiles; adoption resources and links; agency listing.*
**http://www.birthmother.org**

### CambodianAdoptions

*Cambodian adoptions issues; Yahoo group.*
**http://www.groups.yahoo.com/group/CambodianAdoptions**

### Child of My Dreams                                                703.715.9043

*Infertility and adoption information; links and resources; forum; newsletter.*
**http://www.childofmydreams.com**

### Children To Adopt

*Listing of available children; Yahoo group.*
**http://www.groups.yahoo.com/group/childrentoadopt**

### Christians Using DI for Conception

*Fertility; resources for Christians who are using donor insemination for conception; Yahoo group.*
**http://www.egroups.com/list/di-christians**

### Concerned United Birthparents, Inc.                              800.822.2777

*Birth parents support but also for adoptees, adoptive parents and professionals; local support groups; links to related topics, articles and news media; forum.*
**http://www.cubirthparents.org**
Encinitas, CA

### Families for Russian and Ukrainian Adoptions                    703.560.6184

*Former Soviet Union support network for adoptive families; information; chat room; newsletter; non-profit.*
**http://www.frua.org**

### Families Through Adoption

*Support group; share the joy of building families through adoption.*

**http://groups.yahoo.com/group/Familiesthroughadoption**

### Family First Fertility

*Egg donor information and fertility resources including legal; fertility agencies and clinics by state; forum and chat room.*

**http://www.familyfirstfertility.com**

### Fertile Thoughts

*Adoption, infertility, pregnancy, surrogacy and parenting.*

**http://www.fertilethoughts.net**

### Hannah's Prayer Ministries

*Fertility challenges; Christian support network; Yahoo group.*

**http://www.groups.yahoo.com/group/hannahs**

### InterNational Council on Infertility Information Dissemination, Inc.

703.379.9178

*Infertility fact sheets; forums including fertility over forty, miscarriage, endometriosis; reproductive technologies; infertility specialists.*

**http://www.inciid.org/interinfertility.html**

### Learning Center

*Information, resources and links; encyclopedia.*

**http://www.adoptnet.org**

### Military Families Adopting Military Children

*Military personnel can post available adoption situations where they want other military families to adopt their children; Yahoo group.*

**http://groups.yahoo.com/group/militaryfamilies adoptingmilitarychildren**

### National Parenting Center

800.753.6667

*Guidance for parents, comprehensive, from the world's most renowned child-rearing authorities; articles and chat room.*

**http://www.tnpc.com**

New Beginnings Adoption
*Forum that covers many aspects of adoption.*
**http://server5.ezboard.com/bnewbeginningsadoption**

Parentsoup Adoption Central
*Adoptive parents, adult adoptees, and birth parents.*
**http://www.parentsoup.com/adoption**

Positive Adoptive Parent Support
*Adoption issues; Yahoo group.*
**http://dir.groups.yahoo.com/dir/1600042055**

Shared Journey
*Infertility, miscarriage, surrogacy, pregnancy after infertility, living child-free and adoption; chat room and forum.*
**http://www.sharedjourney.com**

Ultimate Baby Community Boards
*For those interested in pregnancy and parenting.*
**http://www.ultimatebaby.com/boards**

# Adoption Facilitators

A Baby from Heaven                                  714.771.5777
*Waiting family profiles; information and support for birthparents and adoptive parents.*
**http://www.babyfromheaven.com**
CA

**A Loving Alternative**                                    949.366.4500
*Waiting family profiles; information for birth parents and adoptive parents.*
**http://www.alovingalternative.com**
San Clemente, CA

**Adopt Link**                                              408.353.4522
*Domestic and international: children from Mexico, Russia, Guatemala and Bulgaria; counseling; nationwide agency listing and other resources.*
**http://www.adoptlink.com**
Los Gatos, CA

**Adopt with Love**                                         916.332.9905
*International: children from Russia, Ukraine and Kazakhstan; waiting children photo listing; financial information.*
**http://www.adoptwithlove.com**
Antelope, CA

**Adoption Abroad Agency**                                  510.235.5393
*International: children from Russia and Kazakhstan; waiting children photo listing; medical, financial and travel information.*
**http://www.adoptionabroad.com**
Richmond, CA

**Adoption Circle, Inc.**                                   818.360.7322
*Domestic infants; support through the adoption process; waiting family profiles; newsletter.*
**http://www.adoptioncircleinc.com**
Valley Village, CA

**Adorable Adoption**                                       415.305.6381
*International: children from Russia and Kazakhstan; waiting children photo listing; travel, medical and financial information.*
**http://www.adorableadoption.com**
Stockton, CA

**Angel Adoption, Inc.**                                     847.462.8874

*Domestic infant adoption; African American children program; works in conjunction with an Illinois licensed adoption agency; birth parents resources; counseling.*

**http://www.angeladoption.net**
Cary, IL

---

**Angels Adoption Services**                                 925.673.3035

*International: children from Russia, Ukraine and Kazakhstan; waiting children photo listing; financial information; non-profit.*

**http://www.angelsadoption.com**
Concord, CA

---

**Aurora International Adoption, Inc.**                       916.369.5228

*Waiting children photo listing; children from Ukraine; non-profit.*

**www.russianadoptions.org**
Sacramento, CA

---

**Babies R Blessings**                                       661.836.1475

*Domestic infants; birth mother counseling and crisis line; advertises in ten states.*

**http://www.babiesrblessings.com**
Bakersfield, CA

---

**Heart 2 Heart Connection**                                 800.618.1113

*Waiting family profiles; works with adopting couples and birth mothers throughout the country.*

**http://www.hearttoheartadoption.net**
OH

---

**Island Coast International Adoptions**                      941.574.4590

*International: children from Asia, Latin America and Eastern Europe; waiting children photo listing; adoptive family stories.*

**http://www.islandcoastinternationaladoptions.com/**
Cape Coral, FL

---

**Lee Slater Adoption Services**                             808.988.9214

*International adoptions, children from Eastern Europe; in-country services.*

**http://www.geocities.com/adoptwithlee**
Honolulu, HI

---

### Lifetime Adoption Services

530.271.1740

*Domestic; birth parent services; waiting family and birth mother listings; biracial adoptions; financial information; nationwide services; newsletter.*

**http://www.lifetimeadoption.com**
Grass Valley, CA

---

### Limiar

210.479.0300

*International: children from Brazil; profile of Brazil with sights, sounds and travel notes; newsletter; information in Portuguese; non-profit.*

**http://www.limiar.org**
San Antonio, TX

---

### Link

704.792.2229

*Connects Christian adoptive couples with birth parents; attorney referrals; non-profit.*

**http://www.linkadoption.com**
Concord, NC

---

### New Families, Inc.

305.254.8425

*International: children from Guatemala and Mexico; waiting children photo listing.*
Miami, FL

---

### Russian Adoption Facilitation Service (R.A.F.S.)

415.567.1232

*International adoption of infants, toddlers and older children from Russia, Ukraine, Bulgaria and Georgia; nationwide services.*

**http://www.adoption-international.com**
San Francisco, CA

---

### Unique Adoptions, Inc.

909.600.2575

*Domestic adoptions; birth mother and adoptive parents services; waiting families profiles.*

**http://www.uniqueadoptions.com**
Wildomar, CA

### Universal Family Services 415.388.3561
*International: children from Mexico, Russia and Armenia; newsletter.*
**http://www.adoptsearch.com**
Mill Valley, CA

### Ysabel Llerena International Adoptions 818.894.4628
*International, specializes in children from Guatemala; general information;*
*single parents; non-profit.*
**http://www.adoption1.com**
North Hills, CA

# Family Support Services

### Adopted Korean Connection 612.532.9913
*Korean support network; educational, cultural and social events; information;*
*newsletter; stories; articles.*
**http://www.akconnection.com**
Maple Grove, MN

### Adoption Forum, Inc. 215.238.1116
*Emotional support to the adoption triad; local support groups; forum; articles;*
*agencies; links; suggested reading; other resources; non-profit.*
**http://www.adoptionforum.org**
Emmaus, PA

### Adoption Information & Direction 715.345.1290
*Support, information and resources for the adoption triad.*
**http://www.uwsp.edu/psych/dh/aidinf.htm**
Stevens Point, WI

### Adoption Network Cleveland 216.881.7511
*Promoting truth and honesty in adoption practice, policy and law; resources,*
*support, forum, education and advocacy; non-profit.*
**http://www.adoptionnetwork.org**
Cleveland, OH

### Adoption Resource Network, Inc.     716.924.5295

*Birth mother support; local groups; adoption resources; workshops; newsletter; links; non-profit.*

**http://www.arni.org**
Pittsford, NY

### Adoption Support and Information Group (ASIG)

*Guidance and information to persons interested in adoption; local support meetings in Encino.*

**http://www.adoptlaw.com/supadopt.html**
Encino, CA

### Adoption Triad Outreach Chat Rooms     414.483.3533

*Support and resources for the adoption triad; legal information; newsletter.*
**http://www.adoptiontriad.org**

### Adoptive Families and Friends

*Local community support for the adoptive family; social events and workshops relating to the adoption process; newsletter.*

**http://www.members.aol.com/Dwasserba/info.html**
Knoxville, MD

### Adoptive Families Coalition     518.448.5295

*Adoption information and support; networking, social events, educational seminars; quarterly newsletter.*

**http://timesunion.memlink.com/default.aspx**
Glenmont, NY

### Adoptive Families Network, Inc.     410.553.0889

*Local support groups; social events; education and advocacy; newsletter.*
**http://www.erols.com/giconklin**
Columbia, MD

### Adoptive Families of Older Children, Inc.     718.380.7234

*Peer counseling meetings for parents, monthly; special needs resources; parenting information; cultural children's activities; social events.*
Flushing, NY

**Adoptive Families Today**                                847.382.0858

*Support group, local; annual conference; newsletter; resources; social activities; non-profit.*

**http://www.adoptivefamiliestoday.org**

Barrington, IL

**Adoptive Families Together, Inc.**                       617.929.3800

*Parent support meetings, local; post-adoptive information, education, and support for all people touched by adoption; newsletter; non-profit.*

**http://www.adoptivefamilies.org**

Boston, MA

**Adoptive Family Therapeutic & Educational Resource**     408.573.8222

*After-adoption assistance to families; support, therapeutic services, advocacy and education.*

**http://www.afteradoption.org**

San Jose, CA

**Adoptive Parents Committee, Inc.**                       212.304.8479

*Support groups, local in New York and New Jersey; advocacy for humanitarian improvements in the adoption and foster care system; non-profit.*

**http://www.adoptiveparents.org**

Bellmore, NY

**AdoptNet**                                               352.377.6455

*Local monthly support groups for the adoption triad; education and information.*

**http://www.geocities.com/Heartland/Ranch/2641**

Gainesville, FL

**Angels Support Network, Inc.**                           585.234.1864

*Local support group in New York and Rochester; for the adoption triad as well as siblings, friends and relatives.*

**http://www.nyadoption.org/angels2.htm**

North Chili, NY

**Asian Adult Adoptees of Washington**                     206.525.1409

*Asian/Pacific adoptee community activities; social events; teen mentorship; scholarship.*

**http://www.aaawashington.org**

Seattle, WA

### Association of Korean Adoptees, AKASF

*Korean adoptee support network; monthly meetings and social events in the San Francisco Bay area; newsletter; non-profit.*

**http://www.geocities.com/Tokyo/Garden/3947**
San Francisco, CA

### Casey Family Program                                   206.282.7300

*Services for children and youth with foster care as its core; adoption, guardianship, kinship care (being in extended family's care) and family reunification; locations in many states.*

**http://www.casey.org**
Seattle, WA

### Center for Adoption Support and Education, Inc.        703.533.7950

*Counseling, individual and family; parenting program; training for professionals; peer group counseling program for children; non-profit.*

**http://www.adoptionsupport.org**
Falls Church, VA

### Center for Family Connections                          617.547.0909

*Services to all touched by adoption, foster care, kinship and guardianship; training, education, consultation, advocacy and clinical treatment.*

**http://www.kinnect.org/index.html**
Cambridge, MA

### Christian Adopt

*Support, encouragement and information to Christians by Christians; e-mail list with 150 families who have adopted and want to share their experiences.*
**http://www.ilovejesus.com/missions/adopt**

### Concerned United Birthparents, Inc.                    800.822.2777

*Birth parents support but also for adoptees, adoptive parents and professionals; local support groups; links to related topics, articles and news media; forum.*

**http://www.cubirthparents.org**
Encinitas, CA

### Eastern European Adoption Coalition, Inc.
*Eastern Europe adoptive families support; agency listing; 19 different Internet mailing list groups; education; bookstore.*
**http://www.eeadopt.org**
Somerset, NJ

---

### Families Adopting in Response (FAIR)
**650.856.3513**
*Adoptive families support, education and advocacy; newsletter; non-profit.*
**http://www.fairfamilies.org**
Palo Alto, CA

---

### Families for Children from China
**503.295.6322**
*Chinese adoption support and education; waiting families support group; cultural resources; parenting resources; newsletter; non-profit.*
**http://www.fcc-oregon.org**
Portland, OR

---

### Families for Private Adoption
**202.722.0338**
*Advocacy for private adoption (non-agency); local support groups and education; legal and parenting resources.*
**http://www.ffpa.org**
Washington, D.C.

---

### Families for Russian and Ukrainian Adoptions
**703.560.6184**
*Former Soviet Union support network for adoptive families; information; chat room; newsletter; non-profit.*
**http://www.frua.org**

---

### Families with Children Adopted from Bulgaria
**425.823.8018**
*Bulgaria adoptive families support; stories and poems; events and resources; newsletter.*
**http://groups.yahoo.com/group/FaCAB1/files/FaCAB.htm**
Kirkland, WA

---

### Families with Children from China
**760.723.8005**
*China adoption community building; information; social and cultural events; language classes; education; newsletter.*
**http://fwcc.org/SanFrancisco/welcome.htm;**
Fallbrook, CA

### Friends of Korea

*Korean support group; proverbs and folktales; meeting birth family resources; cultural events; articles; family exchange program; non-profit.*

**http://209.151.86.53/?menu=links&page=start**

### Inter-National Adoption Alliance　　　615.890.3507

*Support and advocacy; provide resources to domestic and international adoptees and their families; adoption articles; forum.*

**http://www.i-a-a.org**
Murfreesboro, TN

### Jewel Among Jewels　　　317.849.5651

*Educational organization; seminars; online newsletter; adoption related work books; telephone counseling; local support groups in many states.*

**http://www.adoptionjewels.org**
Indianapolis, IN

### Korean American Adoptee Adoptive Family Network　　　916.933.1447

*Asian and Korean adoption support and resources; cultural programs; newsletter; links.*

**http://www.kaanet.com**
El Dorado Hills, CA

### Korean Focus for Adoptive Families

*Korean adoptive families support; education and information; presentations on Korean culture; social events; craft workshops for young children.*

**http://www.koreanfocus.org**
Alexandria, VA

### Latin America Parents Association (LAPA)　　　718.236.8689

*Latin American adoptive families support; cultural information and activities; forum; newsletter.*

**http://www.lapa.com**
Brooklyn, NY

### Open Door Society of Massachusetts, Inc.　　　508.429.4260

*Local support groups; education for the adoptive triad; newsletter; non profit.*

**http://www.odsma.org**
Holliston, MA

**Open Door Society of New Hampshire, Inc.**          603.627.6908

*Local support groups; lending library; social events; conferences; newsletter; non-profit.*

**http://www.odsnh.org**

Derry, NH

**Oregon Adoptive Rights Association**          503.235.3669

*Educates the public in adoption issues; aids in searching for lost family members; monthly meetings and support groups; lending library; non-profit.*

**http://www.oara.org**

Portland, OR

**Oregon Post Adoption Resource Center**          503.241.0799

*Referral, training and support for families adopting through the Department of Human Services (DHS) or any state's foster care system.*

**http://www.orparc.org**

Portland, OR

**Our Chinese Daughters Foundation, Inc.**          309.662.1090

*Chinese adoption resources and support groups; travel information; cultural events; publications; grants for support groups; scholarships.*

**http://www.ocdf.org**

Bloomington, IL

**Post Adoption Center for Education and Research**          925.935.6622

*Support, resources and education for the adoption triad.*

**http://www.pacer-adoption.org**

Oakland, CA

**Single Parent Adoption Network**

*Support for single adoptive parents and children of single adoptive parents; information and resources; links;*

*book list including multicultural books.*

**http://www.members.aol.com/onemomfor2**

**South Carolina Council on Adoptable Children**          803.783.2226

*Waiting children photo listing; education; support groups; resource links; lending library; non-profit.*

**http://www.sc-adopt.org**

Columbia, SC

**Southern Tier Adoptive Families**    607.797.3188

*Education, support and links; membership organization.*

**http://www.tier.net/staf**

Vestal, NY

---

**Stars of David International Inc.**    203.366.5438

*Jewish adoptive family support network; agency listing; fertility resources; email list; chapters in most states.*

**http://www.starsofdavid.org**

Northbrook, IL

---

**Taplink**    215.256.0669

*Support groups; link to resources in Pennsylvania; financial information; forum; newsletter.*

**http://www.taplink.org**

Harleysville, PA

---

# Infertility Resources

**Alison A. Sconyers**    209.579.1978

*Surrogacy, adoption and family law; links to in-depth articles about infertility.*

**http://www.surrogacy.com/lawyer/sconyers.html**

Modesto, CA

---

**American Infertility Association**    718.621.5083

*Infertility and adoption resources; articles and fact sheets; legal information; newsletter; forum and chat room.*

**http://www.americaninfertility.org/**

---

**Child of My Dreams**    703.715.9043

*Infertility and adoption information; links and resources; forum; newsletter.*

**http://www.childofmydreams.com**

Conceptual Options, LLC                              **858.577.0358**

*Center that offers surrogate parenting through gestational or traditional*
*surrogacy, egg donation and/or sperm donation; photo list of donors;*
*legal information.*

**http://www.conceptualoptions.com**
San Diego, CA

Family First Fertility

*Egg donor information and fertility resources including legal;*
*fertility agencies and clinics by state; forum and chat room.*

**http://www.familyfirstfertility.com**

Fertile Thoughts

*Chat room and forum; adoption, infertility, pregnancy, surrogacy*
*and parenting.*

**http://www.fertilethoughts.net**

Hannah's Prayer Ministries: Infertility Resources              **775.852.9202**

*Infertility information; links to resources and fact sheets; Christian links;*
*non-profit.*

**http://www.hannah.org/resources/infertility.htm**
Hanford, CA

Hannah's Prayer Ministries: Men Facing Infertility            **775.852.9202**

*Men's infertility issues.*

**http://www.hannah.org/resources/men.htm**
Hanford, CA

InterNational Council on Infertility Information              **703.379.9178**
Dissemination, Inc.

*Infertility fact sheets; forums including fertility over forty, miscarriage,*
*endometriosis; reproductive technologies; infertility specialists.*
**http://www.inciid.org/interinfertility.html**

### Internet Health Resources 925.284.9362

*Infertility resources and links; publications; over 320 books for consumers and professionals; male infertility.*

**http://www.ihr.com**
Lafayette, CA

### RESOLVE of Atlanta, Inc. 404.233.8443

*Infertility support groups; discussion group, both social and therapist-led; physician referral service; forum; magazine; links to chapters in other states.*

**http://www.resolveofgeorgia.org**
Atlanta, GA

### Resolve of Northern California, National Infertility Association 415.788.6772

*Infertility and surrogacy resources, including local support groups, workshops and referrals to professionals; bookstore; newsletter.*

**http://www.ihr.com/resolve/nchome.html**
San Francisco, CA

### Shared Journey

*Infertility, miscarriage, surrogacy, pregnancy after infertility, living child-free, and adoption; chat room and forum.*

**http://www.sharedjourney.com**

### Stepping Stones c/o Bethany Christian Services

*Christian support for infertility or pregnancy loss; bookstore; newsletter.*

**http://www.bethany.org/step**
Grand Rapids, MI

### Surrogate Mothers Online

*Articles; general information; infertility resources and support groups; related links; forum and chat room.*

**http://www.surromomsonline.com**

# Financial Support Services

### A Chance for a Child                                             645.895.6728
*Assistance for prospective parents in raising money to fund adoption; grants; waiting children photo listing; non-profit.*
**http://www.i-a-a.org/chanceforachild.htm**
Rockvale, TN

---

### A Child Waits Foundation                                        413.499.3992
*Loans with low interest to eligible families for help with adoption costs.*
**http://www.achildwaits.org**
Pittsfield, MA

---

### A Mother's Love
*Fundraising information packets to help defray adoption and infertility costs.*
**http://www.amotherslovefundraising.com**

---

### Adopt Share
*Christian ministry; assistance with adoption costs of special needs children.*
**http://www.geocities.com/janinemomof7/**
**LoansandGrants.html**

---

### Adoption Benefits Guide for Federal Employees
*Leave programs and benefits; tax benefits for adoption; state adoption subsidy programs.*
**http://www.opm.gov/wrkfam/html/adoption.htm**

---

### Adoption Financing Information
*Fundraising ideas; grants and loans; ways to save on adoption travel.*
**http://www.adoptionfinancinginformation.com**

---

### Adoption Services 4 You
*Loans, grants, and more resources for financing adoption.*
**http://www.adoptionservices4you.com**

---

### Adoption4You

*Organizations that offer grants and assistance with adoption; waiting children photo listing; adoption information and links.*

**http://www.praize.com/webmaster/adoption4you**

---

### Adoptions Worldwide, Inc.                                337.626.9009

*Tax credits; grants; loans; nonrecurring adoption programs for adoptive families, including military.*

**http://www.adoptionsworldwide.com/FinancialResources.asp**
Sulphur, LA

---

### Bright Futures Adoption Assistance Foundation

*Grant programs; adoption awareness, education and resources; non-profit.*

**http://www.homestead.com/brightfutures**

---

### Brittany's Hope Foundation                                717.367.9614

*Grant programs, fundraising, loans, tax and employer benefits; non-profit.*

**http://www.brittanyshope.org/financial.html**
Elizabethtown, PA

---

### Casey Family Programs National Center for Resource        202.467.4441
### Family Support (CNC)

*Resources for funding adoption; financial information for potential foster care parents.*

**http://www.casey.org/cnc/support_retention/nav_financial_support.htm**
Washington, D.C.

---

### Childadopt.com

*Extensive financial information; international adoption resources; children from Eastern Europe; travel tips.*

---

### Dave Thomas Foundation for Adoption                        800.275.3832

*Grants; advocates for finding homes for America's waiting children; adoption resource center; non-profit.*

**http://www.davethomasfoundationforadoption.org**
Dublin, OH

---

**Dillon Adoption Financing**                    918.749.4600
*Lifestyle adjustments to help finance the adoption; listing of companies that offer employer benefits for adoptions; tax credits, loans and grants.*
**http://www.dillonadopt.com/Adoption%20Financing.htm**
Tulsa, OK

---

**Federal Citizen Information Center**
*Militarily subsidized adoption information.*
**http://www.pueblo.gsa.gov/cic_text/children/adoption/**
**helpf.html**

---

**For the Children Adoption Ministry**            414.607.1757
*Help to find agencies and resources needed to carry out a successful adoption; numerous resources to help defray adoption costs.*
**http://www.ftchildren.org**
Milwaukee, WI

---

**God's Grace Adoption Ministry**                 209.572.4539
*Financial aid to Christian adoptive families; grants and interest-free loans; non-profit.*
**http://www.ggam.org/main.html**
Modesto, CA

---

**Hebrew Free Loan Association**                  415.546.9902
*Loans, interest-free, for Jewish adults who wish to adopt children domestically or internationally.*
**http://www.hflasf.org/adopt-loans.html**
San Francisco, CA

---

**Internal Revenue Service**                      800.829.3676
*Tax credit; adoption tax identification number information. (Enter the term adoption in the search engine); links to offices nationwide.*
**http://www.irs.ustreas.gov**

---

**International Adoption Center**
*Adoption grants; tips on how to cut adoption expenses.*
**http://www.adoptlaw.org/tiac_htm/7specpro.htm**

**JSW Adoption Foundation**                                      262.268.1386
*Grants to adoptive parents; non-profit.*
**http://www.jsw-adoption.org**
Port Washington, WI

**Kingdom Kids Adoption Ministries**                            509.465.3520
*Christ-centered adoption conferences; assistance for families to raise*
*finances for adoption; local support groups.*
**http://www.kkadoption.com**
Spokane, WA

**Lifetime Adoption Foundation**                                530.271.1756
*Educational scholarships for birth mothers; adoption assistance;*
*referrals and counseling; non-profit.*
**http://www.lifetimefoundation.org**

**NACAC's Adoption Subsidy Resource Center**
*Subsidy fact sheets; definitions and state adoption profiles.*
**http://www.nacac.org/adoptionsubsidy.html**
St. Paul, MN

**National Adoption Foundation**                                203.791.9811
*Financial assistance and services before, during and after the adoption; to*
*families adopting an infant, a child from abroad or a child from foster care.*
**http://www.nafadopt.org/MissionStmnt.htm**
Danbury, CT

**NEFE, National Endowment for Financial Education**
*Affordable adoption information and resources.*
**http://www.nefe.org/adoption**

**Ours by Grace**                                               810.844.0278
*Ministry that raises funds and awareness for the Adoption Community;*
*fundraising events to raise money to distribute as grants to adoptive families*
*needing financial assistance; non-profit.*
**http://www.oursbygrace.com**
Brighton, MI

### Resources to Help Fund Adoption

*Affordable international adoption; in-depth financial information.*
**http://www.angelfire.com/journal/adoptionhelp/adopthelp.html**

---

### United Way International                          703.519.0092

*Assistance for travel with children adopted with illness needing immediate medical attention; applications selectively considered and doctor's statement needed.*
**http://www.uwint.org/services/delta.html**
Alexandria, VA

---

### World Association for Children and Parents (WACAP)    206.575.4550

*Funds and noninterest loans when adopting through the agency; assistance through the government, adoption foundations and bank loans.*
**http://www.wacap.org/FinancialAssistance.asp**
Seattle, WA

---

# General Information & Services

### Adopt Vietnam

*Complete guide to Vietnam adoption; over 200 articles on culture, Vietnam adoption, adoption travel and adoptive parenting.*
**http://www.adoptvietnam.org**

---

### Adopting from Korea

*Korean adoption resources; agency by state; home study information; chat and forum; travel information.*
**http://www.adoptkorea.com**

---

### Adopting.com

*Resources on many aspects of adoption; waiting children photo listing; professional and agency listings; special needs; mailing lists, and forums.*
**http://www.adopting.com**

---

### Adoption Choice Online Service        800.656.6250

*Advertising service, online, for adoptive families; assists in writing a
Dear Birth Mother letter; waiting families photo listing; bookstore.*
**http://www.adoptionchoice.com**
Oceanside, CA

### Adoption Guide

*Advocacy for adoptive families and consumer protection.*
**http://www.theadoptionguide.com**

### Adoption Love Stories

*Adoption stories; share your adoption story and read others; submissions
being accepted for upcoming book.*
**http://www.adoptionlovestories.com**

### Adoption Navigators, LLC.        301.738.1174

*Advocacy service; information about choosing an agency; advantages and
disadvantages of different types of adoption.*
**http://www.adoptionnavigators.com/types.htm**
Rockville, MD

### Adoption Option Committee, Inc.        952.944.0866

*Promotion of adoption as a primary possibility for unplanned pregnancy; birth
mother and adoptive families information; state agency listing; non-profit.*
**http://www.aoci.org**
Minneapolis, MN

### Adoption Professionals

*Professionals; listings of agencies, attorneys, facilitators and social workers
nationwide and by specialty.*
**http://www.adoptionprofessionals.com**

### Adoption Questions

*Commonly asked questions and answers covering every aspect of adoption;
books and newsletter.*
**http://www.adoptionquestions.com**

### Adoption Web Ring

*Educational information, over 400 pages, for the adoption triad.*
**http://www.plumsite.com/adoptionring**

## Adoption.About.com
*Articles, newsletter, information and resources on many aspects of adoption and foster care; chat room and forum.*
**http://www.adoption.about.com**

## Adoption: A Gathering
*Stories and talk about adoption; scrapbook; resources.*
**http://www.pbs.org/weblab/gathering**

## Adoption100.com
*Top 100 professional adoption websites; resources and information; waiting families photo listing.*
**http://www.adoption100.com**

## Africanamericanadoptionsonline.com                    530.271.1740
*African American information; black parenting literature to order; Q & A about the adoption process.*
**http://www.africanamericanadoptionsonline.com**

## All As One (AAO)                                       209.538.8540
*Child welfare organization; school, medical clinic and orphanage in Sierra Leone, West Africa; network with adoption agencies; non-profit.*
**http://www.all-as-one.org**
Ceres, CA

## Alla Adoption                                          209.473.3674
*Waiting children photo listing; children from Kazakhstan and Russia; cultural and travel resources; financial information.*
**http://www.allaadoption.com**
Stockton, CA

## Association of Administrators of the Compact on          202.682.0100
## Adoption & Medical Assistance, AAICAMA
*Technical and legal assistance, training, and information to adoption professionals on issues related to interstate and intrastate adoptions.*
**http://aaicama.aphsa.org**
Washington, D.C.

**Bonding through Touch: Infant Massage for Adoptive Families**    520.878.9222

*Video; infant massage to enhance the bonding process for adoptive families; order online.*

**http://www.thethreehearts.com**
Tucson, AZ

---

**Child Welfare League of America**    202.638.2952

*Protect America's children and strengthen families; adoption fact sheet; tax credits; resources links; foster care and related links.*

**http://www.cwla.org**
Washington, D.C.

---

**China Specific Adoption Information**

*Chinese adoption resources; downloadable visa application; travel info; learn the language; news from China; stories; items to buy for children.*

**http://www.asststork.com/pages/china.html**

---

**Evan B. Donaldson Adoption Institute**    212.269.5080

*Public policy; professional education; research resources; publications; scientific facts about adoption and foster care.*

**http://www.adoptioninstitute.org**
New York, NY

---

**God's Littlest Angels, Inc.**    719.574.7134

*Ministry for premature and malnourished infants in Tahiti; adoption services; outreach ministries for homeless mothers with infants.*

**http://www.gla-missions.org**
West Palm Beach, FL

---

**Heart of God Ministries**    847.870.0977

*Christian; adoption services in Haiti; support and resources; non-profit.*

**http://www.hgm.org/base_frame.htm**
Arlington Heights, IL

**Heaven Sent Adopt**    269.778.9939

*African American and biracial children specialist; referral and networking service; waiting families profiles; chat room.*

**http://www.heavensentadopt.com**
Fulton, MI

---

**I CHILD, India Adoption Resources**

*Indian adoption resources; Internet based, information about adopting from India; waiting children photo listing; agency listing; India related links.*

**http://www.ichild.org**

---

**Independent Ukraine Adoption**

*Ukraine adoption, independent; the adoption process; travel tips; financial information.*

**http://www.adoptukraine.com**

---

**Institute for Adoption Information**

*Educational adoption guide; resources, information and links; non-profit.*

**http://www.adoptioninformationinstitute.org/links.html**
Bennington, VT

---

**International Adoption Consortium, IAC**    540.462.6159

*Consortium of non-profit international adoption professionals promoting the ethical standards of the Hague Convention.*

**http://www.iacgroup.org**
Lexington, VA

---

**International Concerns for Children, Inc.**    303.494.8333

*International adoption resources; monthly updated information on reputable inter-country adoption agencies; newsletter; non-profit.*

**http://www.iccadopt.org**
Boulder, CO

---

**Joint Council on International Children's Services**    703.535.8045

*Advocate for children in need of permanent families; listing of member agencies; overview of agency practice standards; non-profit.*

**http://www.jcics.org**
Alexandria, VA

### Karen's Adoption Links

*Site with multiple links; international, children from Russia, Kazakhstan, Ukraine, & Eastern Europe; funding; Yahoo support groups listed by state.*

**http://www.karensadoptionlinks.com**

### Let's Talk Adoption

*Internet talk radio show that addresses all aspects of adoption; weekly guests; open adoption advocacy; articles and books.*

**http://www.letstalkadoption.com**

### Mardie Caldwell 530.265.4915

*Mardie Caldwell is an adoption professional, author, public speaker and talk show host; articles, CDs, books and newsletter.*

**http://mardiecaldwell.com**
Nevada City, CA

### National Adoption Information Clearinghouse 703.352.3488

*Resource, comprehensive, on all aspects of adoption; directory, professionals; publications; laws; statistics; conferences.*

**http://naic.acf.hhs.gov**
Washington, D.C.

### National Adoption Information Clearinghouse/Military

*Information for the adopting military family.*

**http://www.naic.acf.hhs.gov/parents/special.cfm**

### National Council For Adoption 703.299.6633

*Help children find permanent homes through adoption; in-depth adoption information; agency and attorney listing; literature; non-profit.*

**http://www.ncfa-usa.org**
Alexandria, VA

### North Carolina Center for Adoption Education

*Workshops, conferences, education and counseling for the adoption triad, professionals, legislators and the general public.*

**http://adoptioneducationcenter.homestead.com/indexA.html**
Chapel Hill, NC

### Paraguayan Adoption Resources

*Paraguayan information for families; Internet resources including U.S. Government and news; articles; e-mail lists; shopping online for cultural items.*

**http://www.pyadopt.org**

### Precious in HIS Sight                              608.796.1746

*Waiting children photo listing; links to adoption agencies, facilitators and attorneys; information, resources and publications.*

**http://www.precious.org**

La Crosse, WI

### Precious Kids                                        503.324.7323

*Registry; Christian; advertising for adoptive families to find birth mothers; e-mail lists; home schooling resources.*

**http://www.preciouskids.org**

Banks, OR

### Rainbow Kids

*Publication, online; international adoption information and resource links; waiting children photo listing; adoption community with e-mail lists.*

**http://www.rainbowkids.com**

### Statewide Adoption Network                    717.793.2512

*Network of private and public agencies; consultation, training, referrals, conferences and support services.*

**http://www.diakon-swan.org**

Harrisburg, PA

### United States Office of Personnel Management

*Benefits guide for federal employees.*

**http://www.opm.gov/wrkfam/html/adoption.htm**

### USAadoption.com

*Resources for military families seeking to adopt; articles, books and newsletter.*

**http://www.usaadoption.com**

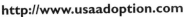

### VitalChek Network, Inc.                                    800.669.8309
*Vital records; birth, death, marriage, divorce; order online by state.*
**http://www.vitalchek.com**

### Welcome Garden
*International resources; links to extensive information on the adoption process; financial information; agency listing.*
**http://www.welcomegarden.com**

### World Clock-Time Zones
*Local times around the world.*
**http://www.timeanddate.com/worldclock**

# Internet Services

### 2adopt
*Internet group; create your own of family and friends to visit and share photographs and news.*
**http://www.groups.yahoo.com/group/2adopt**

### 50 Megs.com
*Web hosting, free e-mail and other web services.*
**http://www.50megs.com**

### America Online, Inc.
*Home page for personalized profiles, free; over 100 templates to choose from.*
**http://hometown.aol.com**

### Bigfoot
*E-mail, free; e-mail and web tools; mobile messaging; domain registration.*
**http://www.bigfoot.com**

**BuyDomains.com**                                              301.439.2900
    *Domain names for purchase.*
    **http://www.thomtech.com/~ati/caf.htm**
    Silver Spring, MD

---

**Christ Art**
    *Christian clipart; free.*
    **http://www.christart.com**

---

**ClipArt.com**
    *Clipart images; more than 2.5 million animations, photos, fonts, and sounds;*
    *add to your personal website.*
    **http://www.clipart.com**

---

**CrossDaily.com**
    *Christian graphics and web hosting.*
    **http://graphics.crossdaily.com**

---

**Direct NIC**
    *Domain registration and hosting; search engine.*
    **http://www.directnic.com**

---

**Dreamwater**
    *Website provider, free; 50 MB of web space.*
    **http://www.dreamwater.com**

---

**e Fuse**
    *Fonts and graphics, free.*
    **http://www.efuse.com**

---

**Essentials of Web Development**
    *Website online course; learn how to create, deploy and maintain a website.*
    **http://www.simpcoms.org/ewd**

---

### Eudora WebMail
*E-mail provider, free.*
**http://www.eudoramail.com**

---

### Excite
*Home page, personalized; free web-based e-mail; chat room.*
**http://email.excite.com**

---

### Free E-mail Providers Guide
*E-mail providers guide; free.*
**http://www.fepg.net**

---

### Freeservers
*Website hosting, free, with 12 MB web space.*
**http://www.freeservers.com**

---

### Free Yellow
*Website hosting, free, with 50 MB of space.*
**http://www.freeyellow.com**

---

### Funtigo
*Create your own photo album; use text and caption capabilities; choose from a full set of background colors; multipictures on each page, and more; free.*
**http://www.funtigo.com**

---

### Homestead Personal
*Website building and hosting.*
**http://www.homestead.com**

---

### Hotmail.com
*E-mail service, free, provided by Microsoft.*
**http://www.hotmail.com**

---

### HTML Made Really Easy
*HTML online training; learn through examples the practical things you need to know to make your own Web pages.*
**http://www.jmarshall.com/easy/html**

---

### Irene's Corner

*Graphics with country flavor for website; download stationery, desktop wallpaper and personal project.*

**http://www.irenescorner.com**

### Jasc Software

*Software and resources for designing websites; order and download online.*

**http://www.jasc.com**

### Keepsake Family Moments                                    908.713.9520

*Videotape materials transfer onto DVD discs; permanent quality, easy access, convenient storage.*

**http://www.keepsakefamilymoments.com**

Clinton, NJ

### Kodak.com

*Kodak prints from your digital camera; instantly share your pictures online.*

**http://www.kodak.com**

### Lifetime Computer Services                                 715.823.5918

*Web design and other computer related services.*

**http://www.bestontheweb.com/LifetimeWebDesign**

Clintonville, WI

### Max Pages Websites

*Website hosting and design services.*

**http://www.maxpages.com**

### My Own E-mail

*Free Web based e-mail; over 200 personalized domain names.*

**http://www.myownemail.com**

### NetColony

*Free Web space; easy homepage creator; fast servers.*

**http://www.netcolony.com**

## Original Country Clipart

*Web graphics and clipart for personal and business web pages, scrapbooks, crafts, desktop publishing and more.*

**http://www.countryclipart.com**

## Picture Trail

*Photo albums, online; make e-cards.*

**http://www.picturetrail.com**

## Shutterfly

*Pictures online with family and friends; order hard-copy prints.*

**http://www.shutterfly.com**

## Sony's Image Station

*Digital images; save to Image Station for easy retrieval, editing, and prints; improve picture taking skills.*

**http://www.imagestation.com**

## TLS Rose's Garden of Web Creation

*Web page creation; online resources.*

**http://www.members.tripod.com/~tlcrose/web.html**

## Top20 Free

*Clipart, free; links to graphics, fonts, samples, fun stuff, software and much more.*

**http://www.top20free.com**

## Top Ten Mistakes in Web Design

*Web design; top 10 mistakes.*

**http://www.useit.com/alertbox/9605.html**

## Web Templates—Top 10 Tips

*Website creation*

**http://www.webtemplates.com/design.html**

## Yahoo! GeoCities

*Website hosting and Internet services.*

**http://geocities.yahoo.com/home**

### Yahoo! Mail
*E-mail service; free.*
**http://mail.yahoo.com**

### ZDNet SiteBuilder
*Website hosting and resources to help build a good website.*
**http://cma.zdnet.com/texis/sitebuilder**

# Legal Resources

### Adoption & Fostering Resource Center
*Statutes and laws in many states; links.*
**http://hometown.aol.com/afresources/frc/adoptionlaw.html**

### Adoption Information, Laws and Reforms
*State codes and international adoption laws; search engines and legal links.*
**http://www.webcom.com/kmc**

### Adoption Solutions
*Birth and adoptive parents resources; registry; legal information and laws;*
*attorney and agency locator by state;*
*waiting children photo listing; forum.*
**http://www.adoptionsolutions.com/general/info_home.htm**

### AdoptionLawyer.com
*Search engine; everything related to adoption law; browse the major search*
*engines to locate legal resources and attorneys.*
**http://www.adoptionlawyer.com**

### American Adoption Law
*Attorney locator; law and state-by-state resources including Canada;*
*downloadable legal books for sale.*
**http://www.americanadoptionlaw.com**

### California Court Self-Help Center

*Legal information; legal terms glossary; ask a Law Librarian in your county; guide to filling out online forms.*

**http://www.courtinfo.ca.gov/selfhelp**

### FindLaw, West Legal Directory

*Lawyer locator by state and city.*

**http://directory.findlaw.com**

### Immigration and Naturalization Service                    800.375.5283

*Immigration services, laws and news.*

**http://www.ins.usdoj.gov**

### Lectric Law Library Lawcopedia

*Family and adoption; legal aspects.*

**http://www.lectlaw.com/tfam.html**

### LII: Legal Information Institute

*Laws of the 50 states, District of Columbia and Puerto Rico; links.*

**http://www.law.cornell.edu/topics/Table_Adoption.htm**

### MegaLaw.com

*Federal and state adoption law statues and regulations; adoption law websites; organizations and resources; listing of agencies.*

**http://www.megalaw.com/top/adoption.php**

### NAIC Adoption Laws

*Federal laws and other adoption legislation.*

**http://naic.acf.hhs.gov/laws/index.cfm**

### Nolo Law for All

*Encyclopedia and dictionary on legal and adoption issues; frequently asked questions about adoption court procedures and legal proceedings.*

**http://www.nolo.com/encyclopedia/articles/kid/pc14.html**

### State Adoption Disclosure Laws

*Disclosure laws by state.*

**http://www.bastards.org/activism/access.htm**

### U.S. Adoption Laws by State
*State adoption statutes, citations and contacts.*
**http://www.abcadoptions.com/uslaw.htm**

### Women Lawyers Directory on the Net
*Women lawyer directory by state; tips on choosing a lawyer.*
**http://www.womenlawyers.com**

## Alabama

**334.269.1515**

### Alabama State Bar
*Directory of members; links and publications; lawyer referral service.*
**http://www.alabar.org**
Montgomery, AL

## Alaska

**907.264.6333**

### Alaska Legal Resource Center
*Law resource center; statutes, codes and constitution.*
**http://www.touchngo.com/lglcntr**
Anchorage, AK

## Arizona

### Arizona State Legislature
*Revised statutes and legal information.*
**http://www.azleg.state.az.us/ars/8/title8.htm**

**602.252.4804**

### State Bar of Arizona
*Lawyer locator and legal information.*
**http://www.azbar.org**
Phoenix, AZ

## Arkansas

**Arkansas Bar Association**                                    501.375.4606
*Lawyer locator and legal information.*
**http://www.arkbar.com**
Little Rock, AR

## California

**FreeAdvice.com**                                             415.331.1212
*Advice, free site, attorney locator.*
**http://www.law.freeadvice.com**
Mill Valley, CA

**State Bar of California**                                    415.538.2000
*Legal information and attorney referral service.*
**http://www.calbar.ca.gov**
San Francisco, CA

## Colorado

**Colorado Bar Association**                                   303.860.1115
*Attorney locator and legal information.*
**http://www.cobar.org**
Denver, CO

## District of Columbia

**American Adoption Congress**                                 202.483.3399
*Reform information; education, advocacy and support; international conferences
and workshops; non-profit.*
**http://www.americanadoptioncongress.org**
Washington, D.C.

ABA Center on Children and the Law                   202.662.1000
*Law and court-related topics affecting children; professional training and*
*education; publications and Internet resources; technical assistance.*
**http://www.abanet.org/child**
Washington, D.C.

Department of State Office of Children's Issues      202.736.7000
*International adoption and other legal resources related to child issues.*
**http://www.travel.state.gov/children's_issues.html**
Washington, D.C.

District of Columbia Bar Association                 202.737.4700
*Resources and attorney locator.*
**http://www.dcbar.org**
Washington, D.C.

Office of Children's Issues                          202.312.9700
*International adoption law.*
**http://www.travel.state.gov/int'ladoption.html**
Washington, D.C.

U.S. Department of State                             202.647.4000
*International adoption information and news.*
**http://www.state.gov**
Washington, D.C.

U.S. Department on Homeland Security
*Naturalization and intercountry adoptions; forms and applications.*
**http://www.dhs.gov/dhspublic/display?theme=23**
Washington, D.C.

## Delaware

Delaware State Bar Association                       302.658.5279
*State codes and attorney referral service.*
**http://www.dsba.org**
Wilmington, DE

## Florida

The Florida Bar                                                    850.561.5600
  *Information and attorney referral service.*
  **http://www.flabar.org**
  Tallahassee, FL

## Georgia

State Bar of Georgia                                               404.527.8700
  *Resources with alphabetical links.*
  **http://www.gabar.org**
  Atlanta, GA

## Hawaii

Hawaii State Bar Association                                       808.537.1868
  *Resources and lawyer locator; non-profit.*
  **http://www.hsba.org**
  Honolulu, HI

## Idaho

Idaho State Bar and Idaho Law Foundation, Inc.                     208.334.4500
  *Resources and directory of attorneys.*
  **http://www.state.id.us/isb**
  Boise, ID

## Illinois

American Bar Association Network                                   312.988.5522
  *Professional association with 400,000 members; law school accreditation,
  continuing legal education, assistance to lawyers and judges.*
  **http://www.abanet.org**
  Chicago, IL

Illinois State Bar Association 217.525.1760

*Legal resources.*

**http://www.illinoisbar.org**

Springfield, IL

## Indiana

Indiana State Bar Association 317.639.5465

*Legal information and links to resources.*

**http://www.inbar.org**

Indianapolis, IN

## Iowa

Iowa State Bar Association 515.243.3179

*Resources and attorney referral service.*

**http://www.iowabar.org**

Des Moines, IA

## Kansas

Kansas Bar Association 785.234.5696

*Resources and attorney referral service.*

**http://www.ksbar.org**

Topeka, KS

## Kentucky

Kentucky Bar Association 502.564.3795

*Resources and attorney referral service.*

**http://www.nkybar.com/**

Frankfort, KY

## Louisiana

Louisiana State Bar Association                    504.566.1600
*Legal services, news and attorney locator.*
**http://www.lsba.org**
New Orleans, LA

## Maine

Maine State Bar Association                    207.622.7523
*Legal information; news and events; lawyer referral service.*
**http://www.mainebar.org**
Augusta, ME

## Maryland

Maryland State Bar Association                    410.685.7878
*Legal information links and resources for finding attorneys.*
**http://www.msba.org**
Baltimore, MD

## Massachusetts

Massachusetts Bar Association                    617.338.0500
*Legal information and attorney referral service.*
**http://www.massbar.org**
Boston, MA

## Michigan

State Bar of Michigan                    517.346.6300
*Information and attorney referral service.*
**http://www.michbar.org**
Lansing, MI

## Minnesota

Minnesota State Bar Association                612.333.1183
> *Information and attorney referral service.*
> **http://www.mnbar.org**
> Minneapolis, MN

## Mississippi

Mississippi State Bar                          601.948.4471
> *Resources and attorney referral service.*
> **http://www.msbar.org**
> Jackson, MS

## Missouri

The Missouri Bar                               573.635.4128
> *Information and attorney locator service.*
> **http://www.mobar.org**
> Jefferson City, MS

## Montana

State Bar of Montana                           406.442.7660
> *Information and attorney locator service.*
> **http://www.montanabar.org**
> Helena, MT

## Nebraska

Nebraska State Bar Association                  402.475.7091
> *Resources and attorney referral service.*
> **http://www.nebar.com**
> Lincoln, NE

## Nevada

State Bar of Nevada Las Vegas Office       702.382.2200
*Information and attorney referral service.*
**http://www.nvbar.org**
Las Vegas, NV

## New Hampshire

New Hampshire Bar Association       603.224.6942
*News and attorney referral service.*
**http://www.nhbar.org**
Concord, NH

## New Jersey

New Jersey State Bar Association       732.249.5000
*Information and attorney referral service.*
**http://www.njsba.com**
New Brunswick, NJ

## New Mexico

State Bar of New Mexico       505.797.6000
*Information and an attorney referral service.*
**http://www.nmbar.org**
Albuquerque, NM

## New York

New York State Bar Association       518.463.3200
*Information and attorney referral service.*
**http://www.nysba.org**
Albany, NY

## North Carolina
. . . . . . . . . . . . . . . . . . . . . . . . . . . . . . . . . . . . . . . . . . . . . . . . . . . . . . . . . . . . . . . . . . . .

North Carolina State Bar                                            919.677.0561
*Information and attorney referral service.*
**http://www.ncbar.org**
Cary, NC

## North Dakota
. . . . . . . . . . . . . . . . . . . . . . . . . . . . . . . . . . . . . . . . . . . . . . . . . . . . . . . . . . . . . . . . . . . .

State Bar Association of North Dakota                               701.255.1404
*Information and attorney referral service.*
**http://www.sband.org**
Bismarck, ND

## Ohio
. . . . . . . . . . . . . . . . . . . . . . . . . . . . . . . . . . . . . . . . . . . . . . . . . . . . . . . . . . . . . . . . . . . .

Adoption Policy Resource Center                                    614.299.0177
*Adoption policy; information and guide.*
**http://www.fpsol.com/adoption/advocates.html**
Columbus, OH

Ohio State Bar Association                                         800.282.6556
*Information and attorney referral service.*
**http://www.ohiobar.org**
Columbus, OH

## Oklahoma
. . . . . . . . . . . . . . . . . . . . . . . . . . . . . . . . . . . . . . . . . . . . . . . . . . . . . . . . . . . . . . . . . . . .

Oklahoma Bar Association                                           405.416.7000
*Legal information and attorney referral service.*
**http://www.okbar.org**
Oklahoma City, OK

## Oregon

Oregon State Bar                                              503.620.0222
*Information and attorney referral service.*
**http://www.osbar.org**
Lake Oswego, OR

## Pennsylvania

Pennsylvania Bar Association                                 717.238.6715
*Information and attorney referral service.*
**http://www.pa-bar.org**
Harrisburg, PA

## Rhode Island

Rhode Island Bar Association                                 401.421.5740
*Information, news and attorney referral service.*
**http://www.ribar.com**
Providence, RI

## South Carolina

South Carolina Bar                                           803.799.6653
*Information and attorney referral service.*
**http://www.scbar.org**
Columbia, SC

## South Dakota

State Bar of South Dakota                                    605.224.7554
*Information and attorney referral service.*
**http://www.sdbar.org**
Pierre, SD

## Tennessee

Tennessee Bar Association      615.383.7421
*Information and attorney referral service.*
**http://www.tba.org**
Nashville, TN

## Texas

State Bar of Texas      512.463.1463
*Information and attorney referral service.*
**http://www.texasbar.com**
Austin, TX

Texas Coalition for Adoption Reform & Education
*Grassroots organization for concerns about adoption issues; access to original birth records; works for improved integrity in adoption law.*
**http://www.txcare.org**
Richardson, TX

## Utah

Utah State Bar      801.531.9077
*Information and attorney referral service.*
**http://www.utahbar.org**
Salt Lake City, UT

## Vermont

Vermont Bar Association      802.223.2020
*Information and lawyer referral service.*
**http://www.vtbar.org**
Montpelier, VT

## Virginia

Christian Legal Society                                        703.642.1070
> *Nondenominational membership organization of legal professionals;*
> *legal resources and referral services.*
> **http://www.clsnet.org**
> Annandale, VA

Virginia State Bar                                            804.775.0500
> *Information and lawyer referral service.*
> **http://www.vsb.org**
> Richmond, VA

## Washington State

Washington State Bar Association                              206.443.9722
> *Lawyer directory and legal information.*
> **http://www.wsba.org**
> Seattle, WA

## West Virginia

West Virginia State Bar                                       304.558.2456
> *Information and attorney locator.*
> **http://www.wvbar.org**
> Charleston, WV

## Wisconsin

State Bar of Wisconsin                                        608.257.3838
> *Information and attorney referral service.*
> **http://www.wisbar.org**
> Madison, WI

## Wyoming

Wyoming State Bar                                307.632.9061
  *Legal information and attorney referral service.*
  **http://www.wyomingbar.org**
  Cheyenne, WY

# Maternity Homes

Harborhouse.org
  *Maternity homes listing; nationwide.*
  **http://www.harborhouse.org/links/maternityhomes.htm**

## Alabama

Alabama Baptist Children's Homes                205.982.1112
  *Housing; crisis pregnancy counseling; adoption information; forum.*
  **http://www.abchome.org/maternity**
  Birmingham, AL

## Arizona

Jesus Cares Ministries                          480.831.1737
  *Christian; housing; live-in; life skill programs for young women that may extend
  from two weeks to three years after the birth of their child.*
  **http://www.jesuscaresministries.org**
  Chandler, AZ

## California

### His Nesting Place Maternity Home — 562.422.2137
*Christian; housing; crisis pregnancy center; Hispanic resources; non-profit.*
**http://www.hisnestingplace.com**
Long Beach, CA

### Mary's Shelter — 714.730.0930
*Maternity home for pregnant minors; teen pregnancy statistics.*
**http://www.teenshelter.org**
Santa Ana, CA

### Villa Majella Maternity Home — 805.683.2838
*Housing; childbirth resources; birth mother support group; counseling.*
**http://www.hometown.aol.com/vmajellace**
Santa Barbara, CA

## Colorado

### Mary's Choice — 303.763.3089
*Birth mother resources; maternity home; newsletter.*
**http://www.tmbf.org/maryschoice**
Bailey, CO

### Shannon's Hope Maternity Home — 303.286.1119
*Christian maternity home; birth mother mentoring; newsletter.*
**http://www.shannonshope.org**
Wheat Ridge, CO

## Florida

### Arbor House — 352.371.2229
*Housing; emergency shelter; family support and counseling; educational resources to pregnant teens and women in crisis.*
**http://www.afn.org/~momhome**
Gainesville, FL

Divine Mercy House    904.268.5422

*Christian; housing; pregnancy counseling.*

**http://stjossphsjax.org/dmhouse/**

Jacksonville, FL

Lifeline Family Center    941.542.4457

*Housing during crisis pregnancy; educational and job training; counseling; parenting classes, and spiritual direction.*

**http://www.lifelinefamilycenter.org**

Cape Coral, FL

## Georgia

The Living Vine Christian Maternity Home    912.352.9998

*Christian ministry; residency to women in crisis.*

**http://www.thelivingvine.faithweb.com**

Savannah, GA

## Iowa

Ruth Harbor    515.279.4661

*Christian home for young birth mothers; adoption counseling; parenting classes.*

**http://www.rutharbor.org**

Des Moines, IA

## Kansas

Bethlehem House

*Housing; pregnancy counseling; education; parenting; birth preparation classes; life skills; forum.*

**http://www.larrydean.com/Bethlehem**

El Dorado, KS

**Mary Elizabeth House**                                    785.625.6800

*Housing; counseling; life skill training programs including birth and parenting.*

**http://www.maryelizabeth.net**

Hays, KS

## Louisiana

**Sellers Maternity Home**                                 318.574.0267

*Housing for pregnant young women while they continue their education.*

**http://www.lbch.org/sellers**

Tallulah, LA

## Maine

**Friendship Homes**                                       207.767.7403

*Christian; housing for pregnant women, women with children in need, and men in need.*

**http://www.friendshiphomes.org**

South Portland, ME

## Massachusetts

**My Father's House**                                      978.251.8191

*Housing, counseling and support services to young women in pregnancy crisis; newsletter, non-profit.*

**http://www.lifesaverministries.org**

North Chelmsford, MA

## Maryland

St. Ann's Infant and Maternity Home                301.559.5500

*Residential emergency placement care to abused or neglected infants, children, pregnant and parenting adolescents.*

**http://www.saint-anns.com**

Hyattsville, MD

## Michigan

Father Pat Jackson House                734.761.1440

*Housing; shelter; educational assistance, independent living skills training; parenting support; non-profit.*

**http://www.comnet.org/local/orgs/fpj**

Ann Arbor, MI

Omega Maternity Home                616.559.0347

*Christian; housing for women experiencing unexpected pregnancies; free counseling; emotional support.*

**http://www.alphawomenscenter.org/OmegaHome.htm**

Grand Rapids, MI

## Minnesota

New Beginnings Maternity Home                320.255.1252

*Housing for pregnant women and their babies while fostering self-esteem, educational growth and skills of living.*

**http://www.newbeginningsmn.org**

St. Cloud, MN

## Missouri

### Bright Futures

*Housing for single adult women who choose adoption for their unborn child; counseling; free legal services; support groups.*

**http://www.maternityhomes.org**
St. Charles, MO

### Highlands Child Placement Services          816.924.6565

*Christian; housing; crisis pregnancy resources; adoption services.*

**http://www.highlands.ag.org**
Kansas City, MO

### LIGHT House Inc.          816.361.2233

*Nonresidential services also available; forum; newsletter.*

**http://www.lighthouse-inc.org**
Kansas City, MO

## North Carolina

### Baptist Maternity Home          828.254.1911

*Housing; prenatal, delivery and postnatal support; adoption counseling.*

**http://www.bchfamily.org/maternity_home.php**
Asheville, NC

### Florence Crittenton Services          704.372.4663

*Housing and nonresidential programs for single pregnant women; adoption support and counseling; pre- and postnatal care.*

**http://www.florencecrittenton.homestead.com/Home.html**
Charlotte, NC

## New Hampshire

### His Mansion Ministries          603.464.5555

*Christian; housing; parenting training; adoption counseling and assistance.*

**http://www.hismansion.com/Pregnant_Women.html**
Hillsboro, NH

## New Jersey

**Friendship Center for New Beginnings**                908.806.4444

*Housing; counseling and pregnancy resource center; parenting classes,
referrals to medical, legal and financial assistance.*

**http://www.friendship-center.org**

Flemington, NJ

## New York

**Brook Haven House**                                     315.376.6278

*Christian; housing for pregnant women.*

**http://www.bhh.org**

Carthage, NY

## Ohio

**Harbor House Maternity Home**                          419.586.9029

*Christian; housing for single pregnant teens; counseling; adoption services.*

**http://www.harborhouse.org**

Celina, OH

**New Life Maternity Home**                              330.856.3616

*Housing, counseling, care and adoption assistance for young women in need.*

**http://www.newlife.8m.com**

Warren, OH

## Oregon

**Grandma's House**                                      541.383.3515

*Housing; educational programs including parenting and life skill training;
counseling; non-profit.*

**http://www.grandmashouseofbend.com**

Bend, OR

Cornerstone Maternity Home                    717.848.5433
*Christian; housing to pregnant teens facing crisis pregnancies.*
York, PA

## Tennessee

Mercy Ministries of America                   615.831.6987
*Christian; maternity home for young women ages 13-28; pregnancy counseling.*
**http://www.mercyministries.com**
Nashville, TN

## Texas

Christian Homes                               915.677.2205
*Christian; housing; counseling and education; adoption services; non-profit.*
**http://www.christianhomes.com/counsel/counsel.html**
Abilene, TX

Christian Homes                               915.677.2205
*Christian; counseling, maternity home, adoption, and foster care to individuals
and families.*
**http://www.christianhomes.com**
Abilene, TX

Hannah's Ministry
*Christian; housing and maternity care; crisis pregnancy services; adoption
referral service and counseling.*
**http://www.tbhc.org/hannah/**
Waxahachie, TX

Mercy House                                   972.641.5835
*Housing during time of pregnancy and for 6 weeks afterwards;
pregnancy care; counseling.*
**http://www.mercyhouse.org**
Euless, TX

Smithlawn Home    806.745.2574

*Housing; adoption assistance; non-profit.*

**http://members.door.net/smithlawn**

Lubbock, TX

## Virginia

Jeremiah House    540.338.2676

*Housing; prenatal care; parenting classes; newsletter; non-profit.*

**http://www.jeremiahhouse.org**

Paeonian Springs, VA

Liberty Godparent Foundation    434.845.3466

*Housing; counseling for young women in crisis pregnancy; China adoptions; home studies; non-profit.*

**http://www.godparent.org/pregnancy.htm**

Lynchburg, VA

Liberty Godparent Foundation

*Christian; maternity home; pregnancy counseling; adoption assistance.*

**http://www.godparent.org**

Lynchburg, VA

## Washington State

Special Delivery    425.485.3582

*Maternity home; support groups; adoption assistance.*

**http://www.specialdelivery.org**

Woodinville, WA

# Medical Information & Resources

### Adoption International                          401.444.8360
*Counseling for international adoptions; potential adopting parents will receive professional "medical clearing house" for international medical records.*
**http://www.adoptionsinternational.com**
Providence, RI

### Adoption Medical News                          202.293.7979
*Experts speak about the unique connections linking adoption and health; newsletter.*
**http://www.adoptionmedicalnews.com**
Washington, D.C.

### AIM-Access for Infants and Mothers
*Low-cost comprehensive health plan for pregnant women and newborns; sponsored by the State of California.*

### The American Academy of Pediatrics              847.434.4000
*General information related to child health; specific guidelines concerning pediatric issues; advocacy, research; medical articles; publications.*
**http://www.aap.org**
Elk Grove Village, IL

### California Health Care Foundation                510.238.1040
*Health insurance information and related topics.*
**http://www.chcf.org**
Oakland, CA

### Centers for Medicare and Medicaid Services      877.267.2323
*Medicaid is the largest program that provides medical and health-related services to America's low income people.*
**http://cms.hhs.gov/medicaid/mover.asp**
Baltimore, MD

**Cord Blood Registry**                                650.635.1420
  *Cord blood stem cells; collection, processing, storage, and retrieval.*
  **http://www.cordblood.com**
  San Bruno, CA

---

**Dr. Jeri Jenista**                                  313.668.0419
  *Specializes in international pediatric medicine; also an adoptive mother.*
  **http://adoptionpros.com/doctors.htm**
  Ann Arbor, MI

---

**Dr. Laurie Miller**                                 617.636.8121
  *Pediatric rheumatologist.*
  **http://adoptionpros.com/doctors.htm**

---

**Genelex**                                           425.825.2850
  *DNA testing; attorney listing; information also in Spanish.*
  **http://www.genelex.com**
  Redmond, WA

---

**Global Voyager Assistance**
  *Medical issues related to adoption from Russia; medical terminology;*
  *other resources links; forum.*
  **http://www.russianadoption.org**

---

**Health-e-App**                                      510.433.9676
  *Health insurance, public, online enrollment for low-income children and*
  *pregnant women.*
  **http://www.healtheapp.org**

---

**International Adoption Medical Support Services**    732.432.7777
  *International adoption medical support service; specializes in adoptions from*
  *the former Soviet Union.*
  **http://www.globalpediatrics.net**
  East Brunswick, NJ

### International Pediatric Health Services, PLLC                212.207.6666
*Pediatrician; specializing in adoption medicine and services for children adopted from abroad; information on common diseases of orphans.*
**http://www.orphandoctor.com**
New York, NY

### March of Dimes                888.663.4637
*Advocacy of healthy born infants; provides information and education to prevent premature births that lead to birth defects and infant mortality.*
**http://www.marchofdimes.com**

### Medi-Cal Policy Institute                510.286.8976
*Medi-Cal policies and legislation in California.*
**http://www.medi-cal.org**
Oakland, CA

### Medlineplus Health Information
*Database, comprehensive, of links to 11 million medical articles in 4,300 journals; drug information and medical news.*
**http://www.nlm.nih.gov/medlineplus**

### Murphy's Unofficial Medicaid Page
*Health insurance for poor and disabled; links to Medicaid sites by state.*
**http://www.geocities.com/medicaid.geo**

### New York Online Access to Health
*Medical information, in-depth; in Spanish and English.*
**http://www.noah-health.org**

### Ronald McDonald House Charities                630.623.7048
*Child-friendly hospital; quality medical care; grants towards reconstructive surgery for children in need; a "home-away-from-home" during treatment.*
**http://www.rmhc.com/**
Oak Brook, IL

### Russian Adoption Medical Services
*Discussion forum for medical issues related to adoptions from Russia.*
**http://www.russianadoption.org/discus**

Schneider Children's Hospital                                   718.470.3000
> *Children's hospital; regional, tertiary care; comprehensive medical, surgical, dental and psychiatric care; non-threatening environment.*
> **http://www.schneiderchildrenshospital.org/**
> Hyde Park, NY

---

Univeristy of Iowa Health Care                                 319.384.8442
> *Women's medical clinic affiliated with University of Iowa; specializing in fertility and high risk pregnancy; in-depth medical information.*
> **http://www.uihealthcare.com/depts/med/obgyn**
> Iowa City, IA

---

# Newsletters & Magazines

Adoption and Fostering
> *United Kingdom journal; subscribers in Europe and North America; articles by social workers, medical practitioners, adopted people and lawyers.*
> **http://www.baaf.org.uk**

---

Adoption for Life
> *Addresses adoption questions on finance, law and more. Inspirational stories, advice and support.*
> **http://www.adoptionforlife.com**

---

Adoption Helper
> *Canada's national adoption publication that helps people adopt domestically and internationally.*
> **http://www.familyhelper.net/ad/ahsub.html**

---

Adoption Quarterly                                             800.342.9678
> *Addresses ethical, biological, financial, social and psychological aspects of adoption as well as issues that are important to both practitioners and researchers.*
> **http://www.haworthpress.com/store/product.asp?sku=J145**
> Binghamton, NY

---

### Adoption Related Newsletters and Magazines/Journals
*Site with adoption magazines and newsletters.*
**http://www.calib.com/naic/pubs/r_mag.cfm**

### Adoption TODAY Magazine         970.663.1185
*Magazine by adoptive parents and professionals; forum for stories, knowledge and experiences; domestic and international adoptions and foster care.*
**http://www.adoptinfo.net**
Loveland, CO

### Adoptive Families Magazine         646.366.0830
*Magazine, national; adoption information for families before, during and after adoption; subscription form.*
**http://www.adoptivefam.com**
New York, NY

### American Baby
*Magazine for expectant and new parents; pre-conception, baby and parenting information; magazine subscription.*
**http://www.americanbaby.com**

### Babytalk.com
*Information for expectant and new parents; from health and safety issues to the latest and greatest products for baby.*
**http://www.parenting.com/parenting/magazines/babytalk.html**

### Black Parenting Today Magazine         215.474.8183
*African American parenting resources; adoption and foster care; educational alternatives; cultural diversity; help for special needs children.*
Philadelphia, PA

### Child Welfare Journal
*Articles that cover all aspects of children's welfare; health, education and psychological; examines theoretical concepts as well as practical ideas and strategies.*
**http://www.cwla.org/pubs/pubdetails.asp?PUBID=P101**

### Children's Voice Magazine

*Advocates for the well-being of families; articles addressing the practical needs of professionals, agency executives, foster and adoptive parents.*

**http://www.cwla.org/pubs/pubdetails.asp?PUBID=P301**

### Fostering Families Today Magazine

*Magazine explores issues that affect families and children of foster care and domestic adoption.*

**http://www.adoptinfo.net**

### Future of Children    650.917.7110

*Translates research into better policy and practice for children; each issue examines a single topic of importance from a multidisciplinary perspective.*

**http://www.futureofchildren.org**
Los Altos, CA

### PACT—An Adoption Alliance

*Quarterly magazine that addresses issues of race and adoption; lively and thought-provoking articles, including contributions from a host of national experts.*

**http://www.pactadopt.org/press**

### Parenting.com

*Fertility, pregnancy, baby, toddler and preschool and parenting resources; subscribe online.*

**http://www.parenting.com**

### Rainbowkids.com

*Publication, international; general information; waiting children photo listing; agency listing; forum.*

**http://www.rainbowkids.com**

### Raising Black and Biracial Children Magazine    800.787.1414

*Topics not usually covered in mainstream parenting publications with a sensitivity for the child's African-American heritage; for parents and professionals.*

**http://www.magazinesubscriptionbox.com/raising-black-and-biracial-children.html**

Red Thread Magazine                                    877.837.1992
*Quarterly magazine for families that have adopted from China; culture,*
*children's health, single parenting, disabilities; children stories and more.*
**http://www.redthreadmag.com**
Whitehall, PA

# Open Adoption Information

American Association of Open Adoption Agencies
*Articles; in-depth information on all aspects of open adoption, especially the*
*advantages; national conference.*
**http://www.openadoption.org**

Insight                                                248.543.0997
*Resources, support and information; books and tapes.*
**http://www.r2press.com**
Royal Oak, MI

Let's Talk Adoption
*Internet talk radio show that addresses all aspects of adoption; weekly guests;*
*open adoption advocacy; articles and books.*
**http://www.letstalkadoption.com**

Open Adoption                                          530.271.1740
*Open adoption articles; information and resources; birth mother hotline and*
*services; newsletter and books.*
**http://www.openadoption.com**
Nevada City, CA

Open Adoption & Family Services, Inc.                  503.226.4870
*Adoption services; home studies; fears and facts about open adoption; free info*
*packets; newsletter; also in Washington state and Canada.*
**http://www.openadopt.com**
Portland, OR

### Open Adoption Services    425.861.4772

*Resources; brings birthmothers and qualified adoptive parents together; waiting family profiles.*

**http://www.open-adoption-services.com/adopt**

Redmond, WA

# Parenting Resources

### ABC's of Parenting

*Parenting, adoption, infertility and much more; resources and links; forum.*

**http://www.abcparenting.com**

### Adoptive Breastfeeding Resource Website

*Breastfeed an adopted infant; related articles and links; forum.*

**http://www.fourfriends.com/abrw**

### Babies Online

*Birth announcement system, automated; fetal development information with pictures; free Web page building with pictures of your baby; forum.*

**http://www.babiesonline.com**

### Baby Name Chooser

*Baby names listing and the name's meaning.*

**http://www.babynames.com**

### Co-Abode, Single Mothers House Sharing

*Single mothers house sharing and pooling of resources and finances with other single moms; online book club; parenting articles.*

**http://www.co-abode.com**

Santa Monica, CA

### Dr. Ray Guarendi

*Radio show on effective child raising, nationwide; father of 10 children, clinical psychologist, author, public speaker.*

**http://www.drray.com**

### Family.com

*Activities and ideas for the family; crafts; home and garden; e-cards; parties; travel and more.*

**http://www.family.com**

### KidSource

*Parenting resource; health and safety articles, book reviews, newsletter and more.*

**http://www.kidsource.com**

### La Leche League International    847.519.7730

*Breastfeeding advocacy and information including adoptive nursing; accessories, supplies, books and more; worldwide network.*

**http://www.lalecheleague.org/NB/NBadoptive.html**
Schaumburg, IL

### Lact-Aid International, Inc.    423.744.9090

*Breastfeeding support and resources; accessories, supplies, books and more.*

**http://www.lact-aid.com/webmap.htm#webmap**
Athens, TN

### LifeServ    312.573.0343

*Pregnancy, parenting, baby's first year, and much more including online florist and gifts for her.*

**http://www.babyserv.com**
Chicago, IL

### National Parenting Center    800.753.6667

*Guidance for parents, comprehensive, from the world's most renowned child-rearing authorities; articles and chat room.*

**http://www.tnpc.com**

### Parenthood.com

*Parenting and pregnancy resources and much more.*

**http://www.parenthoodweb.com**

### Parenting.com

*Fertility, pregnancy, baby, toddler and preschool resources; search engine.*

**http://www.parenting.com**

### Single Parent Central

*Resources for single parents; articles; kid's page; advanced earned income tax credit; news; research, studies, reports; legislation.*

**http://www.singleparentcentral.com**

### Watoto World

*African-American resources; parenting tips; online publication for children; African heritage books.*

**http://www.melanet.com/watoto**

# Search Engines

### 100.com

*Listing of 100 top search engines.*

**http://www.100.com**

### Adoption Information, Laws and Reforms

*State codes and international adoption laws; legal search engines and links.*

**http://www.webcom.com/kmc**

### All the Web

*Web catalog consists of 2.1 billion documents.*

**http://www.alltheweb.com**

### AltaVista

*Search engine; allows searches in different areas by keywords or categories.*

**http://www.altavista.com**

### Ask Jeeves

*Pose a question and Jeeves will retrieve the answer.*

**http://www.ask.com**

## CNET Search.com
*Search engine provided by CNET.*
**http://www.search.com**

## Childslife.com
*Parenting resource search engine; information sorted by state regions.*

## CitySearch
*Guides, interactive, to major U.S. cities and other places in the world.*
**http://www.citysearch.com**

## Ditto
*Visual search engine; search by using pictures, not text; directs users to the originating website on which the pictures are located.*
**http://www.ditto.com**

## DMOZ Open Directory Project
*Web directory; large and comprehensive; human-edited.*
**http://www.dmoz.org**

## Dogpile
*Search multiple search engines at once, therefore twice as fast.*
**http://www.dogpile.com**

## Excite
*Search engine with news and more.*
**http://www.excite.com**

## Findarticles.com
*Archive of published articles, free; constantly updated; dating back to 1998 from 300 magazines and journals.*
**http://www.findarticles.com**

## Go-Girl
*Search engine for young women; girl's stuff.*
**http://www.go-girl.com**

Go.com
> Web guide with extensive search capabilities.

**http://www.go.com**

Google
> Large and current database.

**http://www.google.com**

HotBot
> Popular search engine.

**http://www.hotbot.lycos.com**

Ivillage.com
> Search engine with chat room and forum.

**http://www.ivillage.com**

KinderStart.com
> Children, adoption and foster care information links.

**http://www.kinderstart.com**

LookSmart
> Large professionally edited directory with 2.5 million URLs organized into more than 250,000 categories.

**http://www.looksmart.com**

Lycos
> World wide search engine; e-mail provider.

**http://www.lycos.com**

Mamma
> Meta-search engine; searches a series of other search sites at the same time.

**http://www.mamma.com**

Neonteen.com
> Teenager popular search engine; chat room and forum.

**http://www.neonteen.com**

### Northern Light

*Business library comprising 7,100 trusted, full-text journals, books, magazines, newswires, and reference sources; available for a minimal fee.*

**http://www.northernlight.com**

### Questia.com

*Library, online; 70,000 books, journals and articles.*

**http://www.questia.com**

### Teoma

*Looks at the World Wide Web in terms of subject-specific communities; the third most widely used search technology in the U.S.*

**http://www.teoma.com**

### Top10Links

*Best websites; editors have selected the top 10 websites in hundreds of categories.*

**http://www.toptenlinks.com**

### Vivisimo

*Breakthrough technology that automatically categorizes textual information into crisp, meaningful, hierarchically sorted category folders.*

**http://www.vivisimo.com**

### Volunteer Search Network

*Adoptee search engine and resources.*

**http://www.vsn.org**

### WebCrawler

*The results returned include commercial (sponsored) and noncommercial results; designed to identify the intent of a user's search.*

**http://www.webcrawler.com**

### Webhelp.com

*Search assistance real-time with a live expert.*

**http://www.webhelp.com/home**

### WiseNut
*Searches over 1.5 million web pages.*
**http://www.wisenut.com**

### Yahoo
*Search engine and web guide.*
**http://www.yahoo.com**

# Shopping Online

### A Baby Gift Store
*Adoption gifts for infants, children, birth parents, adoptive parents and adoption professionals; books with positive adoption messages.*
**http://www.ababygiftstore.com**

### Adoption Lifebooks
617.846.6718
*Lifebooks; a journal you create together with your adoptive child to understand and accept being adopted; lifebook trainings and free tips.*
**http://www.adoptionlifebooks.com**
Winthrop, MA

### American Carriage House Publishing
530.470.0720
*Educational and inspirational adoption books; reports; online order.*
**http://www.americancarriagehousepublishing.com**
Cedar Ridge, CA

### Baby Toytown, Inc.
562.860.5358
*Baby bedding linen, strollers, car seats, seats, furniture, cribs and more.*
**http://www.ababytolove.com**
CA

### Bookswithoutborders.com
*Multilingual books, videos and audiotapes for videos.*
**http://www.bookswithoutborders.com**

**Child Link International**                                    612.861.9048
*Christian; Russian handmade items; newsletter; non-profit.*
**http://www.child-link.com**
Richfield, MN

**Child Star Books**                                           877.504.411
*Personalized books with important information about your child; baby books.*
**http://www.childstarbooks.net**
Loves Park, IL

**Galaxy Mall**
*Shopping mall; arts, computers, family and kids, pets, real estate, travel arrangements and more.*
**http://www.galaxymall.com**

**Heart and Seoul**
*Cultural products: customized mugs, clocks, t-shirts and much more, related to your country of adoption.*
**http://www.heartandseoul.com**

**Imaternity**                                                 888.847.2229
*Maternity clothing and infant needs.*
**http://www.imaternity.com**

**Luv n Stuff**                                                503.228.2266
*Flowers for all occasions.*
**http://www.florists.ftd.com/luvnstuff**
Portland, OR

**Mandy's Moon**                                               707.585.2042
*Multicultural and adoption products including fun stuff for kids and baby clothing.*
**http://www.mandysmoon.com**
Rohnert Park, CA

**Miracle of Adoption**                                        800.741.0711
*Greeting cards and adoption gifts.*
**http://www.miracleofadoption.com**
Cincinnati, OH

Multicultural Kids                                    847.991.2919

*Multicultural: books, videos, arts and crafts, educational resources,*
*ethnic gifts and more.*
**http://www.multiculturalkids.com**
Palatine, IL

---

Orphan Angels, LLC                                    860.291.0326

*Entertainment products for children; CDs, cassettes, books, t-shirts and hats.*
**http://www.orphanangels.com**
East Hartford, CT

---

Paul's Teacher's Pet

*Educational products for teachers and parents.*
**http://www.paulsteacherspet.com**
Williamsville, NY

---

Scrap and Tell

*Scrapbooks and lifebooks; stickers, albums, pens, cutting tools, and*
*scrapbooking supplies.*
**http://www.scrapandtell.com**

---

Stork Drop Delivery Service

*Infant and toddler products.*
**http://www.geocities.com/storkdropditto**

---

The Labor of Love

*Products for those trying to conceive and struggling with infertility issues;*
*ovulation kits, fertility monitors and supplements and more.*
**http://www.thelaboroflove.com**

---

Virtually Shopping

*Just about any products you need, from flowers to footwear.*
**http://www.virtuallyshopping.com**

---

# Sites with Web Links

### ABC's of Parenting

*Parenting, adoption, infertility and much more; resources and links; forum.*

**http://www.abcparenting.com**

---

### Adoption Forum, Inc.                                    215.238.1116

*Emotional support to the adoption triad; local support groups; forum; articles; agencies; links; suggested reading; other resources; non-profit.*

**http://www.adoptionforum.org**

Emmaus, PA

---

### Adoptions from the Heart                               610.642.7200

*Domestic infants and biracial children; international: children from 10 countries; home studies; waiting family profiles; links; newsletter; non-profit.*

**http://www.adoptionsfromtheheart.org**

Wynnewood, PA

---

### Epigee Pregnancy Resource

*Birth control and pregnancy symptoms; pregnancy centers; counseling; online pregnancy test; links.*

**http://www.epigee.org/pregnancyhelp**

---

### Frost International Adoptions                          703.750.9470

*Domestic, infants and special needs children; international adoptions; home studies; financial and travel information; resource links; non-profit.*

**http://www.frostadopt.org**

Falls Church, VA

---

### Institute for Adoption Information

*Educational adoption guide; resources, information and links; non-profit.*

**http://www.adoptioninformationinstitute.org/links.html**

---

### Karen's Adoption Links

*Site with multiple links; international: children from Russia, Kazakhstan, Ukraine, and Eastern Europe; funding;*
*Yahoo support groups listed by state.*

**http://www.karensadoptionlinks.com**

---

### Kid Power—Special Needs Links

*Disability resources; adaptive clothing and housing; assistive equipment and technology; educational alternatives; monetary assistance; online magazines.*

**http://www.geocities.com/Heartland/ Village/9021/links.html**

### Korean American Adoptee Adoptive Family Network

916.933.1447

*Asian and Korean adoption support and resources; cultural programs; newsletter; links.*

**http://www.kaanet.com**

El Dorado Hills, CA

### La Vida Adoption Agency

610.688.8008

*International: children from China and Vietnam; home studies; listing of waiting children; links to in-depth resources; non-profit.*

**http://www.lavida.org**

King of Prussia, PA

### Medlineplus Health Information

*Database, comprehensive, of links to 11 million medical articles in 4,300 journals; drug information and medical news.*

**http://www.nlm.nih.gov/medlineplus**

### New York Online Access to Health

*Medical information, in-depth; information in Spanish.*

**http://www.noah-health.org**

### Pregnancy Help Desk

*Pregnancy and child birth information; links and chat room.*

**http://www.geocities.com/wellesley/1483/tests.html**

### Southern Tier Adoptive Families

607.797.3188

*Education, support and links; membership organization.*

**http://www.tier.net/staf**

Vestal, NY

### Special Kids Links Page

*Special needs resource links.*

**http://www.members.tripod.com/specialkids/links.html**

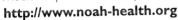 

### Unlocking the Heart of Adoption
*Birth mothers in-depth information.*
**http://www.unlockingtheheart.com**
San Francisco, CA

### Welcome Garden
*International resources; links to extensive information on the adoption process; financial information; agency listing.*
**http://www.welcomegarden.com**

### World Partners Adoption, Inc.                770.962.7860
*International: children from Asia, Eastern Europe and Latin America; resource links; non-profit.*
**http://www.worldpartnersadoption.org**
Lawrenceville. GA

# Social Workers

### Bill Betzen, LMSW, ACSW
*Child placement specialist; helpful checklist to select an open adoption agency; resources and links.*
**http://openadoption.org/bbetzen**
TX

### Brian Combs                                253.884.4306
*Counselor who provides home studies, post-placement reports, workshops and consultations.*
**http://ahomestudy.com**
WA

### Diane M. Keller, LMSW/AP                    214.341.9016
*Home studies; update of a previously completed home study; post-adoption supervision.*
**http://adoptionhomestudiesdallas.bigstep.com**
TX

**Dr. Elaine Kindle, Ph.D., LCSW**                    626.330.7990
    *Licensed clinical social worker experienced in issues of adoption.*
    **http://lifefocuscenter.com/adoption.htm**
    Hacienda Heights, CA

---

**Dr. Joseph Crumbley**                    215.843.5987
    *Post-adoptive therapy, chemical dependency, couples therapy, physical and*
    *sexual abuse; kinship care and transracial adoptions.*
    **http://drcrumbley.com**
    Philadelphia, PA

---

**Gerald A. Bowman, LCSW, ACSW**                    +(49) 89.5601.7944
    *International home studies; licensed clinical social worker; maintains a private*
    *practice; services to U.S. citizens that reside abroad.*
    **http://www.geraldbowman.com**
    Munich, Germany

---

**Jane Santos LCSW, MSM**                    +(49) 6130.919768
    *Independent social worker for Americans living abroad; home studies.*
    **http://randybarlow.com**
    Germany

---

**Marlou Russell**                    310.829.1438
    *Psychologist and Marriage & Family Therapist; specializes in adoption issues;*
    *also an adoptee; author of numerous adoption articles and a book.*
    **http://marlourussellphd.com**
    Santa Monica, CA

---

**National Association of Social Workers**                    202.408.8600
    *Organization with 150,000 members; provides content expertise and informs*
    *members about current trends and policy issues.*
    **http://socialworkers.org**
    Washington, D.C.

---

**North American Association of Christians in Social Work**    888.426.4712
    *Christian membership organization; articles by members; bookstore;*
    *national conferences; home study training programs; newsletter.*
    **http://nacsw.org**
    Botsford, CT

---

Randy Barlow, MSW, MA    +(49)6227.859528

*Independent social worker for Americans living abroad; home studies; experienced in working with adopting military families.*

**http://randybarlow.com**

Germany

Susan P. McKay, LMSW/ACP    214.341.9016

*Home studies; post-adoption supervision; stepparent adoptions specialists.*

**http://adoptionhomestudiesdallas.bigstep.com**

TX

# Special Needs Resources

Abandoned Infants Assistance Resource Center    510.643.8390

*Technical assistance, research and resources for professionals who serve infants and young children affected by drugs or HIV, and their parents.*

**http://socrates.berkeley.edu/~aiarc**

Berkeley, CA

Adaptive Clothing

*Clothing and accessories for special needs children and young adults; links.*

**http://www.allhealthnet.com/Child+Health/Special+Needs/Adaptive+Clothing**

AIDB, e-Conference on Deafness

*E-mail conference moderated by Alabama Institute for the Deaf and Blind, free; Yahoo group.*

**http://www.groups.yahoo.com/group/aidb-deafness**

American Academy of Child and Adolescent Psychiatry, AACAP    202.966.7300

*Developmental, behavioral, and mental disorders; information, fact sheets, treatment, education, research and publications.*

**http://www.aacap.org**

Washington, D.C.

American Christian Voice Article                    407.294.4704

*Free medical equipment program; medical equipment and supplies to those in need.*

**http://wwcol.com/con/voice/medequip.html**
Orlando, FL

---

American Speech-Language-Hearing Association        800.638.8255

*Communication disorders; resources for individuals and professionals; articles; links.*

**http://www.asha.org**
Rockville, MD

---

Attach                                              866.453.8224

*Attachment disorder resources; education of general public about attachment; support for professionals; treatment case monitoring; non-profit.*

**http://www.attach.org**
Columbia, SC

---

Attachment Disorder Network                         913.897.1900

*Reactive attachment disorder network; information and resource links.*

**http://www.radzebra.org**
Stilwell, KS

---

Attachment Disorder Site

*Attachment disorder resources; information, articles, links and forum.*
**http://www.attachmentdisorder.net**

---

Attachment Disorder Support Group

*Attachment disorder support and resources; seminars and workshops; articles and testimonies; forum and chat room; links.*

**http://www.syix.com/adsg**
South Bend, IN

---

B. Bryan Post, PhD, LCSW, DAPA                      580.347.2210

*Emotional disorder resources; family treatment; educational material; articles; suggested reading.*

**http://www.bryanpost.com**
Mountain View, OK

### Cascade Center for Family Growth                    801.229.2218

*Attachment disorders; specializes in children with severe behavioral disorders; treatments, articles and resources.*

**http://www.attach-bond.com**
North Orem, UT

### Center for Family Development                       716.810.0790

*Attachment difficulties; assessment and treatment for children; Counseling; intensive treatment programs; home studies; helpful articles.*

**http://www.center4familydevelop.com**
Williamsville, NY

### Child Advocate Resource Exchange

*Foster parent resources; library with books on special needs, teens and kids; links to associations, government sites and agencies.*

**http://foster-parenting.adoption.com/**

### Children's Disability List of Lists

*Mailing lists for families of children with disabilities and special needs.*

**http://www.comeunity.com/disability/speclists.html**

### Deaf Connection                                     425.742.8194

*Deaf or hard of hearing family member volunteer organization; festivals, events and classes; newsletter.*

**http://www.deafconn.com**

### Deafness/Hard of Hearing at About.com

*Deafness and hard of hearing resources; links to articles and personal pages of families that have adopted deaf children; forum and chat room.*

**http://www.deafness.about.com/cs/adoption**

### Developmental Delay Resources                       301.652.2263

*Support of children with developmental sensory motor, language, social, and emotional delays; research; network of parents and professionals.*

**http://www.devdelay.org**
Bethesda, MD

### Down Syndrome: Health Issues

*Great resource site for children with Down Syndrome; numerous articles and links to sources of information.*

**http://www.ds-health.com/ds_sites.htm**

### Families by Design    970.984.2222

*Attachment and emotional disorder resources; educational material; seminars; has an 85 percent success rate with high-risk children.*

**http://www.nancythomasparenting.com**

Glenwood Springs, CO

### FAS Family Resource Institute    253.531.2878

*Fetal alcohol syndrome; support groups; information packets; workshops; newsletter.*

**http://www.fetalalcoholsyndrome.org**

Lynnwood, WA

### Fetal Alcohol Syndrome Community Resource Center

*Fetal alcohol syndrome; facts, information and links.*

**http://www.come-over.to/FASCRC**

### Foster Parent Community

*Foster care and special needs resources, extensive; forum, chat room, e-mail discussion groups; articles and links; foster parent associations by state.*

**http://www.fosterparents.com**

### Foster Parent Talkabout

*Foster care; articles, links and resources; educational and medical news; legal news watch; trans-cultural issues; forum, chat room and more.*

**http://fostercare.org/FPHP/news.htm**

### Foundation for Medically Fragile Children    770.951.6111

*Advocacy and funding for unmet health care needs of medically fragile children; newsletter; non-profit.*

Atlanta, GA

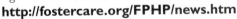

### Hannah and Her Mama

*Attachment and bonding issues; older child adoption; single parent resources; information for kids; agency listings; bookstore, forum.*

**http://www.hannahandhermama.com**

---

### Heal the Hearts Foundation, Inc.                909.788.5966

*Reactive attachment disorder education and resources; online and local support group meetings; periodic workshops; reading list.*

**http://www.healtheheart.org**

Riverside, CA

---

### Hearing Health Magazine                       202.289.5850

*Publication of the Deafness Research Foundation; educate people on the effects of hearing loss on health and quality of life; articles; newsletter.*

**http://www.hearinghealthmag.com**

Washington, D.C.

---

### Institute For Attachment & Child Development        303.674.1910

*Attachment disorder resources; treatments, advocacy, education and research.*

**http://www.attachmentcenter.org**

Kittredge, CO

---

### Kid Power—Special Needs Links

*Disability resources; adaptive clothing and housing; assistive equipment and technology; educational alternatives; monetary assistance; online magazines.*

**http://www.geocities.com/Heartland/Village/9021/links.html**

---

### Kids And Youth Foundation                       608.273.2888

*Education and advocacy services; therapy, respite care, financial and emotional support; for families coping with emotional disorders; non-profit.*

Madison, WI

---

### N.I.C. for Children and Youth with Disabilities        800.695.0285

*Information and referral center on disability-related topics regarding children and youth; state-by-state resources; publications; information in Spanish.*

**http://www.nichcy.org**

Washington, D.C.

**National Foster Parent Association**    253.853.4000

*Advocacy to improve the foster care system; education; publications; networking among foster parents; foster parent associations; links; non-profit.*

**http://www.nfpainc.org**

Gig Harbor, WA

---

**National Respite Network and Resource Center**

*Respite locator service, national; lending library; fact sheets; articles and links.*

**http://www.chtop.com/archbroc.htm**

---

**Northwest Media**

*Books and videos; learning for foster and adoptive parents; finding practical solutions for difficult behavior.*

**http://www.northwestmedia.com**

Eugene, OR

---

**PACER Center**    952.838.9000

*Parenting advocacy focused on children and young adults with disabilities and their families; articles and newsletter.*

**http://www.pacer.org**

Minneapolis, MN

---

**Parent Network for the Post Institutionalized Child, PNPIC**    724.222.1766

*Support network for understanding the needs of children adopted from institutions throughout the world; articles, books, newsletter; research; non-profit.*

**http://www.pnpic.org**

Meadowlands, PA

---

**Parent to Parent of Georgia, Inc.**    770.451.5484

*Support and information to parents of children with disabilities; special needs database containing over 4,000 resources in over 100 categories.*

**http://www.parenttoparentofga.org**

Atlanta, GA

---

**Post Adoptive Resource Project**    920.885.6903

*Special needs support and information for adoptive families with children with emotional or mental disorders; chat room.*

**http://www.geocities.com/syaroch.geo**

Beaver Dam, WI

### Practical Attachment

*Reactive attachment disorder in-depth information.*

**http://home.att.net/~practicalAttachment**

### Registry of Interpreters for the Deaf

*Deafness, information and news; Yahoo group; chat room.*

**http://www.groups.yahoo.com/group/OCRID**

### Sensory Integration International  310.787.8805

*Sensory integrative dysfunction disorder resources; non-profit.*

**http://www.home.earthlink.net/~sensoryint**

Torrance, CA

### Special Kids Links Page

*Special needs resource links.*

**http://www.members.tripod.com/specialkids/links.html**

### St. Joseph Institute for the Deaf  636.532.3211

*Teaching deaf children to listen, read and speak.*

**http://www.stjosephinstitute.org**

Chesterfield, MO

### Stepping Stone Medical Equipment Bank  407.649.4100

*Medical equipment and supplies to those in need, regardless of ability to pay; non-profit.*

**http://www.steppingstonefoundation.org**

Orlando, FL

### Teen Reform Services  877.231.9475

*Specializes in helping parents find the right school or program for their troubled teen; information on all types of youth treatment centers.*

**http://www.teenreform.com**

### WarmLine Family Resource Center  916.922.9276

*Special needs resources in four Northern California counties; links.*

**http://www.warmlinefrc.org**

Sacramento, CA

Wide Smiles                                                    209.942.2812
  *Cleft lip and palate resources; photo gallery of children before and after surgery.*
  **http://www.widesmiles.org**
  Stockton, CA

---

Wisconsin Attachment Resource Network                         262.965.5170
  *Reactive attachment disorder information and links.*
  **http://www.w-a-r-n.com**
  Dousman, WI

---

Yahoo Special Needs
  *Mailing list for parents of children with special needs; parents can get together to dis-*
  *cuss their fears and concerns; friends, relatives and professionals are welcomed.*
  **http://groups.yahoo.com/group/specialneeds**

---

# Foster Care Services

AdoptUSKids                                                   888.200.4005
  *National waiting children photo listing; special needs children;*
  *search by state.*
  **http://www.adoptuskids.org**

---

Open Arms Foster Care Association Inc.
  *Foster care; special needs, children waiting photo listing; articles and links;*
  *chat room; non-profit.*
  **http://www.geocities.com/open_arms_fostercare**

---

## Alabama
. . . . . . . . . . . . . . . . . . . . . . . . . . . . . . . . . . . . . . . . . . . . . . . . . . . . . . . . . . . . . .

Family Finders
  *Recruitment and preparation of foster parents and special needs adoptive*
  *homes; adoption and foster care services; special needs children; home studies;*
  *waiting children photo listing; newsletter.*
  Birmingham, AL

## Alaska

Adoption Advocates International　　　　　　　　　360.452.4777

*Domestic special needs children; international: children from Haiti, Asia and Africa; home studies; news and articles; main office in Washington state, but they are licensed in Alaska as well; non-profit.*

**http://www.adoptionadvocates.org**

## Arizona

Aid to Adoption of Special Kids of Arizona　　　　602.254.2275

*Domestic special needs children; waiting children photo listing; foster care services; adoptive parent training; home studies; international services; non-profit.*

**http://www.aask-az.org**
Phoenix, AZ

Children with AIDS Project of America (CWA)　　480.774.9718

*Advocacy for children infected or affected by AIDS and drug exposed infants who need foster or adoptive families; adoption family registration form.*

**http://www.aidskids.org**
Tempe, AZ

## Arkansas

Project Loving Homes　　　　　　　　　　　　　870.534.6192

*Recruits families for older children and youth; educates prospective parents and the public about the adoption process; dispels myths and misconceptions about adopting older children; non-profit.*

**http://www.lovinghomes.org**
Pine Bluff, AR

## California

### A Better Way                                510.601.0203
*Domestic special needs children; foster-to-adopt program; foster children services; adoptive parents support groups; home studies; non-profit.*
**http://www.abetterwayinc.net**
Berkeley, CA

### AASK Adopt A Special Kid                      510.553.1748
*Preparation and training of families for children waiting in the California foster care system; placement of special needs children; home studies; non-profit.*
**http://www.adoptaspecialkid.org**
Oakland, CA

### All As One (AAO)                              209.538.8540
*Child welfare organization; school, medical clinic and orphanage in Sierra Leone, West Africa; networks with adoption agencies; non-profit.*
**http://www.all-as-one.org**
Ceres, CA

### California Kids Connection                    510.272.0204
*Waiting children photo listing; special needs children; forum.*
**http://www.cakidsconnection.com**
Oakland, CA

### Catholic Charities Adoption Agency           619.231.2828
*Domestic including transracial adoptions; adoption information; pregnancy counseling; information in Spanish; office also in San Francisco.*
**http://www.ccdsd.org/preg.html**
San Diego, CA

### Family Alliance                               916.364.8910
*Treatment foster family agency that assists in adoption; special needs children; foster care services; home studies; steps and requirements to become a foster parent; support groups; counseling; newsletter; non-profit.*
**http://www.familyalliance-sac.org**
Sacramento, CA

### Future Families, Inc.     888.922.5437

*Domestic special needs children; foster care services; home studies;*
*training and support; financial information; non-profit.*
**http://www.futurefamilies.org**
San Jose, CA

### Help One Child     650.917.1210

*Christian; recruits and supports foster parents; special needs children;*
*education for potential foster parents; newsletter; non-profit.*
**http://www.helponechild.org**
Los Altos, CA

### Holy Family Services, Adoption & Foster Care     626.578.1156

*Domestic infants and special needs children; interim infant foster care;*
*home studies; non-profit.*
**http://www.holyfamilyservices.org**
Pasadena, CA

### Lilliput Children's Services     916.923.5444

*Domestic; foster children; home studies; education, resources and links; reading*
*list; local support groups; offices in other cities; non-profit.*
**http://www.lilliput.org**
Sacramento, CA

### SF Child Project     888.732.4453

*Waiting children photo listing; special needs and biracial children;*
*works only families within California.*
**http://www.sfchild.org**
Oakland, CA

### Vista Del Mar Child and Family Services     310.836.1223

*Domestic infants and special needs children; international services; foster care;*
*pregnancy counseling; monthly support groups.*
**http://www.vistadelmar.org**
Los Angeles, CA

## Colorado

Adoption Alliance                                                      303.584.9900

*Domestic infants and special needs children; international adoptions;*
*foster care services; home studies; birth parent services;*
*training and support; non-profit.*
**http://www.adoptall.com**
Denver, CO

---

Colorado Adoptive Family Resource Registry (AFRR)        303.755.4756

*Registry; allows families with home studies to sign up for adoption of special*
*needs child from Colorado.*
**http://www.afrr.org**
Aurora, CO

---

Lutheran Family Services of Colorado                          303.922.3433

*Domestic infants and special needs children; international: children from Asia,*
*Eastern Europe and South America; home studies; foster care services; non-profit.*
**http://www.lfsco.org**
Denver, CO

---

## Connecticut

Adoption Services of Lutheran Social Services of           860.257.9899
New England

*Domestic infants and special needs children; international: children from Asia*
*and Eastern Europe; home studies; non-profit.*
**http://www.adoptlss.org/conn.html**
Rocky Hill, CT

---

Boys Village Youth and Family Services, Inc.                 203.877.0300

*Education for special needs students, teaching them both academic and*
*social skills; foster care; adoption services; shelters; newsletter.*
**http://www.boysvill.org**
Milford, CT

Connecticut Department of Children and Families     860.550.6578
*Waiting children photo listing; foster care; adoption information;
interstate compact, articles.*
**http://www.state.ct.us/dcf/Foster_Adoption/
Foster_Adoption.htm**
Hartford, CT

Downey Side Families for Youth     860.257.1694
*Domestic special needs children; placement of older homeless children;
education and support; legal information; home studies; newsletter; non-profit.*
**http://www.downeyside.org**
Rocky Hill, CT

Family and Children's Agency, Inc.     203.855.8765
*Domestic special needs children; international: children from Russia, Ukraine,
Taiwan, Vietnam, Korea and China; home studies; newsletter.*
**http://www.familyandchildrensagency.org**
Norwalk, CT

Thursday's Child Adoption Agency     860.242.5941
*Domestic and international infants and older children from Bulgaria, China,
Guatemala, Russia, Vietnam and India; home studies; non-profit.*
**http://www.tcadoption.org**
Bloomfield, CO

## District of Columbia

Lutheran Social Services, National Capital Area     202.723.3000
*Domestic infants and special needs children; international services; foster care;
home studies; pregnancy and birth parent counseling non-profit.*
**http://www.lssnca.org**
Washington, D.C.

## Florida

Children's Home Society of Florida                    407.895.5800

*Pregnancy counseling; foster care; special needs children; home studies; waiting children photo listing; more than 200 offices in the state; non-profit.*

**http://www.chsfl.org**

Orlando, FL

Jewish Adoption and Foster Care Options, Inc.          954.749.7230

*Domestic infants and special needs children; foster care services; home studies; training; post-adoption support; non-profit.*

**http://www.jafco.org**

Sunrise, FL

Kids In Distress, Inc.                               954.390.7654

*Abused and neglected children advocacy; family counseling clinic; foster care resources.*

**http://www.kidsindistress.org**

Fort Lauderdale, FL

## Georgia

Families First                                      404.853.2800

*Adoption services; home studies; foster care; links to family related services.*

**http://www.familiesfirst.org**

Atlanta, GA

Georgia AGAPE                                       770.452.9995

*Christian; unplanned pregnancy assistance and counseling; domestic healthy infants; foster care and special needs children; non-profit.*

**http://www.georgiaagape.org**

Atlanta, GA

Georgia Youth Advocate Program, Inc.                706.774.6404

*Foster-to-adopt services; special needs children; home studies; links to related*
*organizations and affiliations nationwide; non-profit.*

**http://www.gyap.org**
Augusta, GA

---

Giving Tree, Inc                                    404.633.3383

*Recruits, educates and supports adoptive parents; special needs children.*

**http://www.thegivingtree.org**
Decatur, GA

---

Lutheran Ministries of Georgia                      404.875.0201

*Domestic, infants and special needs children; international services;*
*foster care services; home studies; non-profit.*

**http://www.lsga.org/Programs/adoption.htm**
Atlanta, GA

---

## Illinois

Generations of Hope                                 217.893.4673

*Matches special needs children with families in their program; foster care services;*
*home studies; intergenerational neighborhood in support of children; non-profit.*

**http://www.generationsofhope.org/**
Rantoul, IL

---

Lutheran Social Services of Illinois               847.635.4600

*Domestic newborns and special needs children; international adoption;*
*foster care services; pregnancy counseling; home studies; non-profit.*

**http://www.lssi.org**
Des Plaines, IL

## Indiana

Children's Bureau of Indianapolis                            317.264.2700

*Specializes in special needs adoption; also domestic infants; foster care services;*
*home studies; outreach to recruit African American adoptive parents;*
*teen pregnancy services.*

**http://www.childrensbureau.org**
Indianapolis, IN

Lutheran Social Services of Indiana                          260.426.3347

*Domestic infants of all ethnicities; home studies; international services; transracial*
*educational adoption seminars twice a year; non-profit.*

**http://www.lssin.org**
Fort Wayne, IN

## Iowa

Kidsake Foster/Adopt Iowa                                    800.243.0756

*Recruits Iowa foster and adoptive parents; photo listing of Iowa's waiting children.*

**http://www.iakids.org**
Ankeny, IA

## Kansas

Adoption Centre of Kansas                                    316.265.5289

*Domestic infants; birth mother counseling services; home studies.*

**http://www.adoptioncentre.com**
Wichita, KS

Kansas Children's Service League                             877.530.5275

*Domestic infants and special needs adoption; foster care; home studies;*
*child advocacy; statewide services in many locations; non-profit.*

**http://www.kcsl.org**
Topeka, KS

## Kentucky

**Adoption and Home Study Specialists**   502.423.7713

*Christian; focus on minority children; international services; home studies; post-placement services; support groups; non-profit.*

**http://www.iglou.com/kac/adoption_homestudy_specialists.html**
Louisville, KY

---

**Kentucky Baptist Homes for Children**   800.928.5242

*Christian; domestic infants and special needs children; foster care services; home studies; pregnancy services; counseling; adoption classes and training; non-profit.*

**http://www.kbhc.org**
Louisville, KY

---

**St. Joseph's Children's Home**   502.893.0241

*Child-caring facility; residential treatment program; foster care and child development center; links; newsletter; non-profit.*

**http://www.sjkids.org/oldindex.html**
Louisville, KY

---

## Louisiana

**Caring Alternatives, a Maternity and Adoption program of**   800.535.9646

*Volunteers of America of Greater New Orleans, Inc. Domestic infants and special needs children; home studies; international and post-placement services; non-profit.*

**http://www.caringalternatives.org**
Metairie, LA

---

## Maine

**A Family for ME**   877.505.0545

*Raises awareness and provides information about foster care and adopting through Maine's foster care system; waiting children photo listing.*

**http://www.afamilyforme.org**
Gardiner, ME

## Massachusetts

Adoption Services of Lutheran Social Services of New England    508.791.4488

> *Domestic infants and special needs children; international: children from Asia and Eastern Europe; home studies; non-profit.*
> **http://www.adoptlss.org/mass.html**
> Worcester, MA

Downey Side    413.781.2123

> *Domestic special needs children; placement of older homeless children; education and support; legal information; home studies; newsletter; non-profit.*
> **http://www.downeyside.org**
> Springfield, MA

Florence Crittenton League    978.452.9671

> *International adoptions: children from China, Guatemala and Eastern Europe; home studies; counseling; non-profit.*
> **http://www.fcleague.org**
> Lowell, MA

Home for Little Wanderers    617.428.0440

> *Domestic infants and special needs children; international: children from Asia, Central America and Eastern Europe; home studies; non-profit.*
> **http://www.thehome.org**
> Boston, MA

## Michigan

D.A. Blodgett Services    616.451.2021

> *Domestic infant, special needs and international adoptions; link to waiting children photo listing; post-adoption services.*
> **http://www.dablodgett.org**
> Grand Rapids, MI

### Eagle Village Family Living Program     231.832.2234

*Domestic infants and special needs children; foster care services; residential treatment; assessment and post-placement services; home studies; non-profit.*

**http://www.eaglevillage.org**

Hersey, MI

---

### Family and Children's Service     269.965.3247

*Human service agency; foster care and adoption services; family intervention services; non-profit.*

**http://www.bcunitedway.org/fcs.htm**

Battle Creek, MI

---

### Family Counseling and Children's Services     517.265.5352

*Domestic infants and special needs children; home studies; pregnancy services; foster care program; international services; non-profit.*

**http://www.fccservices.org**

Adrian, MI

---

### Family Matchmakers, Inc.     616.243.1803

*Domestic special needs children from other states; foster-to-adopt services; home studies; international services; newsletter; non-profit.*

**http://www.familymatchmakers.org**

Grand Rapids, MI

---

### Hands Across the Water     734.477.0135

*Domestic infants and special needs children; international: children from Guatemala, Eastern Europe and Brazil; home studies; education and resources; non-profit.*

**http://www.hatw.org**

Ann Arbor, MI

---

### Lutheran Adoption Services     248.423.2770

*Domestic infants and special needs children; international adoptions; home studies; post-placement services; non-profit.*

**http://www.lasadoption.org**

Southfield, MI

---

Spaulding for Children/National Resource Center          248.443.7080

*Special needs adoption; foster care services; adoption resources and support;*
*links; training for adoption professionals.*

**http://www.spaulding.org**
Southfield, MI

---

St. Vincent-Sarah Fisher Center          248.626.7527

*Special needs adoptions; foster care services; support, education and resources.*

**http://www.svsfcenter.org**
Farmington Hills, MI

---

Teen Ranch Family Services          517.635.7511

*Christian; adoption and foster care services; special needs children.*

**http://users.netonecom.net/~christal/ranch/**
Marlette, MI

## Minnesota

African American Adoption and Permanency Planning          651.659.0460

*Domestic special needs children; foster care services; home studies; recruitment*
*of African-American and adoptive parents; education; non-profit.*

**http://www.afadopt.org**
St. Paul, MN

---

Downey Side          320.240.1433

*Domestic special needs children; placement of older homeless children; education*
*and support; legal information; home studies; newsletter; non-profit.*

**http://www.downeyside.org**
St. Cloud, MN

---

Lutheran Social Services          651.642.5990

*Domestic infants and special needs children; international services; home studies;*
*pregnancy counseling; post-adoption services; non-profit.*

**http://www.lssmn.org**
Minneapolis, MN

North American Council on Adoptable Children          651.644.3036
*Advocacy organization for special needs children; information on adoption*
*subsidy; adoptions and parent support groups; transracial parenting;*
*the most comprehensive adoption conference in U.S.*
**http://www.nacac.org**
St. Paul, MN

Permanent Family Resource Center          218.998.3400
*Domestic infants and special needs children; foster care services; home studies;*
*information and resources; non-profit.*
**http://www.permanentfamily.org**
Fergus Falls, MN

## Mississippi

Mississippi Children's Home Society          601.352.7784
*Domestic infants, special needs and biracial children; home studies; international*
*adoption services; non-profit.*
**http://www.mchsfsa.org/adoption.html**
Jackson, MS

## Missouri

Downey Side Families for Youth          314.457.1358
*Domestic special needs children; placement of older homeless children; education*
*and support; legal information; home studies; newsletter; non-profit.*
**http://www.downeyside.org**
St. Louis, MO

Lutheran Family and Children's Services          314.787.5100
*Christian; domestic infants and special needs children; international adoption; home*
*studies; pregnancy counseling; publication; non-profit.*
**http://www.lfcsmo.org**
St. Louis, MO

## Montana

Lutheran Social Services                                        406.761.4341

*Christian; domestic infants; international and domestic home studies;*
*pregnancy counseling; post-adoption studies; non-profit.*
**http://www.lssmt.org**
Great Falls, MT

## Nebraska

Lutheran Family Services                                        402.342.7038

*Christian; domestic, infants and special needs children; international: children*
*from Eastern Europe and Asia; waiting children photo listing;*
*home studies; non-profit.*
**http://www.lfsneb.org**
Omaha, NE

Nebraska Children's Home Society                               402.451.0787

*Domestic infants and special needs children; pregnancy education and support,*
*behavioral intervention program; foster care; home studies; non-profit.*
**http://www.nchs.org**
Omaha, NE

## New Hampshire

Adoption Services of Lutheran Social Services of               603.224.8111
New England

*Domestic, infants and special needs children; international: children*
*from Asia and Eastern Europe; birth parent services;*
*home studies; non-profit.*
**http://www.adoptlss.org/new_hampshire.html**
Concord, NH

## New Jersey

**Children's Aid and Family Services, Inc.**                    201.261.2600
   *Domestic infants and special needs children; foster care services; home studies;*
   *pre- and post-adoption counseling; non-profit.*
   **http://www.cafsnj.org**
   Paramus, NJ

**Downey Side Families for Youth**                            609.538.8200
   *Domestic special needs children; placement of older homeless children; education*
   *and support; legal information; home studies; newsletter; non-profit.*
   **http://www.downeyside.org**
   Ewing, NJ

**Lutheran Social Ministries of New Jersey**                  609.386.7171
   *Christian; domestic infants and special needs children; international adoption;*
   *birth parent counseling; adoption and post-placement services; home studies;*
   *non-profit.*
   **http://www.lsmnj.org**
   Burlington, NJ

## New York

**Adoption S.T.A.R.**                                        716.691.3300
   *Domestic infants, at-risk and special needs children; African-American program;*
   *home studies; counseling; adoptive parents educational training; non-profit.*
   **http://www.adoptionstar.com**
   Amherst, NY

**Ametz Adoption Program of JCCA**                           212.558.9949
   *Home studies; post-placement services; consultations and education for all parties*
   *in an adoption; foster care services; non-profit.*
   **http://www.jewishchildcareny.org**
   New York, NY

**Downey Side Families for Youth**                    212.714.2200
*Domestic special needs children; placement of older homeless children; education
and support; legal information; home studies; newsletter; non-profit.*
**http://www.downeyside.org**
New York, NY

**Little Flower Children's Services**                  718.875.3500
*Foster-to-adopt services; foster parent education.*
**http://www.littleflowerny.org**
Brooklyn, NY

**New York Council on Adoptable Children**            212.475.0222
*Adoption of abused, neglected, and hard to place children in the NYC foster
care system; links to related sites.*
**http://www.coac.org**
New York, NY

**New York State Citizens' Coalition for Children**   607.272.0034
*Recruitment of families for waiting children; reforms; administrative and legislative
advocacy; community education; parent group development and support services.*
**http://www.nysccc.org**
Ithaca, NY

**Spence-Chapin Services to Families and Children**   212.369.0300
*Domestic, infants, special needs and biracial children; international: children from
Eastern Europe, Asia and Latin America; home studies; non-profit.*
**http://www.spence-chapin.org**
New York, NY

**Vida Special Needs Adoption**                       518.828.4527
*Domestic special needs children; international: children from Latin America, Asia
and Eastern Europe; home studies; travel information; non-profit.*
**http://members.aol.com/vidaadopt/vida.html**
Hudson, NY

## North Carolina

Lutheran Family Services in the Carolinas          919.832.2620
  *Foster care and special needs children; home studies; information;*
  *Post-placement services; serves both North and South Carolina.*
  **http://www.lfscarolinas.org**
  Raleigh, NC

## North Dakota

Lutheran Social Services of North Dakota          701.235.7341
  *Christian; domestic special needs children; foster care services; international;*
  *home studies; pregnancy counseling; non-profit.*
  Fargo, ND

## Ohio

Adopt America Network                             419.534.3350
  *Special needs children in the foster care system; waiting children photo listing;*
  *home studies; adoption specialists by state; newsletter; non-profit.*
  **http://www.adoptamericanetwork.org**
  Toledo, OH

Adoption at Adoption Circle                        614.237.7222
  *Domestic; specializes in newborns and children up to six months of age;*
  *biracial and special needs children; home studies; non-profit.*
  **http://www.adoptioncircle.org**
  Columbus, OH

Catholic Social Services of the Miami Valley      937.223.7217
  *Domestic infants and special needs children; international adoptions; pregnancy*
  *counseling; local support groups; education and training; home studies; non-profit.*
  **http://www.cssmv.org**
  Dayton, OH

**Homes for Kids**                                         330.544.8005

  *Foster care services; special needs children; newsletter; non-profit.*

  **http://www.hfk.org**

  Niles, OH

---

**Lutheran Children's Aid and Family Services**           216.281.2500

  *Domestic infant and special needs adoption; international: children from Russia, China, Guatemala, Colombia, Mongolia and Bulgaria; infant foster care; home studies; non-profit.*

  **http://www.bright.net/~lcafs**

  Cleveland, OH

---

## Oregon

**Christian Family Adoptions**                            503.232.1211

  *Domestic infants and special needs children; home studies; international services; birth parent counseling; non-profit.*

  **http://www.christianfamilyadoptions.org**

  Portland, OR

---

**Heritage Adoption Services**                            503.233.1099

  *Domestic infants and transracial children; international: children from China, Guatemala and Haiti; special needs program; home studies; newsletter; non-profit.*

  **http://www.heritageadoption.org**

  Portland, OR

---

**The Boys and Girls Aid Society of Oregon**              503.222.9661

  *Domestic infants and special needs children; home studies; foster care services; pregnancy counseling; newsletter; non-profit.*

  **http://www.boysandgirlsaid.org**

  Portland, OR

---

**Tree of Life Adoption Center**                          503.244.7374

  *Domestic infants and special needs children; international: children from Eastern Europe; waiting children photo listing; home studies; non-profit.*

  **http://www.toladopt.org**

  Portland, OR

## Pennsylvania

........................................................................................

### Adoption ARC, Inc.                                            215.748.1441
*Specializes in special needs and biracial children; pregnancy counseling; adoption services; online gift store; non-profit.*
**http://www.adoptionarc.com**
Philadelphia, PA

### Adoption World, Inc.                                          215.271.1361
*Home studies; counseling; emphasis on education of all parties involved in adoption.*
**http://www.adoptionworld.org**
Philadelphia, PA

### Brittany's Hope Foundation                                    717.367.9614
*Aid to and facilitating of special children from around the world; family registry; non-profit foundation.*
**http://www.brittanyshope.org**
Elizabethtown, PA

### Council of Spanish Speaking Organizations                     215.627.3100
*Advocates for Latino representation in organizations serving the community; adoption and foster care services; home studies; non-profit.*
**elconcilio.net/Concilio/services.htm**
Philadelphia, PA

### Diakon Lutheran Services                                      717.845.9113
*Domestic infants and special needs children; international adoptions; foster care services; pregnancy program; home studies; non-profit.*
**http://www.diakon.org**
York, PA

### Lutheran Children and Family Service                          215.881.6800
*Domestic special needs children; international: children from Eastern Europe, Asia and Latin America; foster care services; home studies; post-adoption services; non-profit.*
**http://www.lcfsinpa.org**
Roslyn, PA

## Rhode Island

Adoption Rhode Island                           401.724.1910
*Special needs children; home studies; waiting children photo listing; resource
links; non-profit.*
**http://www.adoptionri.org**
Pawtucket, RI

Adoption Services of Lutheran Social Services of        401.785.0015
New England
*Domestic infants and special needs children; international: children from Asia
and Eastern Europe; home studies; non-profit.*
**http://www.adoptlss.org/ri.html**
Cranston, RI

Children's Friend & Service                      401.276.4300
*Foster care and special needs adoption; pregnancy counseling; publications and
newsletter; educational resources.*
**http://www.childrensfriendservice.org**
Providence, RI

## South Carolina

Children Unlimited, Inc.                         800.822.0877
*Domestic special needs children; home studies; waiting children photo listing;
reactive attachment and related disorder resources; newsletter; non-profit.*
**http://www.children-unlimited.org**
Columbia, SC

Special Link                                     864.233.4872
*Clearinghouse and national linking network for adoption of African-American
and biracial infants; support groups; newsletter; non-profit*
Mauldin, SC

## South Dakota

Lutheran Social Services of South Dakota                605.336.3347
*Adoption and foster care services; special needs children; non-profit.*
**http://www.lsssd.org**
Sioux Falls, SD

## Tennessee

International Assistance and Adoption Project           423.886.6986
*International: children from Vietnam and China; link to waiting children photo
listing; special needs children resources and numerous other links.*
**http://www.iaapadoption.com**
Signal Mountain, TN

## Texas

Adoption Access                                        214.750.4847
*Infants and older children of all ethnicities; focus on counseling for birth mothers;
birth father support; general information; non-profit.*
**http://www.adoptionaccess.com**
Dallas, TX

Buckner Adoption and Maternity Services Inc.           214.381.1552
*Domestic infants and special needs children; international adoptions;
home studies; limited foster care services; non-profit.*
**http://www.buckner.org**
Dallas, TX

DePelchin Children's Center                            713.730.2335
*Domestic infant and special needs adoption; home studies; foster care;
teen pregnancy counseling; pre- and post-adoption services; non-profit.*
**http://www.depelchin.org**
Houston, TX

**Marywood Children and Family Services**  512.472.9251

*Domestic infants and special needs children; international services;*
*pregnancy counseling; foster care services; home studies; non-profit.*

**http://www.marywood.org**

Austin, TX

---

**Methodist Mission Home**  210.696.2410

*Christian; international and domestic adoptions; infants and special needs*
*children; home studies; post-adoption services.*

**http://www.mfrs.org**

San Antonio, TX

---

## Vermont

**Vermont Children's Aid Society**  800.479.0015

*Domestic infants and special needs children; international: children from China,*
*Korea, Russia and Guatemala; home studies; non-profit.*

**http://www.vtcas.org**

Winooski, VT

---

## Virginia

**Children's Home Society of Virginia, Inc.**  540.344.9281

*Domestic infants and special needs children; home studies; international services;*
*pregnancy and birth counseling; foster care services; non-profit.*

**http://www.chsva.org**

Roanoke, VA

---

**Coordinators/2, Inc.**  800.690.4206

*Domestic infants; international: children from Eastern Europe, Latin America and*
*Asia; special needs adoptions; home studies; education and training; non-profit.*

**http://www.c2adopt.org**

Richmond, VA

### Lutheran Family Services, Inc.                804.288.0122
*Christian; domestic infants and special needs children; international: children from Asia, Eastern Europe and Guatemala; home studies; non-profit.*
**http://www.lfsva.org**
Roanoke, VA

### Northern Virginia Family Service            703.385.3267
*Services for families in need to achieve and maintain self-sufficiency; foster care services; family counseling programs; teen services; non-profit.*
**http://www.nvfs.org**
Oakton, VA

### United Methodist Family Services of Virginia    804.353.4461
*Domestic infants and special needs children; international services; foster care program; home studies; crisis pregnancy counseling; non-profit.*
**http://www.umfs.org**
Richmond, VA

## Washington
. . . . . . . . . . . . . . . . . . . . . . . . . . . . . . . . . . . . . . . . . . . . . . . . .

### Adoption Advocates International             360.452.4777
*Domestic special needs children; international: children from Haiti, Asia and Africa; home studies; news and articles; also licensed in Alaska; non-profit.*
**http://www.adoptionadvocates.org**
Port Angeles, WA

### Christian Family Adoptions                  360.892.1572
*Domestic infants and special needs children; home studies; international services; birth parent counseling; non-profit.*
**http://www.adventistadoption.com**
Vancouver, WA

### Medina Children's Services                  206.260.1700
*Domestic infant and special needs adoptions; abused, neglected, abandoned children; home studies; pregnancy counseling; non-profit.*
**http://www.medinachild.org**
Seattle, WA

One Church, One Child doing business as UJIMA    **206.760.3456**
Community Services

*Domestic special needs children; home studies; support of foster care families;*
*children of African-American descent; non-profit.*

**http://www.ococujima.org/pages/806757/index.htm**
Seattle, WA

## Wisconsin

Acres of Hope, Inc.    **715.765.4118**

*Advocacy and education for special needs adoptions; biracial children; referral*
*service; maternity home; emotional support; financial assistance; non-profit.*

**http://www.acresofhope.org**
Mason, WI

Catholic Charities—Diocese of La Crosse    **608.782.0710**

*Domestic infant and special needs adoption; international; home studies;*
*pregnancy counseling; non-profit.*

**http://www.catholiccharitieslax.org**
La Crosse, WI

Family Services of Northeast Wisconsin, Inc.    **920.436.4360**

*Variety of services for individuals, families and children including*
*post-adoption services.*

**http://www.familyservicesnew.org**
Green Bay, WI

Special Needs Adoption Network    **414.475.1246**

*Waiting children photo listing; special needs; newsletter and resources.*

**http://www.wiadopt.org**
Milwaukee, WI

# Support Services

### Adoptive Families Coalition

*Adoption information & support, networking, social events, educational seminars, and a quarterly newsletter.*

**www.timesunion.com/memlink.com/default.aspx**

### Angels Support Network, Inc

*New York, Rochester—local support group for the adoption triad as well as siblings, friends and relatives.*

**www.nyadoption.org/angels2.htm**

### Giving Tree, Inc

*Recruits, trains and supports families for the adoption of children from foster care.*

**www.thegivingtree.org**

### Open Door Society of Massachusetts, Inc.

*Educational & support programs for the adoptive triad, newsletter, non profit.*

**www.odsma.org**

### Open Door Society of New Hampshire, Inc.

*Adoption information, support groups, deaf adoption news service, non-profit.*

### Oregon Post Adoption Resource Center

*Support, education & resources: a lending library, assistance in developing respite resources.*

**www.orparc.org**

### PACT, an Adoption Alliance Los Angeles

*Support for the adoption triad, serve children of color; newsletter; non-profit.*

**www.pactadopt.org**

## Parent Network for the Post Institutionalized Child, PNPIC

*Support network for adoptive parents of special needs children from all over the world, resources, newsletter & publications.*

**www.pnpic.org**

## Parent to Parent of Georgia, Inc.

*Support & information to parents of children with disabilities; special needs database containing over 4,000 resources in over 100 categories.*

**www.parenttoparentofga.org**

## Post Adoption Center for Education and Research

*Support, resources, and education to the adoption triad.*

**www.pacer-adoption.org**

## Precious Kids

*Advertising network service for adoptive families, support for adoptive parents to find birth mothers, home schooling resources.*

**www.preciouskids.org**

## RESOLVE of Atlanta, Inc.

*Infertility support groups—discussion/social & therapist-led; physician referral service; bulletin board; magazine, links for chapters in other states.*

**www.resolveofgeorgia.org**

## Safe Havens of Kornerstone

*Texas—Christian, foster parent support and resources, placement of special needs children.*

**www.safehavens.org/Default.htm**

## South Carolina Council on Adoptable Children

*Waiting children photo list; non-profit organization; education and support groups; resource links; in South Carolina.*

**www.sc-adopt.org**

## Spaulding for Children/National Resource Center

*Special needs adoption, foster care, adoption resources and support, links, in Michigan.*

**www.spaulding.org.**

### Stars of David International, Inc.

*Non-profit organization; support network for Jewish adoptive families; listing of adoption agencies; fertility resources; e-mail list; in Illinois; chapters in most states.*

**www.starsofdavid.org**

### Taplink and NACAC

*Support groups, link to resources in Pennsylvania, financial information, fourm, and a newsletter.*

**www.taplink.org**

# Travel Resources

### Adoption Travel.com

*Articles, tips and resources including travel agency listing.*

**http://www.adoptiontravel.com**

### Cheap Tickets                                          888.922.8849

*Booking of flights, rental cars and lodging.*

**http://www.cheaptickets.com**

### Federal Travel Adoption Services                954.942.8666

*Arrangements for travel; specialize in adoption and family travel.*

**http://www.federaltravel.com**

Lighthouse Point, FL

### Hotwire.com

*Airfare, hotels and cars.*

**http://www.hotwire.com**

### Life in Korea

*Korean travel guide; online reservations to airlines, car rentals, hotels, restaurants, tours and lots more.*

**http://www.lifeinkorea.com**

**LowTicket**                                                817.284.0776
  *Full service travel site; low airfare prices; vacation packages; hotel, rental cars and cruises.*
  **http://www.lowticket.com**
  Bedford, TX

---

**Northwest Airlines Special Delivery Adoption Program**    800.322.4162
  *Significant fare discounts for international adoptions.*
  **http://www.nwa.com/features/adopt.shtml**

---

**Priceline.com**
  *Bargain travel services.*
  **http://www.priceline.com**

---

**The Preston Group Adoption Air Fare**
  *Discounts on adoption travel.*
  **http://www.prestongrouptravel.com/adopt.htm**
  Salt Lake City, UT

---

**The Ties Program**                                         800.398.3676
  *Travel program for adoptive families visiting their child's country of birth: experience the culture and reconnect with significant people and places related to their adoption.*
  **http://www.adoptivefamilytravel.com**
  Wauwatosa, WI

---

**Traveler's Health**                                        877.394.8747
  *International travel; preparation, health, disease, and vaccination information; other related resources.*
  **http://www.cdc.gov/travel**

---

**Trip.com**
  *Arrangements and resources; flights, lodging, condos, cars and last minute trips.*
  **http://www.trip.com**

---

*We are always updating our data base. If you know of any sites that were left out, please feel free to send us an e-mail at submit@adoptingonline.com*

# Adoption Glossary

Used by social workers, attorneys, facilitators and other adoption professionals who may apply slightly different meanings in international adoption and in the various states.

**abandonment:** Desertion of a child by a birth parent or guardian with no provisions for continued care or evidence of intent to return. When he/she has not had contact for an amount of time specified in state law which varies by state. See also **legalized abandonment.**

**adopt:** To take (a child of other parents) as one's own in affection and law.

**adoptee:** A child or an adult who is adopted and joins a family through adoption.

**adoption:** A permanent social and legal process which establishes the relationship of parent and child between people who did not give birth to the child. Adoption allows the same rights and obligations that exist between children and their biological parents.

**Adoption Assistance Program (AAP) or Adoption Assistance Payment:** Also called adoption subsidies or Title IV-E. Providing financial assistance, including help with medical care to families who adopt children who would otherwise remain in long term foster care. AAP continues until the child reaches 18 or 21 if the child has a mental or physical disability which requires continuation of benefits. Children not covered under Title IV-E may be eligible for state subsidies. Contact your social service agency for details.

**adoption agency:** Licensed by a state, either public, private for-profit or private not-for-profit; providing services to birth parents, adoptive parents and adoptive children. Agencies can do all or some of the required legal and social work, including home studies. Some agencies offer full service adoptions, preparing the home study, handling the intakes of birth families and the placement of the child(ren) in the adoptive family's home. Some agencies now provide home studies for independent adoptions, allowing families to find their own birth mother with the help of an attorney or adoption facilitator.

**adoption assistance:** Any financial help given to adoptive parents. See AAP.

**adoption attorney:** An attorney who specializes in adoption law and is experienced with filing, processing and finalizing adoptions in a court having jurisdiction. Some lawyers provide assistance on how to locate a child, speak to birth parents, request medical records, network with an attorney in the birth mother's state and provide all services to finalize your adoption—except the home study. Some attorneys prefer to process only the adoption paperwork. Some attorneys work with adoption facilitators to locate the birth mothers for their clients or ask the prospective family to find a birth mother on their own through other resources.

**adoption benefits:** An employee benefit offered by some employers to adoptive parents, often comparable to maternity leave. Benefits may include monetary reimbursement for the expenses of adopting a child, financial assistance or parental or family leave in connection with the adoption.

**adoption consultant:** See **Adoption Facilitator.**

**adoption decree:** The document signed by a judge and issued by the court upon finalization of an adoption stating that the adoptee is the legal child of the adoptive parents, who now possess legal custody.

**adoption disruption:** The interruption of an adoption plan prior to finalization where the child leaves the adoptive home. This may occur because the adoptive parents change their minds for some reason, also known as a failed adoption. Or because the birth parents revoke consent before finalization occurs, also known as a reclaim. It may be that the adoptive parents are felt to be endangering the child or are not complying with requirements set by the agency, also known as a failed placement.

**adoption dissolution:** An adoption that has been legally finalized and then subsequently dissolved by the current adoptive family. The child can be placed in a new home. This requires court action and can be initiated by the adoptive parents or the courts, but not the birth parents.

**adoption exchange:** Programs offered by organizations by which they help facilitate adoption placements. They assist in the matching of children and families by sharing information about waiting children seeking an adoptive family. Exchanges may provide advocacy, training, support and resource services, as well as referrals for adoption agencies and adoptive families.

**adoption facilitator:** One who helps bring together members of birth families and prospective adoptive parents for the purpose of arranging an adoption plan for a child; an adoption professional whose business includes connecting prospective birth parents and adoptive parents for a fee. Attorneys may be facilitators. Not all states allow the payment of an adoption facilitator, also known as an adoption consultant or intermediary.

**adoption home study report:** A detailed written report about the prospective adoptive family, including their life experiences, family life and upbringing, home, health, life style, values, beliefs and interests. It may also cover family support systems, adoption and parenting style and preparation for adoption. A home study includes a background check completed for all the adults living in the home. An FBI and/or state fingerprint check is normally included.

**adoption insurance/adoption cancellation insurance:** Insurance that protects against financial loss incurred when an adoption proceeding has begun but the birth parents change their minds and decide not to place their child for adoption. Not always available and usually only to those families working with approved agencies or attorneys.

**adoption laws:** Each state has laws that are based on that states' statutes and case law enacted by the state legislature which regulates adoptions. Birth parents, adoptive parents and adoption professionals must comply with adoption laws and regulations. The state in which the birth mother resides or gives birth may have different laws than the state of residence for the adoptive family. An adoption attorney should be consulted when legal questions arise.

**adoption petition:** A legal document and request for approval in which prospective adoptive parents appeal to the state court for permission to adopt a specific child.

**adoption placement:** The time when a child starts to live with prospective adoptive parents before the adoption is finalized.

**adoption plan:** Commonly used term in adoption referring to when biological parents or birth parents make a distinct and individual plan for the adoption of their child. Often includes the decision to place their child in an adoptive home, the type of family they wish to adopt the child, who will be at the birth and the amount of contact between the adoptive parents, adoptee and birth parents following the adoption.

**adoption profile/resume:** In independent domestic adoptions; an outline of the prospective adoptive parent's life in written form with photos and descriptions of their family, hobbies, home life etc., which is used by the birth parent to select parents for their child.

**adoption reversal or reclaim:** Occurs when birth parent(s) have a change of heart regarding a child who had been voluntarily placed with adoptive parents. Each state has specific laws, which define the time limits, and under what circumstances a child may be reclaimed.

**Adoption Service Provider (ASP):** A licensed social worker who is certified by the state to assist birth parents and adoptive parents with the placement of a child in an independent adoption placement.

**adoption subsidy:** See AAP—Adoption Assistance Payment.

**adoption tax credits:** A tax credit, which may reduce taxes owed by adoptive parents who claim adoption expense reimbursement. This can be claimed on federal taxes and in some states with similar legislation, on state taxes. The credit can include adoption fees, court fees, attorney fees, and travel expenses. Currently at $10,000 per adoption.

**adoption tax credit exclusions:** The IRS has provisions in the federal tax code allowing adoptive parents to exclude any cash or adoption benefits for qualifying adoption expenses received from an employer when computing the family's adjusted gross income for tax purposes.

**Adoption Tax Identification Number:** A temporary identification number for the child you are adopting, which is issued until a Social Security Number can be obtained. An ATIN is not a permanent valid identification number. This ATIN number is used on your federal income tax forms to identify the child while the adoption is pending. This allows you to claim your adoptive child as a dependent and, if eligible, claim a child care credit.

**adoption triad:** The three parties (three or more people) involved in an adoption: birth parents, adoptive parents and adopted child/children. Also referred to as adoption triangle or adoption circle.

**adoptive parent:** A person or persons who become the permanent and legal parents through a court approved adoption with all the legal rights and social and moral responsibilities of a biological parent.

**adult adoption:** The adoption of a person over the age of majority as defined by state law. In most states, an adult can be legally adopted by another adult as long as that adult is at least ten years older than the person being adopted. Adult adoption cannot be done for illegal reasons such as immigration.

**agency adoption:** Adoptive parents can work with either public agencies or private agencies that are licensed by the state and that offer a variety of services. Programs and services vary between agencies. Most provide home study services to prospective adoptive parents, counseling to birth parents, birth parent relinquishment services (though some have an attorney do this for them) and post-placement follow-up. A social worker screens prospective adoptive parents and supervises the placement of children in adoptive homes until the adoption is finalized. Some agencies are full service and have specialties such as special needs adoptions. Others provide both domestic and international adoption programs. Requirements and services can vary amongst programs within the same agency.

**agency assisted adoption:** An agency that will help the prospective adoptive parents with the completion of the adoption once a child is identified. Other agencies may screen calls from birth mother inquires and provide services to the birthmother and the adoptive parents. Prospective adoptive parents network and advertise or work with an adoption facilitator to locate a birth parent. Once a birth mother is identified, the agency will handle the paperwork and finalization of the adoption. Many agencies today provide this type of service for domestic adoptions.

**alleged birth father:** The father of a child born out-of-wedlock. Referred to in some states as a putative father or reputed father. A man is the alleged or putative father of the child if the birth mother alleges he is the father and the putative father, by written affidavit at any time or by surrender and release executed within one year of the relinquishment of the child by the birth mother or termination of parental rights of the birth mother, acknowledges being the child's biological father.

**amended birth certificate:** A document issued after a child has been adopted indicating the adoptive parents' names as parents of the adopted child. This certificate states the name the adoptive parents chose for the child. Some states allow an adoptee to obtain an uncertified copy of their birth record prior to adoption by submitting a notarized written request. State laws vary and change yearly.

**apostille:** Used in international adoptions. A process similar to certifying a document at the state level. A notarized document is taken to the secretary of state's office for verification of the notary's signature. The apostille is then stapled to the original document. See **Hague Convention.**

**authentication:** In international adoptions, a procedure in which the notarized and certified documents are viewed and approved by the consulate or embassy of the country the adoptive child is from.

**birth fathers' adoption registry:** Created to allow putative fathers to register and thus receive notice from the court if plans to place the child for adoption are made. A man may register before the child is born, but must register within a specific period of time required in the state of the child's birth to ensure that his rights are protected. Not all states have father's registries.

**birth parent:** A child's biological parent or genetic parent. The parents who conceived and gave birth to a child.

**child abuse clearances:** A method of checking to see if a person has a history of child abuse. This is used as part of the home study process for prospective adoptive and foster parents. These clearances must be updated annually while adopting.

**closed adoption:** An adoption in which the birth parents and adoptive parents do not share any identifying information; in some types of closed adoptions, no information is shared at all. In a true closed adoption, total confidentiality is maintained, with sealed records and no contact or ongoing relationship between the triad.

**compact administrator:** The commissioner of the Department of Children and Families ICPC (Interstate Compact on the Placement of Children) as designated by law, is appointed by the governor in their state to carry out the provisions of the interstate compacts. See **interstate compact.**

**consent:** Consent refers to the agreement by a birth parent, or a person or agency acting in place of a parent, to relinquish a child for adoption and release all rights and responsibilities with respect to that child. A birth parent(s) can legally change their minds at any point before the birth and up to the time their rights are terminated. Check with your state's laws on consent, as states differ on when this consent may be given and withdrawn.

**cooperative adoption:** Often provides an adoption where the birth parents and adoptive parents agree voluntarily on postadoption contact and communication between the child and members of the birth family. Birth parents may realize that they cannot parent their children, but want a completely open and ongoing adoption arrangement. A wide range of possibilities and options are possible and are determined by all the parties involved.

**criminal clearances:** Part of the home study process, a clearance through the state police department to determine if a person has a criminal record. Each state can supply appropriate forms. In many states, the clearances must be updated on an annual basis. In adoptions, all adults living in an adoptive parent residence are required to obtain criminal and child abuse clearances prior to a child being placed in the adoptive parents' home.

**Department of Human Services (DHS):** The state agency that handles adoptions and foster care for children in custody of the state. Social service workers who do home studies usually work for this agency. The name varies by state. DHS may also be called DHSS—Department of Health and Social Services or DSS—Department of Social Services.

**designated adoption:** The birth mother specifies the adoptive placement of her child to a particular family. The designation is often made on the recommendation of a professional (lawyer, doctor, clergy, facilitator or counselor or acquaintance) known mutually by the birth parent(s) and prospective adoptive family. The adoption can be completed by an agency or can be an independent adoption, done by an attorney, depending on the state laws.

**dossier:** A collection of papers providing detailed information about the adoptive parents. A variety of legal documents used in an international adoption to process a child's adoption or assignment of guardianship in the foreign court.

**domestic adoption:** The adoption of a child living in the United States by adoptive parents residing in the United States.

**disruption:** An interruption in an adoption plan where a child leaves the adoptive home before the finalization of the adoption. Disruption can occur when a) the birth parents revoke their consent to the adoption, b) the adoptive parents decide not to continue with the adoption plan, or c) the agency or court representative feels it is not in the best interest of the child to complete the adoption. This may be due to the families' non-compliance with requirements of the court or if the child is endangered in some way.

**employer adoption assistance:** When an employer offers adoption benefits to employees. This may include cash assistance to cover adoption expenses, reimbursement of approved adoption expenses, paid or unpaid family leave.

**finalization:** The final legal step in the adoption process; involves a court hearing during which the judge orders the adoption decree that the adoptive parents become the child's legal parents, permanently, and legally. In different states, this court hearing will occur after a specific time, according to the laws of the state.

**facilitator:** Also known as an adoption facilitator. An organization or individual working with adoptive parents and birth parents to come together and create an adoption between the parties. Facilitators usually locate birth mothers or birth parents seeking adoption. The services vary greatly. Some include services for advertising only to help find a child for a prospective adoptive family and others will follow an adoption to finalization. Facilitators are not licensed but some are bonded. They do not perform any legal services or home studies. Some offer counseling by outside licensed counselors. Laws vary state to state regarding the payment and use of facilitators by a prospective adoptive family. In many cases, a well qualified and experienced facilitator has proven to be a valuable asset in the adoption field, as an adoption professional can guide and assist families in completing adoptions.

**foster-adoption/fostadopt:** A form of adoption where a child who is unlikely to be returned to his or her birth family is placed into a home as a foster child and is eventually, legally adopted by the foster parents. A child placement in which the birth parents' rights have not yet been severed by the court or in which birth parents are appealing the court's decision but foster parents agree to adopt the child if/when parental rights are terminated. The main purpose for making such a placement is to keep the child from being moved from home to home. Also called legal-risk adoption

**foster care:** Temporary or long-term care, informal or arranged through a social services agency or court, in which persons other than the birth parents care for a child for a period of time.

**guardian:** A person who is legally responsible for the care and management of a minor child. The court or birth parents may continue to hold some authority over the child. Guardianship is subject to ongoing supervision by the court and ends at the child's majority or by order of the court. Guardians do not have the same shared rights of inheritance as birth or adoptive parents.

**guardian ad litem:** A volunteer citizen or paid attorney who becomes a representative for the best interests of an assigned child. The guardian ad litem is a representative for the child before the court and social service agencies. The legal protective status of a guardian ad litem will exist only within the confines of the particular court case in which the appointment was made, such as an adoption.

**Hague Convention:** The convention will apply to all adoptions between countries becoming parties to it. An adoption may take place only if : 1) The country of origin has established that the child is adoptable, that an intercountry adoption is in the child's best interests and that after counseling, the necessary consents to the adoption have been given freely. 2) The receiving country has determined that the prospective adoptive parents are eligible and suited to adopt and that the child they wish to adopt will be authorized to enter and reside permanently in that country. Every country must establish a national government-level central authority to carry out certain non-delegable functions, which include cooperating with other central authorities, overseeing the implementation of the convention in its country, and providing information on the laws of its country.

**home study:** Required in most states before a child can be placed for adoption or foster care. Generally, the home study will include visits to the adoptive parents' home and must be completed before a child is placed in the home. The home study is conducted by a licensed social worker in the adoptive families' state. The process of adoption is explained. Home studies include medical reports, financial statements, family background information and a number of interviews. Fingerprints and an FBI investigation for child abuse or criminal background may also be required by the state in which the birth mother or the adoptive parents lives.

**identified adoption:** For adoptive parents who wish to locate a birth mother or birth parents on their own, with the help of friends, family, a physician, or an adoption professional such as an attorney or a facilitator. The adoptive parents and birth parents find each other and then have an agency or attorney complete the legal paperwork process.

**independent adoption:** An adoption facilitated by those other than caseworkers associated with an agency. Handled by attorneys or adoption facilitators. Independent adoption is not allowed in all states.

**Indian Child Welfare Act:** A federal law regarding the placement of Native-American children which establishes the tribe's sovereignty as a separate nation over the welfare of children who are tribal members or who are eligible for tribal membership. Permission must be granted (and often is) for adoption of children with any Indian heritage.

**INS:** Immigration and Naturalization Service is a U.S Federal agency that oversees all visas issued to allow entry into the United States. This agency is responsible to review documents and issue approval for a child adopted from a country outside the U.S. to immigrate to the United States. Many changes have occurred in this agency since 9/11.

**institutionalization:** Children placed in hospitals, institutions or orphanages. Experts agree that placement in institutions during a child's early critical developmental periods and for lengthy periods may be connected with developmental delays due to environmental deprivation, nutrition, inadequate staff-child ratios, or lack of early stimulation.

**intercountry or international adoption:** The adoption of a child who is a citizen of one country, by adoptive parents who are citizens of a different country. Legal work through immigration services must be completed to authorize an international adoption. For safety reasons, international adoptions should be arranged through a qualified adoption agency versus independently. Both domestic and foreign governments must give approval.

**interstate adoption:** An adoption in which the baby is born in one state and the adoption is finalized in a different state. The placement of a child across state lines for adoption is protected, regulated and monitored by the Interstate Compact on the Placement of Children. This uniform law establishes procedures for the interstate placement of children as well as defines the responsibilities for all involved persons.

**Interstate Compact on the Placement of Children:** Known as ICPC or Interstate Compact. Has state law in all fifty states, the District of Columbia and the Virgin Islands. An agreement regulating the placement of children across state lines. The ICPC must give its approval for any child before it can be moved from one state to another for the purpose of adoption, foster care or temporary care. The adoption plan must be approved by both the child's state of origin—the sending state—and the state where the child will reside—the receiving state—before the child can legally cross state lines. In an interstate adoption, the agency with custody or attorney for the adoptive parents is responsible for processing the interstate paperwork. The ICPC does not apply to placement to or from foreign countries, except as applicable in some intercountry adoptions or to placements into or from Puerto Rico or Guam.

**involuntary termination of parental rights:** A legal procedure in which the legal rights of the birth parents of a child are terminated by the court without the birth parents' signed consent. Decisions for such action are based on the best interest of the child and include abandonment, repeated or severe abuse and neglect.

**legalized abandonment:** Some states have passed laws that legalize the anonymous abandonment of infants at predetermined drop centers, such as hospitals and fire departments.

**legal risk adoption:** An adoption where the child to be adopted is placed with the prospective adoptive parents prior to the termination of the birth parents rights. This means that the birth parents could revoke their consents to the adoption and the child would have to be returned to the birth parents. The legal risk period is determined by each states' law.

**legally free:** A child who is available for adoption when the birth parents' rights have been legally terminated.

**matching:** An adoption match is the process of locating and connecting a birth mother and an adoptive family who is interested in completing an adoption plan for the birth mother's child; not to be confused with "placement."

**nonrecurring adoption costs:** One-time adoption expenses, which through the provisions of the Adoption Assistance and Child Welfare Act of 1980, may be at least partially reimbursed by the state to parents adopting children with special needs. Allowable expenses for this reimbursement benefit may include the home study cost, adoption fees, court costs, attorney fees, physical and psychological examinations, travel to visit with the child prior to the placement and other expenses related to the legal adoption of a child with special needs.

**open adoption:** the adoption plan that allows the birth mother or birth family to have a choice about the family that adopts their child. In open adoption, a wide range of alternatives are available, which may include but are not limited to meetings between families before or after the birth of the child, allowing adoptive parents to attend the birth, and the continuation of relationship between families through various combinations of letters, photos, videos, e-mails or visits.

**orphanage:** An institution that houses children who are orphaned, abandoned, or whose parents are unable to care for them. They are more frequently found in other countries. Foster homes and group homes have replaced orphanages in the United States.

**orphan:** A child under 18 whose parents have died, have relinquished their parental rights, or whose rights have been terminated by the courts.

**paternity testing:** Genetic testing that can determine the identity of a child's biological father, often paid for by the birth parents.

**photo listing book:** Resources either online or in a book form that contain photos and descriptions of waiting children who are available for adoption.

**post-placement supervision:** Adoption supervision provided to the adopted parents and adopted child before the adoption is legally finalized in court. It often includes pre-placement visits by a social worker prior to the child's placement. Reports are drawn up to finalize the adoption in the court of jurisdiction.

**precertification:** When prospective adoptive parent/s submit to the court their home study, references, child abuse clearance, fingerprints, medical status, employment verification and other documents for the court to review. The court then approves the prospective adoptive parents and issues a certificate that the person/s can adopt a child. This paperwork is submitted by an attorney. The same paperwork is usually required by an agency adoption. The certificate stays with the court.

**private or independent adoption:** Privately funded by the adoptive parents, these adoptions often are arranged without the participation of an agency. Facilitated by an intermediary, adoption facilitator, attorney or privately funded agency, these can be open adoptions, although not always. Private/independent adoptions should not be confused with private agency adoptions.

**private agency adoption:** Placements made by licensed agencies that screen prospective adoptive parents and supervise the placement of children in adoptive homes until the adoption is finalized; birth parent relinquishments are taken, services are offered for both birth families and adoptive families and the agency can be for profit or not for profit.

**public agency adoption:** The public agency known as the Department of Human Services, Office of Children and Youth Services or a similar name. This is a publicly supported agency that places children who come into their care either voluntarily or involuntarily. Public agencies are accountable for most adoptions of older children and for handling cases where children have been abused, neglected or abandoned by their birth parents. Take relinquishments from birth parents.

**putative father:** Legal term for the alleged or supposed father of a child. A man who may be a child's biological father, but who is either not married to the child's mother on or before the date that the child was or is to be born, and/or has not established paternity of the child in a court proceeding. See **putative father registries.**

**putative father registries:** Registry system in some states helping ensure a birth father's rights are protected. Some states require that birth fathers register, while other states presume a birth father does not wish to pursue paternity rights if he doesn't initiate any legal action. States generally require a putative father to register or acknowledge paternity within a specific timeframe in order to receive notice of such a pending adoption. Many states have putative father registries. Several, however, only mandate by law that a putative father file a notice of his paternity claim within a certain period of time. Failure to register or file may prohibit the right to notice of termination or adoption proceedings.

**relinquishment:** Legal process by which birth parents voluntarily terminate their parental rights in order to free their child for adoption. In some adoptions, referred to as a surrender or making an adoption plan for their child. Relinquishment is a legally binding, permanent procedure involving the signing of legal documents and court proceedings.

**reunification:** The attempt to return foster children to the custody of their birth parent(s) after they have been placed outside of their home.

**revocation of consent:** A legal process in which a birth parent revokes the adoption consent they signed and requests the child be returned to his/her custody. All states allow the birth parent to exercise this option within a specific and limited period of time. State laws vary and are constantly changing.

**semiopen adoption:** An adoption in which the adoptive parents and birth parents establish some continuing contact that the birth parents will have with the child. The options range from letters and photos, e-mails and anything in between which is mutually agreed upon. Some semiopen adoptions have no contact after placement.

**special needs adoption:** The adoption of a special needs child. Special needs children include older children; sibling groups, children facing physical, emotional or intellectual challenges, children of minorities and mixed race children of all ages. This adoption commonly includes a more extensive training and often involves lower or no fees. When adopting a child with special needs, ask your adoption professional about the availability of federal and state subsidies.

**SSI benefits:** Social Security Administration program provides financial support to persons, including children with specifically defined handicaps. After an adoption is finalized, SSI benefits are tied to the adoptive parent's income.

**subsidy:** See AAP—Adoption Assistance Payment.

**surrender:** See Relinquishment.

**system:** Known as "The public child welfare system;" A network of governmental agencies and services provided for children in its community or region.

**termination of parental rights:** A court hearing in which a judge enters a decree permanently ending a birth parent's legal parental rights to a child. This can be voluntary or involuntary and must happen before a child is legally free for adoption.

**traditional adoption:** Typically refers to a domestic infant adoption in which confidentiality is preserved, known also as closed adoption.

**traditional agency adoption:** An agency that locates a birth mother, counsels her and provides assistance for an adoption plan to occur. Some agencies may or may not allow the birth parent to choose the prospective adoptive parents from profile/resumes. The adoptive parents may or may not have contact with the birth parents.

**U.S. adoption laws:** Those considering adoption must comply with adoption laws specific to state laws and regulations in the state in which the adoptive parents live and in some adoptions the state in which the placing birth parent resides. State adoption laws are comprised of laws from state statutes and state case law.

**voluntary placement agreement:** An agreement made through the courts or a social service agency with the birth parent(s) of a child who needs to be in foster care while the family meets certain requirements specified in the agreement. The child may be permanently removed and placed for adoption, if the agreement and plan are not fulfilled by the birth parents in a specific timeframe.

**voluntary termination of parental rights:** The birth parents of a child voluntarily, of their own desire and choice, make an adoption plan for a child and relinquish their legal rights to the child, making the child legally free for an adoption.

**waiting children:** Children who are waiting to be adopted into permanent, loving families. Typically, these children are older, in the public child welfare system and cannot return to their birth families. Can also be another term for children with special needs.

**waiting period:** The time after an adoptive family is approved for adoption by an adoption professional until a child is placed in their family.

**waiver of confidentiality:** A document filled out by a person allowing for disclosure of records or identifying information to another person about themselves or an adoption.

# Index

# Quick Order Form

**Email orders:** info@carriagehousepublishing.com

**Fax orders:** 1-877-423-6783

**Telephone orders:** Call Toll Free 1-877-423-6785. *Have your credit card ready.*

**Postal orders:** American Carriage House Publishing, PO Box 1130, Nevada City, CA 95959. USA Telephone: 530-470-0720

Please send the following Books, Discs or Reports.

_____

_____

_____

Please send more FREE information on:

❏ Other books    ❏ Speaking/Seminars    ❏ Consulting

Name:_____

Address:_____

City_____State_____Zip_____-_____

Telephone:_____

Email address:_____

**Sales tax:** Please add 7.75% for products shipped to California addresses.

**Shipping by air:**

**US:** $4.00 for the first book or disk and $2.00 for each additional product.

**International:** $9.00 for 1st book or disk; $5.00 for each additional product (estimate).

**Payment:** ❏ Check

❏ Credit card: ❏ Visa  ❏ MasterCard  ❏ AMEX  ❏ Discover

Card number:_____

Name on card:_____Exp. date:____/_____

*See http://www.americancarriagehousepublishing.com*

Contact the publisher for volume discounts for seminars, support groups or fund raisers.

# My Notes

# Quick Order Form

**Email orders:** info@carriagehousepublishing.com

**Fax orders:** 1-877-423-6783

**Telephone orders:** Call Toll Free 1-877-423-6785. *Have your credit card ready.*

**Postal orders:** American Carriage House Publishing, PO Box 1130, Nevada City, CA 95959. USA Telephone: 530-470-0720

Please send the following Books, Discs or Reports.

_____

_____

_____

Please send more FREE information on:

❏ Other books    ❏ Speaking/Seminars    ❏ Consulting

Name:_____

Address:_____

City_____State_____Zip_____-_____

Telephone:_____

Email address:_____

**Sales tax:** Please add 7.75% for products shipped to California addresses.

**Shipping by air:**

**US:** $4.00 for the first book or disk and $2.00 for each additional product.

**International:** $9.00 for 1st book or disk; $5.00 for each additional product (estimate).

**Payment:** ❏ Check

❏ Credit card: ❏ Visa ❏ MasterCard ❏ AMEX ❏ Discover

Card number:_____

Name on card:_____Exp.date:____/_____

*See http://www.americancarriagehousepublishing.com*

Contact the publisher for volume discounts for seminars, support groups or fund raisers.

# My Notes